Zorba the Buddha

Zorba the Buddha

*Sex, Spirituality, and Capitalism
in the Global Osho Movement*

Hugh B. Urban

UNIVERSITY OF CALIFORNIA PRESS

University of California Press, one of the most
distinguished university presses in the United States,
enriches lives around the world by advancing scholarship
in the humanities, social sciences, and natural sciences. Its
activities are supported by the UC Press Foundation and
by philanthropic contributions from individuals and
institutions. For more information, visit www.ucpress.edu.

University of California Press
Oakland, California

Library of Congress Cataloging-in-Publication Data
Urban, Hugh B., author.
  Zorba the Buddha : sex, spirituality, and capitalism in
the global Osho movement / Hugh B. Urban.
    p. cm.
  Includes bibliographical references and index.
  ISBN 978-0-520-28666-5 (cloth, alk. paper) —
  ISBN 978-0-520-28667-2 (pbk., alk. paper) —
  ISBN 978-0-520-96177-7 (electronic)
    1. Osho, 1931-1990. 2. Gurus—Biography.
3. New Age movement—Oregon—History—20th
century. 4. New Age movement—India—History.
I. Title.
  BP605.R344U73 2015
  299'.93—dc23
                                              2015017708

Manufactured in the United States of America

24 23 22 21 20 19 18 17 16 15
10 9 8 7 6 5 4 3 2 1

In keeping with a commitment to support
environmentally responsible and sustainable printing
practices, UC Press has printed this book on Natures
Natural, a fiber that contains 30% post-consumer waste
and meets the minimum requirements of ANSI/NISO
Z39.48-1992 (R 1997) (*Permanence of Paper*).

Contents

Illustrations

Preface

Writing about Osho-Rajneesh; or, the Art of Being Driven Nuts

I have been consistently inconsistent so that you will never be able to make a dogma out of me.

You will simply go nuts if you try. I am leaving something really terrible for scholars; they will not be able to make any sense out of me. They will go nuts—and they deserve it, they should go nuts!

—Osho, *Autobiography of a Spiritually Incorrect Mystic*

This book is based on research conducted in India and the United States between 1995 and 2013, which was supported by generous grants from the American Academy of Religions and the National Endowment for the Humanities. A great many people deserve thanks for their invaluable help with this book. These include colleagues and mentors such as Corinne Dempsey, Wendy Doniger, Eugene Holland, Andrea Jain, Jeffrey Kripal, Jeffrey Lidke, Bruce Lincoln, Amanda Lucia, Smriti Srinivas, Tulasi Srinivas, and David Gordon White; journalists such as Les Zaitz and Milt Ritter; librarians such as the curators of the Oregon Historical Society and the University of Oregon Special Collections; and current and former members of the Osho-Rajneesh community, such as Swami Amrito, Swami Prabodh Dhanyam, Aneesha Dillon, William Foster, Swami Anand Teertha, and Swami Satya Vedant.

Finally, I am grateful to Osho (aka Bhagwan Shree Rajneesh or Osho-Rajneesh), for his endlessly provocative, ever fascinating, often humorous, and at times infuriating body of work. As he himself put it, any scholar who tries to make too much sense of his teachings will inevitably be "driven nuts" by his playful, ironic, and consistently inconsistent methods. With that in mind, I have avoided trying to impose too much order or coherence onto the Osho-Rajneesh movement, instead simply offering my own humble and admittedly incomplete commentary on its complex role amid the shifting global networks of the last five decades.

Introduction

Gurus, God-Men, and Globalization

My concept of the new man is that he will be Zorba the
Greek and he will also be Gautam the Buddha: the new man
will be Zorba the Buddha. He will be sensuous and physical,
in the body, in the senses, enjoying the body and all that the
body makes possible, and still a great consciousness. . . . He
will be Christ and Epicurus together.

—Bhagwan Shree Rajneesh, *Zorba the Buddha*

Max Weber's famous metaphor in *The Protestant Ethic* of
religion striding into the marketplace of worldly affairs and
slamming the monastery door behind it becomes further
transformed in modern society with religion placed very
much in the consumer marketplace alongside other meaning
complexes.

—Mike Featherstone, *Consumer Culture and Postmodernism*

Most Americans today probably remember Bhagwan Shree Rajneesh
(aka Osho) as "that Indian guru" who became hugely controversial
during the 1980s, when he created an enormous utopian commune in
central Oregon, collected a fleet of ninety-three Rolls-Royces, and
taught a radically sex-friendly form of spirituality before being arrested
and deported in 1985. Personally, I first remember hearing about
Rajneesh while watching an episode of the ABC news program *60 Minutes* in 1985, which played a clip of the notorious "Guru of the Rich."
"I *sell* contentment. I *sell* enlightenment," he said in the now infamous
segment, which made him the media's poster child of the charismatic,

enormously wealthy, yet seemingly unscrupulous New Age guru (see fig. 1).[1]

The story of Rajneesh's rise to celebrity and dramatic fall into infamy in the United States is indeed a remarkable tale to tell. Despite its brief existence, the Oregon commune was one of the largest and most successful religious experiments in American history, covering more than 64,000 acres and housing over 2,500 residents, even as some $130 million flowed through its gates.[2] Far ahead of its time in the practice of organic farming, recycling, and land reclamation, the Rajneesh community transformed an arid, overgrazed piece of Oregon desert into a utopian experiment that impressed journalists, scholars, and lawmakers alike. The collapse of the Oregon experiment, however, was even more spectacular than its rise, as the tensions between the Rajneesh community and local residents quickly escalated into all-out war that involved an array of almost surreal guerrilla tactics. In addition to being one of America's most successful religious experiments, the Rajneesh community holds the dubious distinction of launching the largest biological terrorist attack on American soil, one of the largest illegal wiretapping operations in American history, and the largest immigration fraud ever recorded—in addition to the numerous other charges of arson, burglary, and attempted murder filed against members of the community.[3] As the *Atlantic* recently put it, the Oregon experiment seems like a kind of "bizarre, made-for-Hollywood episode."[4]

However, the real story of the Rajneesh movement extends both well before and well after the brief yet spectacular episode of the Oregon ranch in the 1980s. Arguably the first truly global guru of the twentieth century, Bhagwan Shree Rajneesh began teaching in India during the 1960s and 1970s, as new waves of global tourists, spiritual seekers, and eventually capitalist investors began to pour into a rapidly changing South Asian landscape. His early community in Pune was one of the first attempts to combine Indian meditation techniques with Western psychology, becoming a major hub of global spiritual experimentation during the 1970s. And ironically, Rajneesh became even *more* popular after the scandalous collapse of the Oregon community and his arrest and deportation from the United States. Returning to India and assuming the title Osho, he established a new and explicitly global religious community in Pune, now known as the Osho International Foundation. Offering a vast array of spiritual practices drawn from East and West in a luxurious setting, the new Osho resort has become a global tourist hub that attracts a vast international audience of spiritual seekers.

Indeed, the "Osho Multiversity" in Pune now claims to be "the largest center in the world for meditation and personal growth processes," offering a dizzying array of spiritual practices from around the world and encompassing "all the current western therapy approaches, the healing arts of East and West, esoteric sciences, creative arts, centering and martial arts, Tantra, Zen, Sufism, and Meditative Therapies."[5]

all healing in one place

As such, Osho-Rajneesh and the movement he inspired represent something far more interesting that just another curious anecdote from Reagan's America of the 1980s. Rather, they offer profound insights into the larger processes of globalization and the transnational flow of people, ideas, tourism, and capital in the late twentieth and early twenty-first centuries. Not only was this arguably the first truly transnational religious movement of the modern era, tracing a complex global circuit from India to America and back to India again, but this was also perhaps the first to explicitly unite spirituality and capitalism, wedding the ideal of otherworldly transcendence to the unapologetic pursuit of material wealth.[6] This ideal is embodied in Osho-Rajneesh's central concept of "Zorba the Buddha," the perfectly integrated person who could combine the materialism of Zorba the Greek with the spirituality of the Buddha, uniting sensuality and worldly enjoyment with other-worldly transcendence.[7] While this ideal ended in a spectacular collapse in Oregon during the 1980s, it has been reborn and now circulates worldwide in the new Osho movement of the twenty-first century.

Despite the colorful history and remarkable success of the Osho-Rajneesh movement, however, there has been no significant scholarship on it since the late 1980s.[8] Its absence from scholarship is doubly unfortunate, I would suggest, not simply because of the fascinating history of this controversial movement but more importantly because of the unique insights it gives us into the broader transformations of religious ideas in the context of globalization and capitalism.

A HISTORY OF A GLOBAL MOVEMENT: KNOTS AND NODES IN A TRANSNATIONAL SPIRITUAL NETWORK

In this book, I will retrace the complex history of the Osho-Rajneesh movement from its early days in India to its surprising success and rapid collapse in the United States to its return to India and rebirth as the Osho International Foundation. I have no interest in producing another exposé or sensationalist account of this complex movement—of which there are already several.[9] Instead, I approach it methodologically as a

FIGURE I. "Bhagwan Shree Rajneesh Raises His Hands." Max Gutierrez photo, Oregon Historical Society, bb 001267.

historian of religions, in Bruce Lincoln's sense of the phrase.[10] That is, I will situate this complex spiritual movement very concretely in its specific historical contexts, from India of the 1960s to Oregon of the 1980s to a transnational religious and economic context today. My own interest in Osho-Rajneesh began in the late 1990s, when I became fascinated by his remarkable synthesis of eclectic spirituality, irreverent humor, and unapologetic embrace of capitalism; and over the last fifteen years, I have done extensive archival and field research in India and the United States, including interviews with current and former members of the movement, Indian and American journalists, and local citizens.[11]

The Osho-Rajneesh movement, I will argue, not only reflects but critically embodies some of the most important economic and spiritual currents of the last forty years, emerging within and adapting to an increasingly interconnected and conflicted late capitalist world order. With its explicit fusion of spirituality and materialism, its ideal of Zorba the Buddha, its radically eclectic practices, and its wide global following, the Osho-Rajneesh movement is a microcosm of these broader transnational religious and cultural forces. Indeed, Osho-Rajneesh's eclectic, parodic, and iconoclastic teachings embody what Paul Heelas calls a kind of "postmodern spirituality" and a "spiritual marketplace," uniquely adapted to the shifting religious tastes of a global audience of consumers.[12] Adapting a phrase from Fredric Jameson, I will suggest that this movement is thus a striking illustration of the complex and contradictory "spiritual logic of late capitalism."[13]

As such, the Osho-Rajneesh movement poses a significant challenge to most of the existing literature on religion and globalization. To date, much of the scholarship on religion and globalization has tended to focus on religious violence (particularly on radical Islam),[14] and on various forms of global Christianity (such as Pentecostalism and Catholicism).[15] To cite but one of many telling examples, Frank Lechner and John Boli's widely used volume, *The Globalization Reader*, contains a large section on "religion and globalization" that focuses entirely on radical Islam and various forms of global Christianity.[16] With a few notable exceptions,[17] there is surprisingly little work on global religious movements coming out of India or other parts of Asia. And yet, as Tulasi Srinivas has persuasively argued in her work on the Sathya Sai Baba movement, Indian-based movements offer a powerful alternative to the usual narratives of globalization. Cultural ideologies, she suggests, flow *everyone is involved* not simply from "the West to the rest" but also from India and other parts of Asia, revealing a far more dynamic and multidirectional global flow of religious forms.[18]

Going still further, I will suggest that the Osho-Rajneesh movement is neither a mere response to Western-style globalization nor simply a global movement that simply happens to have emerged from South Asia; rather, borrowing a phrase from Arjun Appadurai, I will argue *a central connecting point* that this movement is better understood as a crucial *node* in a far more complex, fluid, and shifting transnational network of people, ideas, and capital now emanating from multiple sites across the globe.[19] Indeed, the Osho movement is not only a transnational but an explicitly "postnational movement," in Appadurai's sense.[20] Yet with its fluid transnational organization and its enthusiastic embrace of materialism, the Osho movement is also uniquely adapted to the increasingly "deterritorialized" nature of contemporary global capitalism.

Rather than mere by-products of globalization, charismatic religious movements like this might be better described as something like *hyphal knots* in the networks of globalization. Here I am adapting a phrase from the field of mycology, where "hyphal knots" are those key intersections amid the complex networks of mycelia that spread subterraneously throughout the ecosystem and play critical roles in the circulation of resources and information between organic and inorganic matter.[21] In the context of this book, I think of charismatic religious groups as roughly analogous to hyphal knots amid the complex global networks of people, ideas, and capital, playing critical roles in the circulation of resources and information that often go well beyond the boundaries of the nation-state.

GURUS AND GLOBALIZATION

Osho-Rajneesh was not, of course, the first international guru to emerge from India. Rather, he is just one of the more recent—but, as I will argue, one of the most *explicit* and *self-conscious* —examples of influential transnational spiritual figures who have emerged from South Asia and played a critical role in the refashioning of global spirituality since the early nineteenth century. One of my key arguments in this book is that charismatic gurus such as Rajneesh are by no means simply curious artifacts or marginal figures in the processes of globalization.[22] As epicenters of tourism, travel, cultural exchange, spiritual experimentation, and big business, these charismatic gurus and their followers are not simply passive reflections of globalization but often its active *drivers*. In this sense, I am more Weberian than Marxist in my approach, since I am interested more in the "transformative force of certain religious ideas" than in the role of religious ideas as masks, mystifications, or dissemblances of economic and social interests.[23]

As Amanda Lucia observes, this central role of the global guru was already beginning to emerge in the early 1800s, with figures such as Rammohun Roy (1772–1833), the Bengali reformer who helped redefine modern Hinduism in the face of British colonial rule, reframing it in a more palatable way for an American and European audience.[24] But it reached perhaps its early peak in the late nineteenth century in Swami Vivekananda (born Narendranatha Datta; 1863–1902), who helped bring Hindu philosophy and yoga to an American and British audience. The disciple of the enigmatic Bengali saint Shri Ramakrishna (1836–86), Vivekananda achieved international fame during his visit to the first World's Parliament of Religions conference, held in Chicago in 1893, where he delivered a tremendously influential speech that helped introduce and also define Hinduism for a global audience. Perhaps more than any other single figure, Vivekananda helped to re-present Hinduism as a truly "global" religion. The term "Hinduism," most scholars agree, is itself a relatively recent invention that is used as a broad label to refer to a tremendously diverse, complex, and heterogeneous body of texts, traditions, rituals, and sects that spread throughout South Asia for over 2,500 years.[25] Vivekananda was a key figure in the modern reimagining of Hinduism not simply as a unified, coherent "ism," but also as a uniquely universal religion. In Vivekananda's persuasive reformulation, Hinduism is a religion rooted in the ideals of inclusivism and universal truth, and thus the one philosophy that could integrate all the world's many traditions through the monistic idea that all religions come from the same source and all spiritual paths are headed toward the same goal.[26]

> The other great idea that the world wants from us today . . . is the eternal grand idea of the spiritual oneness of the whole universe. . . . This is the dictate of Indian philosophy. This oneness is the rationale of all ethics and all spirituality. Europe wants it today just as much as our downtrodden masses do, and this great principle is even now unconsciously forming the basis of all the latest political and social aspirations that are coming up in England, in Germany, in France and in America.[27]

Vivekananda had an aggressive and ambitious vision for the global spread of Hinduism. Coming as he did from the British colonial context, and having experienced the oppressive presence of imperial power and Christian missionary activity, Vivekananda called for a kind of "reverse colonialism." While "Western" nations had conquered India with superior military might and material power, India should now rise up and conquer the globe with its superior spiritual power—with the strength of its ancient religious traditions and sophisticated philosophical thought:

> Up, India, and conquer the world with your spirituality! . . . Now is the time to work so that India's spiritual ideas may penetrate to the West. . . . We must go out, we must conquer the world through our spirituality. . . . The only condition of national life, of awakened and vigorous national life, is the conquest of the world by Indian thought.[28]

different view from Christian colonialism

However, Vivekananda also recognized the advantages of certain aspects of Western power. Above all, he admired the effective organizational structure and missionary zeal of Christian groups such as the Baptist Missionary Society, which he directly emulated in the creation of the "Ramakrishna Mission." Calling upon his disciples to take up their own "Gospel of Shri Ramakrishna" and aggressively proselytize, he declared, "What I want is a band of fiery missionaries.[29] The Swami also respected the material, scientific, and technological advances of the

West, and was one of the first modern gurus to imagine a kind of East-West synthesis in which the best of Indian spirituality would be wedded to the best of European and American social advances and scientific thought: "The Hindu should make the organizational abilities, the pragmatic orientation, the work ethic, the social virtues, and the scientific power of Europe . . . their own. They should overcome their lethargy and advance to new vigor and self-confidence."[30]

Finally, Vivekananda was also one of the first Indian gurus to frankly acknowledge the financial relationship between himself and his American audiences. If the "West" was materially prosperous but spiritually impoverished, India was spiritually rich but materially poor. So it only made sense to bring Americans religious treasures and take their money in exchange: "I have come to America, to earn money myself, and then return to my country and devote the rest of my days to the realisation of this one aim of my life. As our country is poor in social virtues, so this country is lacking in spirituality. I give them spirituality, and they give me money."[31]

While the influence of early figures such as Vivekananda was huge and formative, it was really during the 1960s and 1970s that India-based gurus began to play a more central role in the complex new networks of globalization that were rapidly stretching across Asia, Europe, and the United States. A key figure during these decades was Maharishi Mahesh Yogi (1918–2008), who developed one of the most widely practiced forms of meditation in the world today, Transcendental Meditation (TM). In many ways, the Maharishi was also the first international guru to recognize the incredible potential of mass media and the power of celebrity spokespersons. "He appeared on the various talk shows. . . . He hired PR men and began to court personalities in the movies, TV, and sports. Mia Farrow, then married to Frank Sinatra, became a meditator."[32] The Maharishi's teachings became even more popular in the United States in the 1970s when TV talk-show host Merv Griffin began to speak openly about the benefits of the technique, which created what some called the "Merv wave" of TM.

One of the key moments in the global circulation of spirituality, tourism, and popular culture occurred in 1968, when all four members of the Beatles—at that point easily the biggest musical group in the world—traveled to Rishikesh, India, to stay at the Maharishi's ashram. There they were joined by Mia Farrow and by fellow musicians Donovan and Mike Love of the Beach Boys. Although the Beatles left India just a few months later after disagreements with the Maharishi, their journey helped spark a massive flood of spiritual seekers from the United Kingdom, the United States, and Europe. As Philip Goldberg notes, this "may have been the most momentous spiritual retreat since Jesus spent those forty days in the wilderness," opening a new global superhighway between "the West" and the romanticized idea of a mystical India.[33] Indeed, the Beatles' trip to the "exotic Orient" helped inspire a whole new wave of spiritual tourism to India that continues to this day.[34] Even now, one can see thousands of American and European young people following in the Beatles' footsteps by traveling to Rishikesh, hanging out with sadhus, and meditating next to the Ganges in the foothills of the Himalayas.

Although the Beatles parted ways with the Maharishi, George Harrison would forge a new relationship with the second great global guru of the 1960s, Swami Prabhupada, the founder of the International Society for Krishna Consciousness (ISKCON), better known as Hare Krishna. In 1965, the elderly Swami (1897–1976) traveled from his native Calcutta to the United States, bringing the simple message of devotional love of the Hindu god Krishna. Arriving at the perfect place at the perfect time—New York and then San Francisco at the dawn of the countercultural revolution—Prabhupada quickly attracted thousands of young people from across the United States, England, and Europe.[35] An ISKCON center opened its doors in Haight Ashbury in the very midst of the "summer of love," making a direct appeal to young Americans who were seeking alternatives to traditional religious and cultural values. Prabhupada's movement is also a truly global religious hybrid. With the slogan "Stay high forever," ISKCON appealed directly to many young Americans and Europeans who had become disillusioned with the drugs and sex of the counterculture and were seeking a more permanent sort of altered consciousness.[36]

While most Americans today associate these sorts of global gurus with the counterculture of the 1960s and 1970s, their influence has not only continued but arguably has become even more significant on a transnational stage in the twenty-first century. Thus we find hugely popular figures such as Sathya Sai Baba (1926–2011), whose following not only spread rapidly all over South Asia, America, and Europe, but also to Africa, South America, and East Asia. As Tulasi Srinivas has persuasively argued, the Sai Baba movement offers powerful evidence that globalization is by no means simply a "Western" phenomenon and by no means simply a matter of the "East" responding reactively to ideas and goods flowing from America and Europe.[37] Rather it is a far more decentralized, multifocal, and multidirectional process emerging from countless points across a shifting, interconnected network:

> Whereas globalization was incontrovertibly dominated by Western economic and ideological structures, in actuality the data suggested that India had "emitted" cultural goods, ideologies and ways of being regularly into the network—that cultural goods, services and ideas flowed *out* of India—though little attention was paid to analyzing how cultural ideologies and forms *from* India engaged and affected the global network.[38]

We could easily cite an array of other influential global gurus here, ranging from founders of new international yoga movements such as B.K.S. Iyengar to American importers of Tantric yoga such as Pierre Bernard to hugely popular female figures such as Amma, the "hugging mother," who has drawn a massive global audience into her maternal embrace.[39] Yet Osho-Rajneesh, I will argue, was in many ways the first self-consciously global guru of the modern period, offering key insights not simply into contemporary spirituality but also into broader shifts in global capitalism itself over the last four decades.

A POSTNATIONAL, LATE CAPITALIST, AND POSTMODERN RELIGIOUS MOVEMENT

The Osho-Rajneesh movement, I would suggest, is perhaps best understood as a uniquely *postnational, late capitalist,* and *postmodern* movement, one that reflects—in almost exaggerated form—several broader global currents of the last several decades. With its wildly eclectic practices and its global following drawn from every corner of the planet, this is a movement that is not simply "transnational" but also quite "postnational" in Appadurai's sense of the term. As Appadurai suggests, we are increasingly living in a postnational world, in which new forms of sodality and new forms of community are emerging that "frequently operate beyond the boundaries of the nation."[40] The multinational corporation is just one example of a postnational formation; it now exists alongside other transnational entities, including new globalized religious and spiritual movements, which often exist within, beside, and between the structures of late capitalism.

Although he did not use the exact term "postnational" himself, Osho-Rajneesh articulated a similar ideal already as early as 1978. Over a decade before Appadurai's work, he had announced the death of the nation and the emergence of a new kind of community, of which his own ashram would be one prime example:

[handwritten marginalia: universal brotherhood]

The days of the nation are over, the days of divisions are over, the days of the politicians are over. We are moving into a tremendously new world, a new phase of humanity—and this phase is that there can only be one world now, only one single humanity. And then there will be a tremendous release of energies. . . .

Now there is no need to ask for another world; we are capable of creating paradise here on this earth.[41]

Yet at the same time, with its fluid transnational organization and its unapologetic embrace of materialism, the Osho-Rajneesh movement is also uniquely adapted to the current economic system, which has been variously called "late," "deterritorialized," or "disorganized capitalism." The phrases "late capitalism" and "deterritorialized capitalism" have, of course, been used in many different ways;[42] but here, I find authors such as David Harvey and Fredric Jameson particularly helpful. As Harvey suggests, there was a fundamental shift from the early "Fordist" model of monopoly capitalism, which was predominant until the 1950s, toward the new forms of extremely fluid, protean, and global capitalism that emerged during the late 1960s and 1970s. Harvey uses the phrase "flexible accumulation" to describe this shift to a "late" or postmodern form of capitalism, meaning ever more flexible labor processes, markets, means of production, and patterns of consumption. On a cultural level, this shift was accompanied by a profound sense of "space-time compression," as new means of transportation, travel, and electronic communications accelerated the global circulation of capital, making it faster and faster if not instantaneous.[43] *capitalizing religion*

However, as Jameson points out, late capitalism is by no means a "post-capitalist" system, but rather an even "purer" and more intense form of *hyper-capitalism*, which expands the processes of commodification to more and more aspects of human culture and life—including religion itself. Even "sacred spaces," in other words, become absorbed into the ostensibly "secular" space of the marketplace, as Mike Featherstone puts it in the passage cited at the beginning of the introduction.[44]

In the last decade or so, much of the discussion of late or disorganized capitalism has shifted toward a discussion of "neoliberalism." As Marshall Sahlins asks, "Whatever happened to 'Late Capitalism'?" His conclusion is that "it became Neoliberalism."[45] In many ways, late capitalism and neoliberalism are simply two different narrative frameworks for describing the same global economic phenomenon—the latter decidedly more pessimistic than the former.[46]

As Harvey suggests, there has been an emphatic turn toward neoliberalism as the dominant global economic and political ideology since the 1970s and 1980s. Particularly with the rise of Reaganism in the United States and Thatcherism in the United Kingdom, the neoliberal ideals of privatization, deregulation, and an unquestioning faith in the free market have become increasingly hegemonic not just in "the West" but on a global scale: "The deregulation of everything from airlines to telecommunications to finance opened up new zones of untrammeled market freedoms for powerful corporate interests. . . . The market, depicted ideologically as the way to foster competition and innovation, became a vehicle for the consolidation of monopoly power."[47] As a result of this embrace of deregulation and this unquestioned faith in the market, neoliberalism is also characterized as the "commodification of everything," or the idea that everything from goods and services to ideas and cultural knowledge can be regarded as commodities to be exchanged in the open market: "To presume that markets . . . can best determine all allocative decisions is to presume that everything can in principle be treated as a commodity. Commodification presumes the existence of property rights over processes, things and social relations, that a price can be put on them, and that they can be traded subject to legal contract."[48]

No aspect of modern culture has been exempted from this neoliberal faith in the market—not even spirituality. As Jeremy Carrette and Richard King suggest, much of contemporary spiritual life has not only become commodified but has also been co-opted by a neoliberal economy that needs to train happier, more efficient workers: "From feng shui to holistic medicine, from aromatherapy candles to yoga weekends, from Christian mystics to New Age gurus, spirituality is big business. . . . Spirituality as a cultural trope has also been appropriated by corporate bodies and management consultants to promote efficiency, extend markets and maintain a leading edge in a fast-moving information economy."[49]

Of course, the commodification of spirituality is not entirely new. As scholars such as R. Laurence Moore, Diane Wintson, and others have shown, this process had already begun in the nineteenth-century United States, as religious groups were increasingly forced to compete within a teeming free market of culture alongside not only other spiritual goods but also a vast array of secular commodities.[50] And by the 1980s, with the triumph of neoliberalism, this expansion of the logic of the market to all aspects of culture and this "commodification of everything" had

liberalism favoring
free-market capitalism

become increasingly hegemonic not just in the United States, but on a global scale.[51]

But whether we choose to call it "late capitalism" or "neoliberalism," this transition in the global economy during the late twentieth century occurred almost *simultaneously* with birth of the Osho-Rajneesh movement. With its open embrace of consumption, its broad transnational audience, and its wildly eclectic practices, the Osho-Rajneesh community embodies a new kind of late capitalist spirituality, uniquely adapted to this new global economic and cultural landscape. Rajneesh and his followers were, in fact, quite explicit about their embrace of the emerging global marketplace of the 1960s and 1970s. As he put it in 1978, at the height of the early community in Pune, "This place is a marketplace. Can you find any other place that is more like the market? I could have made the ashram somewhere in the Himalayas. . . . I want to remain part of the marketplace. And this ashram is run almost as part of the marketplace."[52] During the Oregon communal experiment of the 1980s, Rajneesh was even bolder in his use of the rhetoric of capitalism and the market. His claim to "sell contentment" and "sell enlightenment" is perhaps the epitome of neoliberalism as the "commodification of everything"—including intellectual ideas, personal happiness, and spiritual realization. In the words of his infamous secretary and chief organizer during the Oregon phase, Ma Anand Sheela (aka Sheela Silverman), "Our religion is probably the only religion which has synthesized capitalism and religion. . . . It's wonderful. It works."[53]

Like the phrase "late capitalism," the term "postmodernism" has of course been used in a wide range of conflicting ways and in different disciplines, from architecture and literature to philosophy and economics. Here I use the term, again, primarily as it is understood by Fredric Jameson, David Harvey, and Terry Eagleton, among others. As Harvey suggests, as a cultural phenomenon postmodernism really began in the 1960s and 1970s as a counterpart of the shifts taking place in the global economy. As such it does not represent so much a radical break from modernism, but rather an intensification of certain key features of modernism. Perhaps above all, postmodernism tends to be characterized by its "total acceptance of the ephemerality, fragmentation, discontinuity and the chaotic" over the ideals of purpose, design, and determinacy: "Postmodernism swims, even wallows, in the fragmentary and the chaotic currents of change."[54] It tends, moreover, to accept and affirm rather than resist the chaos of the consumer marketplace. As Eagleton famously put it,

> The typical postmodern artifact is playful, self-ironizing and even schizoid. . . . It reacts to the austere autonomy of high modernism by impudently embracing the language of commerce and the commodity. Its stance toward tradition is one of irreverent pastiche.[55]

It is in this sense that postmodernism can be described as the "cultural logic of late capitalism." As Harvey suggests, postmodernism emerged along with the greater shift from a political economy based on Fordism to one based on flexible accumulation and the rapid global transfer of people, ideas, and capital in the late twentieth century.[56]

It is probably no accident that Osho-Rajneesh began teaching at more or less the same time that postmodernism and poststructuralism were emerging as powerful new intellectual trends in Europe and America; indeed, his own rhetoric often closely mirrors that of French authors such as Gilles Deleuze, Michel Foucault, Jean-François Lyotard, and others. Unlike other contemporary gurus, Osho-Rajneesh not only affirmed but celebrated the ephemeral, fragmentary, inconsistent, paradoxical, humorous, and often absurd nature of existence—and of his own teachings. "I am not concerned whether I am consistent, because that is not the purpose," he remarked, in his characteristically parodic style.

> I don't remember what I have said yesterday, so I cannot bother about being consistent—that is too much worry. I can easily contradict myself because I am not trying to have a communication with your rational mind. . . . I am using words just to create silent gaps. The words are not important so I can say anything contradictory, anything absurd, anything unrelated, because my purpose is just to create gaps."[57]

As we will see, Osho-Rajneesh was a unique postmodern character, with a remarkably fluid, protean, and shifting identity (see fig. 2). Between the 1960s and his death in 1990 he was known by at least seven different names. Born Chandra Mohan Jain, he assumed the titles Acharya Rajneesh, Bhagwan Shree Rajneesh, Maitreya, Zorba the Buddha, Osho-Rajneesh, and finally just Osho. Similarly, his teachings are a remarkable postmodern bricolage drawn from a tremendous array of sources, ranging from yoga, Tantra, Taoism, and Sufism to Nietzsche, Freud, and Reich; and yet his teachings were always delivered with a keen sense of humor, playfulness, and self-mocking irony, which made even the very idea of enlightenment "the greatest joke there is."[58] Even Rajneesh's embrace of the marketplace and conspicuous consumption

FIGURE 2. "Close-Up of Bhagwan Shree Rajneesh." Max Gutierrez photo, Oregon Historical Society, bb 006534.

was presented as a joke or a bit of satire. As he later reflected, his absurd collection of ninety-three Rolls-Royces was an ironic parody of the materialism that runs through American politics and religious life itself, as exemplified by bloated Congressmen and billionaire televangelists: "The Americans think they are the richest people in the world. But I created a simple joke with ninety-three Rolls-Royces, and all their pride was gone. Even the president became jealous, the governors became jealous, the clergymen became jealous. . . . I destroyed the pride of America! I don't need ninety-three Rolls-Royces. It was a practical joke."[59] We will see, of course, that Rajneesh's collection of luxury automobiles was a good bit more complicated than a practical joke; yet his unique postmodern sense of irony, his playfulness, and his unabashed consumerism remain quite clear.

FROM THE "PROTESTANT ETHIC AND THE SPIRIT OF CAPITALISM" TO THE "NEO-TANTRIC ETHIC AND THE SPIRIT OF LATE CAPITALISM"

As a unique sort of postnational, late capitalist, and postmodern movement, the Osho-Rajneesh community embodies some of the most profound shifts in modern capitalism itself during the late twentieth and early twenty-first centuries. If Max Weber was correct in identifying an "elective affinity" between Protestant Christianity and early modern capitalism, we might say there is a similar "elective affinity" between the Osho-Rajneesh movement and the dynamics of postindustrial or disorganized capitalism. Perhaps we could describe this as a shift from the Protestant ethic and the spirit of capitalism to the Neo-Tantric ethic and the spirit of late capitalism.

As Weber argued in his classic work of modern sociology, *The Protestant Ethic and the Spirit of Capitalism,* religious movements are enmeshed in deep and complex ways with economic movements. It would, of course, be far too simplistic to say that Protestantism or any other religious movement directly "caused" modern capitalism; social and religious movements do not create material conditions any more than the latter simply cause or give rise to the former. Rather, Weber suggests, it is more accurate to see early Protestant Christianity and early modern capitalism as having a certain fit or affinity that allowed the two to flourish side by side in reciprocal, partially overlapping, and mutually beneficial ways. This affinity was characterized by an ethic of hard work, thriftiness, austerity, and restraint in consumption, or what Weber called a kind of "inner-worldly asceticism."[60]

Following Weber, I will approach the Osho-Rajneesh movement as having a similar kind of complex, reciprocal, and partially overlapping relationship with the contemporary forms of late or deterritorialized capitalism that have emerged since the end of World War II. I will examine three broad periods in the growth of the Osho-Rajneesh movement as it traveled from India to the United States and back again, each of which had a particular fit or affinity with broader transformations in global capitalism between the 1960s and the present. During the early period of the movement in Pune during the 1960s and 1970s, Rajneesh was among the first and most vocal intellectuals to begin criticizing India's socialist-leaning economics and to call for a turn to American-style capitalism; as such, he was at the forefront of India's own turn away from socialism and toward the global capitalist marketplace in the 1980s and 1990s.[61] During the Oregon period in the 1980s, the Rajneesh community largely accepted many of the policies of neoliberalism that became dominant during the Reagan era, including the belief that "government is the problem," an almost religious faith in the market, and a subsequent "commodification of everything." The Rajneesh empire during this period also evolved into an incredibly elaborate, fluid, and protean transnational network of corporate entities that in many ways epitomized what David Harvey has called "flexible accumulation," the hallmark of postmodern forms of capitalism.[62] Finally, since the 1990s, the new Osho resort in Pune has evolved once again into a hybridized cross between a spiritual retreat and an international luxury hotel, which is perhaps ideally suited to a twenty-first century global audience of tourists, travelers, and spiritual seekers.

Simultaneously, the Osho-Rajneesh movement also reflects shifting attitudes toward the body, sexuality, and consumption that have accompanied these broader economic and cultural shifts in the twentieth and twenty-first centuries. As Bryan S. Turner notes, the early capitalist attitude based on the Protestant work ethic, thriftiness, and inner-worldly asceticism has been progressively displaced by a late capitalist attitude based on consumption, sensual pleasure, and physical enjoyment. In consumer culture, the body ceases to be a vessel of sin or an unruly vessel of desires that must be disciplined; rather, the body is seen as the ultimate source of gratification and fulfillment: "In the growth of a consumer society with its emphasis on the athletic/beautiful body we can see a major transformation of Western values from an emphasis on control of the body for ascetic reasons to the manipulation of the body for aesthetic purposes."[63]

As we will see in the chapters that follow, Osho-Rajneesh was not merely a reflection but an epitome—and arguably even a driver—of this shift from an early capitalist Protestant ethic to a late capitalist consumer ethic. His central ideal of "Zorba the Buddha" is itself the epitome of the broader turn away from inner-worldly asceticism toward the full acceptance of the body, physical pleasure, and material consumption:

> I am a spiritual playboy. . . . I call myself Zorba the Buddha, and that's my whole life effort, to bring Zorba and Buddha closer. I don't want a dichotomy of the spiritual and the material. I want the spiritual and the material as one whole. They are. The division is a schizophrenic state in humanity, and all the religions are criminals in that sense. They have created a split in man. Your body is separate, your soul is separate. You have to fight with the body,

you have to remain celibate, you have to fast. . . . To me this is simply garbage, just nonsense.[64]

Explicitly rejecting the asceticism of traditional religions, including even that of India's national hero, Mahatma Gandhi, Rajneesh turned instead to the more radical path of Tantra for his primary inspiration. Traditional forms of Hindu and Buddhist Tantra in Asia actually have relatively little to do with sex—at least not in the sense of sexual pleasure—focusing more on secrecy, esoteric ritual, and power. But Rajneesh was arguably the most important figure in the modern popularization and redefinition of Tantra (or "Neo-Tantra") as a spiritual path primarily focused on sensual pleasure and physical enjoyment.[65] As Rajneesh described it, the Tantric path is one of total acceptance, the "Zorba the Buddha" path that celebrates both the spiritual and sensual, the otherworldly and the innerworldly, the transcendent and the material aspects of our existence, thus offering a holistic rather than dualistic worldview:

> Tantric acceptance is total, it doesn't split you. All the religions of the world except Tantra have created split personalities, have created schizophrenia. . . . They say the good has to be achieved and the bad denied, the devil has to be denied and God accepted. . . . Tantra says a transformation is possible. . . . Transformation comes when you accept your total being.[66]

At the same time, Osho-Rajneesh's Neo-Tantra also embodied his ideal wedding of spirituality and capitalism, the quest for liberation and the goal of material prosperity. From the "Zorba the Buddha" perspective, there can be no real disagreement between one's spiritual and material aims, even in the acquisition of a fleet of Rolls-Royces. As he put it in his characteristically ironic and self-mocking style in an interview in 1985, "I am the rich man's guru. . . . My conception of a beautiful flowering being is not that of austerity. It is of luxury. . . . To me, all religions of the world up to now have been sado-masochistic. My religion is for the first time life-affirming. . . . All other religions are looking after the poor. At least leave me alone to look after the rich."[67] Again, it would be far too simplistic to describe the Osho-Rajneesh movement as either a direct causal factor or a mere by-product of the shifts in the global economy that took place in the second half of the twentieth century. Rather, following Weber, it is perhaps better understood as having a deep elective affinity with the dynamics of late capitalism.

In this sense, we will see, the Osho-Rajneesh movement also poses some important challenges to many classical sociological models. Weber, for example, had assumed that religious charisma of the sort that we see in leaders such as Osho-Rajneesh is inherently at odds with capitalist bureaucracy. For Weber, "charismatic domination is the very opposite of bureaucratic domination. . . . Charisma rejects all rational economic conduct."[68] From its beginnings in India in the 1970s, however, the Osho-Rajneesh community was a highly charismatic and wildly prolific movement that was also uniquely adapted to the logic and organization of late twentieth-century capitalism. Indeed, the Osho-Rajneesh movement might be described as a "charismatic variant of a multinational corporation" and even as a kind of "re-enchanted capitalism," working fluidly within the flexible new patterns of the global economy.[69]

SOURCES AND METHODOLOGICAL CHALLENGES

With a few exceptions,[70] most of the literature on Osho-Rajneesh and his following has fallen into two categories at two extremes. On the one hand, there are countless works by admirers and followers that celebrate Osho-Rajneesh as a radically new kind of master who inspired a profound form of global spirituality for the modern world, yet was tragically misunderstood by an intolerant and narrow-minded society.[71] On the other hand, there at least as many accounts by journalists, ex-members, and critical scholars that dismiss Osho-Rajneesh as a mere opportunistic retailer of exotic Eastern spiritual wares and regard his following primarily as a bunch of affluent spiritual consumers hoping to combine their search for enlightenment with their quest for material success in a capitalist marketplace.[72]

My own view is that this guru and the movement he inspired are far too interesting and complicated to be reduced to either of these common interpretations. It is surely true that Osho-Rajneesh was a guru who embraced the ideology of capitalism and created a movement that explicitly combined spirituality and business. Yet it is no less true that he was one of the first modern intellectuals to begin speaking about a kind of postnational society and to create a successful transnational movement that undertook incredibly progressive experiments, not just in spiritual practice but in organic farming, land reclamation, and recycling.[73] As such, I will suggest, the Osho movement is a striking illustration of the deep "cultural contradictions of late capitalism" and also of the "split character of globalization"—its potential to inspire both new forms of economic exploitation and new forms of communal experimentation.[74]

The sources for this book have been gathered over a period of fifteen years in the course of both archival and ethnographic work in India and the United States. One of the nice things about studying Osho-Rajneesh is that there is certainly no shortage of material to consider. Osho-Rajneesh himself is credited with an astonishing list of books, audio recordings, and DVDs, numbering in the thousands. The movement also produced an astounding number of personal accounts by both loyal followers and disgruntled ex-members, which provide fascinating insights into the growth of the community from the late 1960s to the present. On top of all that, there is a massive body of magazines, newsletters, brochures, flyers, and now web-based material, and I have spent years wading through the mountain of print matter alone.[75]

Beyond the textual record, however, I have also made use of a vast body of far more interesting—and in some cases more problematic—archival and ethnographic sources. Both the University of Oregon and the Oregon Historical Society have truly remarkable archival collections, including a vast number of legal documents, photographs, and fascinating ephemera (such as safe-sex kits and anti-Rajneesh T-shirts). Most of this has never been examined in any thorough way.[76]

The interview material includes conversations with high-level leaders in the community, such as Osho's former personal physician, Swami Amrito (aka George Meredith), his first official biographer, Vasant Joshi, and younger adherents who have joined the movement since Osho's death, such as cartoonist Sudi Narayanan and others in the new generation of followers. However, this book will also feature accounts from numerous ex-members who left the movement in disillusionment, such as Will Foster, who joined the Oregon commune in 1980s but now regards Osho as a brilliant but deeply unethical figure.

Of course, the use of material derived from both ex-members and current members does raise some difficult methodological questions. Until relatively recently, many scholars of new religious movements have been wary of using the accounts of ex-members, assuming them to be too biased to serve as reliable sources of information. In the opinion of the respected British sociologist Bryan R. Wilson, the ex-member or "apostate" is often so driven by the need for self-justification, vindication, and media attention that his or her narrative cannot be accepted by either the scholarly community or the courts. As Wilson put it in a statement republished by the Church of Scientology (and used in Scientology-related court cases),

> Neither the objective sociological researcher nor the court of law can readily regard the apostate as a reliable source of evidence. He must always be seen

as one whose personal history predisposes him to bias with respect to both his previous religious commitment and affiliations, the suspicion must arise that he acts from a personal motivation to vindicate himself and to regain his self-esteem, by showing himself to have been first a victim but subsequently to have become a redeemed crusader.[77]

More recently, however, authors have begun to challenge this wholesale rejection of ex-members' accounts. After all, all sources of information—including current members—have particular biases, commitments, and axes to grind, so it is not immediately evident that an ex-member's account would necessarily be any more biased than that of a member in good standing. Indeed, as I discovered in the course of my research on Scientology, the accounts of current members of the church were often *far* more problematic and biased than those of ex-Scientologists.[78] As Lewis Carter notes in his discussion of "apostate" or ex-member accounts, "Each source of information—of believers, apostates, ethnographers and opponents—has different strengths and weaknesses." While ex-members will likely be more negative in their views of a given movement, active members have their own agendas and biases, typically "being the most motivated by both perception and by group pressure to emphasize positive aspects of those practices and to censor damaging perceptions."[79] Moreover, it seems odd to dismiss an account simply on the grounds that it comes from an ex-member. After all, few scholars or courts today would dismiss the account of a victim of child sexual abuse simply because s/he happens to be "ex-Catholic."[80] Similarly, few would dismiss the account of a survivor of the Jonestown murder-suicides simply because s/he is an ex-member of Peoples Temple. On the contrary, those ex-member accounts have been critical to reconstructing the complex history of this new religion and its final days.[81]

Thus, more recent scholars such as Tulasi Srinivas have argued that our understanding of many new religions has actually been skewed by ignoring the accounts of ex-members and listening only to those of current believers. As she suggests in her study of the global Sathya Sai Baba movement, a rich and detailed picture of any movement requires that we take seriously, analyze, and critically examine all available narratives—those of former as well as current members: "To understand the construction of identity in this world of conflict . . . we cannot afford to disinclude any particular voice in measuring the locus of disagreements and rival claims."[82]

In short, the narratives of *both* current and former members are potentially valuable and potentially problematic. Both therefore need to be subjected to respectful criticism and a certain "hermeneutics of suspicion" in order to create a rich, nuanced, and multilayered portrait of a particular religious movement.

. . .

This book is organized historically and thematically in six chapters, each of which covers roughly one decade in the development of the Osho-Rajneesh movement from the 1950s to the present. The chapters will also situate this movement very concretely in the shifting social, political, and economic context of these decades, examining the ways in which this community at once reflected and creatively responded to the changing dynamics of Indian society, American culture, and global capitalism in the post–Indian independence/post–World War II era.

Chapter 1, "India's Most Dangerous Guru," will trace the emergence of Bhagwan Shree Rajneesh as a hugely popular but also tremendously controversial spiritual leader in the decades following India's independence. After achieving enlightenment in 1953, Rajneesh quickly established a reputation as the most iconoclastic guru of modern India, mocking national heroes and attacking established religions. With his rejection of all established religious institutions and his critique of mainstream politics, Rajneesh represented in many ways a radical response to the turmoil of Indian religious and political life in the years after independence. Yet with his uniquely protean, shifting, and plural identity, rapidly changing names and adapting his message to new audiences, Rajneesh was also a uniquely "postmodern" sort of guru.

Chapter 2, "Beware of Socialism!" will situate Rajneesh's early movement amid the debates over Indian religion, society, and economy in the late 1960s. Not only did Rajneesh make a name for himself through his iconoclastic spiritual ideas, but he was also an outspoken critic of Indian economics and an early advocate of American-style capitalism. His early book *Beware of Socialism!* was at the forefront of a greater shift in India away from Nehruvian socialism toward an increasing embrace of capitalism and the larger global marketplace. Setting himself up as a kind of "anti-Gandhi," he rejected the asceticism, simplicity, and nationalism of the Mahatma in favor of a full acceptance of sensuality, the body, and the global economy. This antisocialist, anti-Gandhian ideal was also realized in Rajneesh's first spiritual commune in Pune during the 1970s. Attracting a growing following of Americans and Europeans, the Pune ashram became a kind of global node that brought together Western capitalism and Eastern spirituality in a unique new transnational religious experiment.

Chapter 3, "From Sex to Superconsciousness," will examine Rajneesh's teachings on sexuality and Tantra in the early 1970s, which perhaps more than anything else helped propel him to international fame and controversy. Rajneesh's philosophy was a complex hybrid of Hindu Tantra and post-Freudian psychoanalysis, particularly the work of Wilhelm Reich, which Rajneesh cited repeatedly in his lectures. Rajneesh was arguably the most important figure in the modern transformation of Tantra, which he presented as a form of spiritual sexuality and marketed primarily to a European and American audience of spiritual seekers.

Chapter 4, "The Messiah America Has Been Waiting For," will focus on the Rajneesh community's transplantation to the United States in the 1980s and the foundation of the utopian city of Rajneeshpuram in Oregon. While relatively short-lived, Rajneeshpuram was surely one of the most remarkable religious experiments in American history, growing in just a few years into perhaps the largest, most progressive, most lucrative, but also controversial utopian community of the twentieth century. However, Rajneeshpuram was no less remarkable for its spectacular collapse, largely under the leadership of Rajneesh's secretary, Ma Anand Sheela (aka Sheela Silverman), who engaged in a stunning array of criminal acts during an escalating war with the local community of Antelope, Oregon. Ironically, even as Rajneesh railed against President Reagan, his Oregon experiment was in many ways a weird spiritual mirror of Reagan's America and of capitalism itself during the 1980s, reflecting many of the same neoliberal ideals of deregulation and free markets, along with periodic hostile takeovers and financial scandals.

Chapter 5, "Osho," will follow the movement's relocation to India following Rajneesh's arrest and deportation from the United States in 1985. Amazingly, the community became even more successful and prosperous upon its return to Pune, where Rajneesh assumed the new title Osho (derived from the name for a Zen Buddhist priest and also from the "oceanic feeling" of mystical experience). The new Osho community gradually evolved from a spiritual ashram into an "International Meditation Report," embodying the "Zorba the Buddha" ideal by offering a smorgasbord of spiritual practices from all the world's traditions in the luxurious atmosphere of a five-star international hotel.

Chapter 6, "OSHO®?," will then examine the most recent legal, financial, and political struggles over Osho's legacy in India and around the world. Since the guru's death, the Osho community has become increasingly splintered, with a group centered in Pune, led primarily by non-Indian members, and a rival group centered in New Delhi, led primarily by Indian members—thus highlighting the nationalist and transnational tensions within the community. Among other disputes, the two groups have fought major legal battles over the rights to the name Osho itself (which the Osho International Foundation claims to have trademarked), raising much larger and more complex questions about trademark and copyright in a religious movement. Similar legal battles for trademark and copyright have been waged by a wide array of other global spiritual movements, including various forms of yoga, such as Bikram Yoga, new religions, such as the Church of Scientology, and many others.

In the conclusion, I will discuss Osho-Rajneesh's legacy and the impact of his life, teachings, and broader movement on the global dynamics of spirituality in the twenty-first century. Although Osho-Rajneesh himself died over twenty years ago, his influence has not only persisted but is now pervasive throughout much of contemporary spirituality, particularly the loose and eclectic body of spiritual beliefs and practices collectively labeled "New Age." His deliberate fusion of the spiritual and the material, the transcendent and the commercial, is ubiquitous throughout New Age literature, giving rise to what some have called "New Age capitalism." At the same time, Osho-Rajneesh's unique form of Neo-Tantra has been the most important influence in the transformation of traditional Hindu and Buddhist Tantra into the "spiritual sex" that has been so widely popularized since the 1970s. And finally, the most recent struggles over Osho's trademark and copyrights are part of a much larger debate surrounding spirituality and intellectual property that may well become one of the defining issues in twenty-first-century religious life.

The Osho-Rajneesh movement, I will show, is a particularly striking embodiment of what Appadurai calls the "split character of globalization." On the one hand, it exemplifies how globalization opens new possibilities for alternative forms of collective life or postnational communities, such as the Rajneesh experiments in Oregon and Pune; on the other hand, it is an illustration of how globalization also draws individuals and groups ever more into the disciplinary control of global capitalism and the ever-expanding logic of the market.[83]

CHAPTER I

"India's Most Dangerous Guru"

Rajneesh and India after Independence

I teach utter rebellion. . . . If we want to change society,
society is going to be offended.

—Bhagwan Shree Rajneesh

Osho is the most dangerous man since Jesus Christ. . . . He's
obviously a very effective man, otherwise he wouldn't be such
a threat. He's saying the same things that nobody else has the
courage to say. A man who has all kinds of ideas, they're not
only inflammatory—they also have a resonance of truth that
scares the pants off the control freaks.

—Novelist Tom Robbins

From his first public lectures, Rajneesh presented himself and his ideas
as radical, iconoclastic, and dangerous. Never conforming to the traditional model of a "guru" who had sat at the feet of another enlightened
master in a long line of teachers stretching back into the hoary past,
Rajneesh claimed instead to be a self-enlightened being, a radically new
sort of guru who had no teacher of his own, but discovered spiritual
awakening through his own initiative and self-experimentation. Similarly, the message he brought was a powerfully iconoclastic one, mocking the great religions of the past and challenging his followers to find
their own way to inner truth. Known variously as "the fiery teacher
who destroys age-old myths and beliefs, traditions and teachings"[1] and
even as "the most dangerous man in the world,"[2] Rajneesh was famous
for infuriating everyone, from theologians and journalists to politicians
on both ends of the political spectrum. As his first official biographer

Vasant Joshi put it, he "refutes Marx and socialist ideas, criticizes Freud and Jung, cracks jokes at the people in the Vatican . . . and does not disguise his contempt for politicians. The Hindus condemn him as a hedonist, the Communists belittle him as a spiritualist, the journalists describe him as a 'sex guru,' and one scholar called him 'the Hugh Heffner of the spiritual world.'"[3]

In order to understand Rajneesh's iconoclastic religious spirit, however, we need to place him within his larger historical, political, social, and economic context, in the new state of India in the decades after independence. Rajneesh claimed that his enlightenment experience occurred in 1953, just six years after India became independent, at a time of tremendous religious, social, and political turmoil in the fledging democracy.[4] The two nation-states of India and Pakistan had just barely been created, demarcated in large part along religious boundaries, and India was struggling to negotiate its role within the complex Cold War landscape dominated by the United States and the Soviet Union, striving to navigate a middle way between "the capitalist West and the communist soviet block."[5]

Rajneesh's bold and at times abrasive message was in many ways a direct challenge to his Indian audience during the decades of the 1950s and 1960s. Even as modern India was shedding the bonds of its British colonial masters and struggling to negotiate its identity in relation to America and Europe, Rajneesh was calling for a more radical shedding of all bonds to any masters—political, social, or spiritual. And just as India in the postindependence era was beginning to open up to a wide array of non-Indian cultural and intellectual influences, so, too, Rajneesh was sharing his remarkably eclectic teachings, incorporating not only a vast array of ideas drawn from Hinduism, Buddhism, and Sufism, but also elements of European psychoanalysis and philosophy. That these different influences sometimes conflicted with or contradicted one another was not really a problem for Rajneesh. Indeed, his message was in many ways deliberately contradictory, resisting any kind of system, coherent ideology, or dogma: "I am a man who is consistently inconsistent," he noted. "[Consistency] is impossible for me: I live in the moment, and whatsoever I am saying right now is true only for this moment. I have no reference with my past and I don't think of the future at all."[6]

Even Rajneesh's own biography is something of a confusing pastiche. As Lewis Carter notes, the narrative of his life offered by Rajneesh and his followers is less a simple historical document than a kind of "reconstructed

Mythos" that imaginatively re-presents his various transformations of identity, his shifting personas from young Chandra Mohan Jain to "Acharya Rajneesh" to "Bhawgan Shree Rajneesh" to "Maitreya," and finally to "Osho."[7] In this sense, his biography is not unlike those of other new religious leaders, such as L. Ron Hubbard or Madame Blavatsky, who also fashioned a kind of "hagiographic mythology" around themselves, woven of various threads of historical and imaginative narrative.[8]

With his iconoclastic, parodic, and paradoxical teachings and his mytho-historical biography, Rajneesh is thus not just the first truly global guru but also perhaps the first "postmodern guru" of the twentieth century. As we saw in the introduction, the term "postmodernism" has been used in wildly different and often contradictory ways; however, as authors such as David Harvey suggest, postmodernism is characterized above all by its emphasis on play, chance, irony, and indeterminacy over the ideals of purpose, design, and determinacy.[9] And this focus on fragmentation, play, and indeterminacy extends above all to the idea of the self or subject, which is likewise seen as multiple and shifting rather than singular and homogenous. As Michel Foucault famously put it in 1966, "Man is an invention of a recent date. And one perhaps nearing its end," destined to be erased like a face drawn in the sand at the edge of the sea.[10] In the wake of Foucault, a variety of postmodern theorists would continue to deconstruct and dethrone the idea of a unified or "sovereign subject," articulating "an emerging post-humanist epistemic space."[11] As Fredric Jameson observes, "Not even Einsteinian relativity, or the multiple subjective worlds of the modernists, is capable of giving adequate figuration to this process, which . . . makes itself felt by the so-called death of the subject, or more exactly, the fragmented and schizophrenic decentering of this last."[12]

Rajneesh's early following emerged almost *simultaneously* in the 1960s with the postmodern turn and its "incredulity toward metanarratives," along with its embrace of play, irony, and indeterminacy over purpose, design, and determinacy.[13] Yet Rajneesh also challenged the very idea of a fixed, permanent selfhood or identity, instead calling for the birth of a "new man" who would be "a liquid human being," constantly flowing, resisting all fixed attitudes, orthodoxies, and above all religious dogmas.[14] As we will see in chapter 2, this paradoxical ideal of a "liquid" and constantly shifting identity would become the basis for a new, equally "liquid," fluid, and flexible community in the 1970s and 1980s. All of this would make Rajneesh an extremely attractive figure in the rapidly changing young India of the decades after independence, but also one deeply threatening to those who supported the status quo.

FROM CHANDRA MOHAN JAIN TO BHAGWAN SHREE RAJNEESH

Part of the difficulty in reconstructing Rajneesh's biography is that it is in many ways not the story of just one person. Rather, the figure that emerges from Rajneesh's narrative is a fluid, shifting, and often contradictory one, less a singular being than a kind of playful trickster who experimented with multiple identities at different moments for different audiences. As former follower James Gordon recalls, "As I listened to Rajneesh's tapes and read his books, I thought of Proteus, the elusive mythical shape-changer; of Lao-Tzu, the Chinese sage; and of Ba'al Shem Tov, whose ecstatic celebration of the divinity in daily life illuminated the eighteenth century Hasidic movement."[15] Even his posthumous *Autobiography of a Spiritually Incorrect Mystic* describes Rajneesh's many personas as "the many faces of a man who never was," and these faces include his various labels as the "sex guru," the "con man," the "cult leader," the "joker," the "Rolls-Royce guru," and the "Master."[16] In the words of Indian journalist M. V. Kamath, quoted at the end of Rajneesh's first biography, Rajneesh is such an iconoclastic figure that he is better understood not as one man but as multiple, shifting identities:

> There has been no other man like this before. . . . Like Whitman, Rajneesh is an iconoclast, a maverick, a hater of cant, superstition, snobbery and holier-than-thou-ism, and a lover of the good things of life. He will make a most remarkable statement of purpose and philosophy and illustrate it with the most outrageous joke or story picked straight from *Playboy* or *Penthouse*. There is no way one can compartmentalize this man. It would almost seem that he is not one man but many men. . . . Rajneesh is Moses, Walt Whitman, Buddha, Jesus Christ and Ramana Maharshi all rolled into one. . . . It is ridiculous to try to define this man. He challenges definition. His technique is to put everything upside down on its head . . . and make you look at the world from that vantage point. He is a disturbing man because he makes you question the validity of all your principles.[17]

Likewise, Rajneesh's biography is also a complex and shifting sort of postmodern narrative. As Rajneesh himself argued, historical "facts" don't really matter in the creation of a biography; what matters is the deeper spiritual truth and the evolution of an individual's consciousness, which may not necessarily correspond to fact in a historical sense:

The first thing you have to understand is the difference between the fact and the truth. Ordinary history takes care about the facts—what actually happened in the world of matter, the incidents. It does not take care about the truth because truth does not happen in the world of matter, it happens in consciousness. . . . One day we will have to write the whole of history with a totally different orientation, because the facts are trivia—although they are material, they don't matter.[18]

While Rajneesh initially eschewed the idea of writing an autobiography, he did include numerous personal vignettes in his lectures. Many of these were later woven into a biography by Joshi in his 1982 book, *The Awakened One,* and then reworked in various other official narratives.[19] While in Oregon, Rajneesh dictated a series of anecdotes from his early life (from a dentist's chair while under the influence of nitrous oxide, according to one close disciple),[20] which was published in 1985 as *Glimpses of a Golden Childhood.* In 2000, the Osho International Foundation released *Autobiography of a Spiritually Incorrect Mystic,* which edited and repackaged the guru's life story from the perspective of the current Osho movement. The most exhaustive and also most hagiographic biography appeared still later in nine volumes and 3,600 pages in Hindi under the title *Ek Phakkad Messiah* and was later published in a single, abridged English volume as *The Rebellious Enlightened Master* (2006).[21] Finally, there are also a few "dissenting" accounts of Rajneesh's early life, such as the critical narrative provided by his former bodyguard, Hugh Milne. After visiting Rajneesh's family members in the village of Drug, Milne found that they had rather different recollections of the young Rajneesh, which departed significantly from the official accounts.[22]

In sum, Rajneesh's biography is not so much a singular, linear narrative of one individual but rather a far more protean, fragmented, shifting patchwork of multiple narratives and identities. Some of these identities, according to his recollections, even preceded this particular lifetime and included past lives dating back many centuries. For example, he recalled having been a previous spiritual master in the twelfth century, who had established a mystical school in a mountainous area and then died at the age of 106 after a twenty-one-day fast.[23]

In his twentieth-century identity, however, he was born Chandra Mohan Jain in the small village of Kuchwada, Madhya Pradesh, in 1931. Nicknamed Rajneesh, he was raised by his maternal grandparents, an elderly Jain couple, who gave him remarkable freedom and treated him as a "rajah" or king.[24] As his biographer Joshi recalls, Rajneesh was from his earliest years a rebellious and antiauthoritarian figure, who also had a fascination with danger and the limits of mortality: "His school years are described as a period of rebellion against all authority, organizing gangs to terrorize villages and reckless 'experiments' in which he would lead or push others into life-threatening circumstances."[25]

It is perhaps not insignificant that Rajneesh was born to a Jain family and raised during the 1930s. As Christophe Jaffrelot notes, the Hindu Nationalist movement, which had emerged first in the nineteenth century, really began to expand and crystallize as an ideology in the period between the 1920s and 1940s. The same period also witnessed increasing tensions between Hindu nationalists and Muslims, which would help lead in part to India's partition and its violent aftermath.[26] Coming from a Jain background, Rajneesh was not only an outsider to these divisions, but also deeply cynical toward all forms of religious or political orthodoxies throughout his life.

If there is any one recurring theme in the various accounts of Rajneesh's early life, it is his preoccupation with and experience of death. Long before postmodernists and deconstructionists in Europe began to talk about the idea, Rajneesh was fascinated with the possibility of the "death of the subject" (an idea also discussed in the Buddhist tradition 2,000 years earlier, we should note). Thus he recalled that an astrologer had predicted at his birth that it was "almost certain that this child is going to die at the age of twenty-one. Every seven years he will have to face death."[27] So his parents were also said to have been concerned about his possible death throughout his childhood. In his youth, Rajneesh then had several actual encounters with death that would have a profound impact on him. The first was the death of his maternal grandfather when Rajneesh was seven years old, an event that left a permanent emotional scar. He recalled watching his grandfather die slowly for three days, after which he himself refused to eat or get up for three days. As Rajneesh put it, "His death became for me the death of all attachments. Therefore I could not establish a bond of relationship with anyone. . . . Since then, I have been alone."[28] A second early experience was the death of a childhood girlfriend in 1947, which pushed him into a deep state of depression that lasted several years. Preoccupied with the question of mortality, he spent large amounts of time in cremation grounds observing dead bodies and following funeral processes. "Death," he put it, "is such a beautiful phenomenon, and one of the most mysterious"; and from an early age he recalled thinking about the day of his own death.[29]

Rajneesh was also remembered for hurling himself into life-threatening situations, such as jumping into a dangerously flooded river and leaping from a seventy-foot bridge. Yet he is also said to have been fascinated with observing others confront the fact of their own mortality. For example, he recalled holding a friend who was unable to swim under water until he became desperate, and then eagerly asked him about the experience afterward.[30]

As a student, Rajneesh appears to have been constantly butting up against authority and getting into trouble with teachers and university administrators. At age nineteen, he began his studies at Hitkarini College in Jabalpur, but after conflicts with an instructor soon transferred to D. N. Jain College. Here he was apparently so disruptive that he was not required to attend classes but only to take exams, and so he used his free time to work for a local newspaper and begin public speaking. As Rajneesh himself later recalled, he seemed almost compelled to cause trouble and generate arguments with his instructors, even if only for his own entertainment: "With or without reason, I was creating controversies. . . . There seemed even if just for fun a necessity to create controversies."[31]

Rajneesh's first major spiritual transformation took place in the early 1950s. After a long period of intense physical and emotional distress, he underwent a profound experience that he described as full enlightenment. As he later recounted the episode, he had gone through a period of intense questing, during which he challenged and discarded all religions, philosophies, scriptures, and any other systems of truth. Krishna, Buddha, Mahavir, Jesus, the Vedas, the Koran—nothing seemed to provide a stable foundation for certainty, and he was left spiritually adrift in a kind of "dark night of the soul." As he put it, "Questions remained without any answer. . . . I was as good as mad. . . . I was in a deep sea. . . . without any boat or bank anywhere. . . . My condition was utter darkness. It was as if I had fallen into a deep well. . . . My condition was full of tensions, insecurity and danger."[32] He then went through a period of intense asceticism and physical austerity, during which he went for days without feeling hunger or thirst, running five to ten miles every morning and evening, until all those around him also thought he was mad.[33] His distressed parents took him to one physician after another, trying Ayurvedic doctors and religious specialists.

At last, on the brink of complete despair, he simply gave up and stopped struggling. On the seventh day after he had given up his discipline, in March 1953, his enlightenment experience occurred. Like the historical Buddha, who had also first tried extreme asceticism before abandoning that path, he simply allowed his own enlightened nature to manifest itself spontaneously within him. As he later recalled, this experience was a kind of inner explosion that burst inside of him like a ball of blissful energy and illuminated the entire universe around him in an incredible and intoxicating ecstasy (which, interestingly enough, he also described, using Western counterculture language, as being "high"):

> These seven days were of tremendous transformation, total transformation. And the last day the presence of a totally new energy, a new light and new delight, became so intense that it was almost unbearable, as if I was exploding, as if I was going mad with blissfulness. The new generation in the West has the right word for it: I was blissed out, stoned.[34]
>
> And the day the search stopped, the day I was not seeking for something, the day I was not expecting something to happen, it started happening. A new energy arose—out of nowhere. It was not coming from any source. It was coming from nowhere and everywhere. It was in the trees and in the rocks and in the sky and in the sun and in the air. . . . The day effort ceased, I also ceased.[35]

He would also describe this experience as a profound sort of death and rebirth—the dissolution of his old identity and the birth of a new man, in which his entire former body and experience of the world were shattered and replaced by a new selfhood and a new experience of reality. In many ways, this was the culmination of his early obsession with death, now fulfilled in his own experience of psychological death. While postmodernist philosophers of the 1960s and 1970s would later talk about the "death of man" and the "death of the subject" in abstract terms,[36] Rajneesh appears to have undergone his own personal deconstruction of the rational ego and ordinary human consciousness:

> I became non-existential and non-existent. That night I died and was reborn. But the one that was reborn had nothing to do with that which died. . . . The person who had lived for many, many lives, for millennia, simply died. . . . Another being, absolutely new . . . . started to exist.[37]
>
> The whole day was strange, stunning, and it was a shattering experience. . . . I was becoming a nonbeing, what Buddha calls *anatta*. Boundaries were disappearing, distinctions were disappearing. Mind was disappearing; it was millions of miles away.[38]

As Rajneesh himself notes here, the idea of the loss of ego or extinction of the self is a traditional one and lies at the very heart of the Buddhist ideal of *nirvana* (snuffing out). Yet, as we will see, Rajneesh's particular articulation of the death of the self was also in many ways a rather postmodern one, giving birth to a new series of fluid, protean, playful identities that he would experiment with for the next forty years.

It is also significant that Rajneesh's enlightenment experience took place in 1953, less than six years after India's independence. As Ramchandra Guha notes in *India after Gandhi,* this was a period when the fledging nation was struggling with a variety of social conflicts on multiple axes of caste, language, class, and above all religion.[39] Just a few years before, during the anguish of partition, much of the nation had been torn by massive rioting between Hindus and Muslims. Meanwhile, the new democracy was negotiating its complex relationship with the capitalism of America and Europe and the socialism of China and the Soviet Union. As we will see in the following chapters, all of these currents are embodied in Rajneesh's teachings, which at once reject all religious orthodoxies and call for radical reform of India's economic policies.

Ironically, despite having become fully enlightened at the age of twenty-one, Rajneesh actually continued his studies and received his BA and MA in philosophy in 1955 and 1957. He then went on to teach philosophy, first at Raipur Sanskrit College. Already a controversial and widely known figure, Rajneesh continued to antagonize his fellow teachers and superiors. As one administrator at Raipur Sanskrit College put it, "This man is dangerous. He will destroy my students' morality, character, and religion."[40] And Rajneesh himself embraced this "dangerous" image, presenting himself as a radical, provocative, iconoclastic, and refreshingly original teacher who challenged his listeners to remember that the very idea of "God" or "the divine" is itself a potentially threatening thing: "God is very dangerous. There exists no other dangerous word comparable to God. God means to live a life of spontaneity, of nature."[41]

Rajneesh subsequently moved on to teach at Jabalpur University in 1958 and also began traveling and lecturing throughout India under the title Acharya [teacher or professor] Rajneesh. During this period, he began to hone his style as a deliberately provocative, controversial, but also entertaining lecturer, creating his own Indian version of a countercultural revolution that in many ways mirrored the countercultural movements emerging in America, England, and Europe. As James Gordon reflects on this period in Rajneesh's career,

> In the 1960s, Rajneesh's mood, like the times, changed. While a graduate student and lecturer at Jabalpur, he stormed across India, provoking like some itinerant anarchist organizer. These talks revealed Rajneesh's affinity with the contemporary Western rebels who would soon be drawn to him. . . . Like Ken Kesey spiking fruit punch with LSD he was trying to disrupt conventional patterns of thought and behavior.[42]

Rejecting not only the austere Jainism of his family but also all religious orthodoxy, Rajneesh was beginning to craft his own unique brand of iconoclastic spirituality, which would later flourish in the 1970s and 1980s. Indeed, the Jainism of his childhood had become for him really the "prototype for the narrowness and stupidity of all organized religion," and he would later embrace all those things that Jainism had rejected: sensuality, sexuality, material enjoyment, and wealth.[43] At the same time, he would also present himself as a kind of "anti-guru" or "guru-less guru," an enlightened being who came from no established lineage of masters and taught a radically antiauthoritarian message. While most other religious teachers in India had certified themselves by connection to a guru and to a lineage that might stretch back beyond written history, ideally to a deity such as Shiva, Vishnu, or the Goddess, Rajneesh was one of the first to proudly declare that he had no teacher. The true "Master" in his view was not someone who makes you feel better or gives you all the answers, but instead the one who confuses you, makes you question yourself, and creates intense internal conflict:

> When you come to a Master like Jesus you come for peace. You are blissfully unaware that you have come to the wrong person. . . . This is the way you can know a false master from a true Master: a false master is a consolation. He gives you peace as you are; he never bothers to change you. He is a tranquillizer. He is just like sleeping pills. . . . A true Master will create more turmoil, more conflict. He is not going to console you.[44]

By the late 1960s, Rajneesh had indeed become a "Master of conflict," cultivating a national reputation for his irreverent and confrontational style. Thus in 1969, at the Second World Hindu Conference, he took an apparent delight in offending not only Hindu leaders but also almost everyone else, criticizing all organized religions and their self-serving priests. So provocative were his comments that one of Hinduism's most important spiritual authorities, the Shankaracharya of Puri, attempted to have the lecture stopped.[45]

It is not easy to summarize Rajneesh's philosophy, which was rooted in his reading of a vast range of European and Asian philosophy and was articulated through his own deliberately confusing, ironic, and often self-contradictory teaching style. A voracious, eclectic, and wide-ranging reader, Rajneesh quoted freely both from great spiritual figures such as Buddha, Jesus, Kabir, Guru Nanak, and Lao Tzu and from modern philosophers and psychologists such as Nietzsche, Wittgenstein, Freud, Jung, and Reich, fashioning his own unique sort of postmodern bricolage.[46] However, one of his recurring themes was the idea that we are all, at our core, divine beings and even Buddhas: "You are all buddhas," as he put it. "Whether you know it or not, it doesn't matter. . . . At the very core of your soul, you are a Buddha."[47] Yet our inherent divinity has been progressively covered over by layers of conditioning by family, society, politics, and religious institutions, leaving us like sleeping, brainwashed automatons. Therefore, the goal of Rajneesh's bold and often jarring techniques is a kind of *dehypnosis* aimed at shocking us into awakening, often in ways that seem contradictory or confusing: "What is the business of any Buddha? To shake us up. To shock us out of our stupor we mistake for conscious life into a sudden ecstatic awareness of the enlightened consciousness that is our intrinsic nature."[48] In the words of one follower, this process is a kind of *de-programming* or *reverse brainwashing* that undoes the layers of conditioning that have covered our divinity:

> You are programmed by family, acquaintances, institutions. Your mind is like a blackboard on which the rules and other programming are written. Bhagwan writes new rules on the blackboard, he tells you one thing is true and the next day that its opposite is true. He writes and writes new things on the blackboard of your mind until it is a "whiteboard." Then you have no programming left. Bhagwan frees the individual from all prior constraints and norms.[49]

Another follower, Swami Prabodh Dhanyam, put it even more succinctly in an interview in late 2013: "To me [his] message is Freedom: freedom from all the conditioning in your mind, which has been planted there from childhood on."[50] As we will see, however, there is some debate as to whether Rajneesh really freed his disciples from all conditioning or rather imposed new forms of (sometimes more problematic) conditioning.

RAJNEESH AND THE "CRAZY WISDOM" TRADITION

One of the key themes that runs throughout Rajneesh's teachings from his early lectures of the 1960s until his final works before his death is that of "divine madness" or "crazy wisdom." In Rajneesh's view, we are all so programmed and brainwashed by social institutions that any genuine holy man would have to appear "mad" by mainstream social standards. Conversely, only the most outrageously "mad" techniques would help shock and shake us out of our mundane, comfortable lives: "To teach man I have to devise and use all sorts of mad games, so that the accumulated madness could be acted out, catharted out, thrown out."[51] In his opinion, we are all already "insane," so the task of the true Master is simply to help us become "consciously insane" and so purge ourselves of our own insanity:

> Those who repress their neuroses become more and more neurotic, while those who express it consciously throw it out. So unless you become consciously insane, you can never be sane. . . . You *are* insane, so something has to be done about. What I say is to become conscious of it. . . . Allow it to come out; that is the only way toward sanity.[52]

However, Rajneesh's radical and at times offensive style of teaching was always combined with a sharp sense of humor and a love of jokes—even raunchy jokes—as a means of waking up his audience: "I have to tell jokes, because the things that I am saying are so subtle, so deep and profound that if I simply go on telling you those things you will fall asleep, and you will not be able to listen. . . . The more profound the truth I have to tell you, the worse joke I choose for it. . . . Even a dirty joke can be helpful—more so because it can shock you to the very roots, to the very guts. And that's the whole point!"[53] Ultimately, the greatest joke of all is the idea of "enlightenment" or spiritual awakening itself. From Rajneesh's perspective, we are all already Buddhas, we all already Christs, so the idea of going out somewhere looking for enlightenment from someone else is the most laughable thing of all: "Enlightenment, the very idea of enlightenment, is the greatest joke there is. It is a joke because it is trying to get something which is already there. It is trying to reach somewhere you are already. . . . It is an effort which is ridiculous."[54]

More than one observer has noted that Rajneesh's controversial teaching style has much in common with many other iconoclastic spiritual teachers through the ages. The idea of a kind of "holy madness" or "crazy wisdom" runs through many religious traditions, from Indian movements such as the Bauls (the wandering minstrels and "madmen" of Bengal) to Tantric Buddhist masters who are known for their mad and shocking techniques to the Eastern Christian ideal of the "holy fool" to various New Age gurus who appear insane or bizarre by mainstream standards.[55] In many ways, Rajneesh's often shocking ideas have much in common with those of other contemporary "crazy wisdom" teachers, such as the modern Tibetan teacher Chögyam Trungpa, the American guru known as Adi Da, and others who similarly combined spiritual shock tactics with humor, parody, and free sexual experimentation.[56]

FIGURE 3. George Ivanovich Gurdjieff.

One of the most important of these crazy wisdom figures for Rajneesh was the charismatic and controversial Armenian mystic George Ivanovich Gurdjieff (1866–1949; fig. 3). While Rajneesh cited relatively few figures as significant influences on his thinking, he did name Gurdjieff as one of his favorites; and it is not difficult to see many fundamental similarities between the two men.[57] Like Rajneesh, Gurdjieff was a radical, iconoclastic, and controversial figure who took a certain delight in annoying religious and political orthodoxies; like Rajneesh, Gurdjieff was incredibly eclectic, having explored and drawn from a vast array of religious, spiritual, and mystical ideas, ranging from Eastern Orthodox Christianity, Tibetan Buddhism, and Sufism to modern dance and music; and perhaps most like Rajneesh, Gurdjieff's primary task as a spiritual teacher was to "shock" his followers into an intense experience of awakening to their own true and full potentials.

In Gurdjieff's view, most human beings live their lives in a state of "sleep," drifting through the world in a semiconscious state and rarely if ever glimpsing the true possibilities of existence: "The chief feature of a modern man's being which explains everything else that is lacking in him is *sleep*. A modern man lives in sleep, in sleep he is born and in sleep he dies. . . . If a man really wants knowledge, he must first think how to wake."[58] The state of enlightenment is what Gurdjieff called the "fourth state," which lies beyond the normal conditions of sleeping, dreaming, and waking consciousness (which is itself closer to sleep than to actual "waking"). This fourth state is "an objective state of consciousness" in which "a man can see things as they are. . . . In the religions of all nations there are indications of the possibility of a state of consciousness of this kind which is called 'enlightenment.' . . . The fourth state of consciousness in man means an altogether different state of being; it is the result of inner growth and of long and difficult work."[59]

To awaken his followers from their normal slumbering state, Gurdjieff used a variety of "crazy wisdom" techniques aimed at jolting them into a sudden recognition of their true nature and the possibility of enlightenment. Gurdjieff's techniques—called "the Work"—tended to focus on the body and the senses, such as music, physical movement, and manual labor: "He had used ancient Christian chants . . . and meditations learned from Tibetan yogis and dervishes, physical disciplines, sexual excess, and abstinence, exaggerations and lies, even alcohol and violence—anything that worked—to wake his followers from their habitual ways of seeing and reacting to the world around them."[60] Dance also was a central part of the work (as it would also be for Rajneesh), and Gurdjieff often referred to himself as a "teacher of dance." Also known as the "Fourth Way," Gurdjieff's method addresses the totality of the human being. Whereas other spiritual paths focus on just one aspect of the human being, such as the body (the way of the fakir), the emotions (the way of the monk), or the mind (the way of the yogi), the Fourth Way embraces the total human being, offering the most balanced and also most rapid path to enlightenment. Significantly, Gurdjieff also emphasizes that the Fourth Way does not demand that the seeker renounce ordinary life, family, or work. It can be practiced while still "in the world," without sacrificing the usual relations and pleasures of daily social existence. As Gurdjieff's Russian follower and popularizer P. D. Ouspensky described it,

> The fourth way requires no retirement into the desert, does not require a man to give up or renounce everything by which he formerly lived. . . . The beginning of the fourth way is easier than the beginning of the ways of the fakir, the monk, and the yogi. On the fourth way it is possible to work and to follow the way while remaining in the usual conditions of life, continuing to do the usual work, preserving former relations with people, and without renouncing or giving up anything.[61]

Many aspects of Gurdjieff's teachings, we will see, would be absorbed into Rajneesh's eclectic work. The emphasis on the body, the importance of dance, music, and movement, the idea of an integrated "total" approach, the application of radical "crazy wisdom" techniques, and the use of often biting, satirical humor as a teaching method can all be found in Rajneesh's movement from the late 1960s onward. Not only did Rajneesh himself cite Gurdjieff as one of his favorite authors, he used much of the same language of "awakening" and "shocking" his disciples from the "sleep" in normal life; and he similarly enjoyed the fact that his teachings were alarming, controversial, and outrageous to many in mainstream society. In this sense, he embraces the title of a "spiritual terrorist," who uses his shock tactics to jolt us into waking:

> I don't have any weapons, I don't have any nuclear missiles. But I have something greater and something far more effective. It is not to kill. It is to bring life to those who are living almost as if they are dead. It is bringing awareness to those who are daily like somnambulists. Walking in their sleep, talking in their sleep, not knowing exactly what they are doing and why they are doing.[62]
>
> I certainly enjoy disturbing people. Because there is no other way to help them. When somebody is asleep, the only way to wake him up is to disturb, shake him, throw cold water on him. Of course he will be angry . . . I enjoy disturbing people for the simple reason if they are disturbed, then there is a possibility of changing their minds.[63] *heal reaction*

Not surprisingly, the similarities between Gurdjieff and Rajneesh have been noted by many observers and admirers. As novelist Tom Robbins put it, in a quote that continues to be featured on the Osho. com website,

> Wit and playfulness are a tremendously serious transcendence of evil, and this is one thing that Osho understood better than any contemporary teacher that I can think of. Gurdjieff had an element of that in his teachings, but certainly in the past fifty years there has not existed a teacher in the world who understood the value of playfulness and wit quite so well as Osho.[64]

In many ways both more ambitious and more eclectic than Gurdjieff, Rajneesh would soon combine elements of the Fourth Way with a wide array of other spiritual and psychological ideas ranging from Freud to Tantra, weaving them into his own playful new mix.

"RELIGIONLESS RELIGION" AND THE BIRTH OF THE "BHAGWAN"

By the mid-1960s, Acharya Rajneesh had begun attracting a number of important and increasingly affluent followers. While conservative Hindus

FIGURE 4. Rajneesh and Ma
Yoga Laxmi.

saw Rajneesh as an outrageous fraud, a self-styled "guru" who came
from no spiritual lineage and openly mocked India's greatest national and
religious heroes, many of the newer class of upwardly mobile businessmen found his message refreshing, inspiring, and liberating.[65] As Gordon
recalls this period in Bombay, Rajneesh seemed—to some, at least—to be
the new, modern, urban face of India in the 1960s: "Rajneesh's fiery presence and the freshness, indeed the outrageousness of his message attracted
the curious and adventurous. . . . These were Indians whose heterodox
opinions or social concerns or questioning minds were already putting
them in conflict with their religion or their family. They saw Rajneesh as
a modern man, critical, sexually liberated. . . . Cosmopolitans, . . . specu-
lators, bureaucrats, performers, . . . wealthy urbanites—all came to listen."[66] Beginning in 1964, Rajneesh received financial backing from a
group of wealthy businessmen who helped support his teachings and set
up his first meditation camp in the hills of Rajasthan.[67] A group of four
Bombay businessmen, including Ishverlal N. Shah, began to see Rajneesh
"as a comer if not a fully developed commodity," and formed the first
formal Rajneesh organization in 1965—a trust registered as Jivan Jagruti
Andolan or "Life Awakening Movement."[68] Resigning from his academic
post in 1966, Rajneesh took up residence in an apartment in Bombay,
where he began to draw his first long-term devotees.

Foremost among his early disciples was Laxmi Thakarsi Kuruwa, a
well-connected young woman and the daughter of a key supporter of the
Nationalist Congress Party with close ties to Nehru, Morarji Desai, and
other political figures (fig. 4). Laxmi met Rajneesh at a lecture in a small

FIGURE 5. Ma Anand Sheela. Max Gutierrez photo, Oregon
Historical Society, bb 011956.

hall in Bombay and apparently fell in love with him at first sight. His first
real "groupie," Laxmi would become a key figure in Rajneesh's national
emergence as a spiritual leader and his growing appeal among affluent
Indian businessmen in the rapidly growing metropolis of Bombay.[69]
Another key figure in the early days (later displacing Laxmi in the 1980s)
was Sheela Patel, who had been sent to school in New Jersey and married
a wealthy American named Marc Silverman. Later taking the name Ma
Anand Sheela, she would bring significant resources to the movement as
each of her three husbands also became followers of Rajneesh (fig. 5).

With Laxmi's business savvy and Sheela's connections, Rajneesh
began to draw not only wealthy Indian followers but also a growing

number of European and American tourists, who found his mix of
Indian spirituality, Western psychology, and attacks on the establishment to be a refreshing alternative to their own troubled lives back
home. While the United States was still in the throes of the anti-Vietnam
protests and the end of the 1960s counterculture, Rajneesh seemed to
offer something wildly new and exciting. Like other new religious movements of this period (such as ISKCON, TM, and many others), the early
Rajneesh movement appealed in particular to young people who had
experimented with psychedelic drugs, radical politics, and other countercultural ideas but were still searching for a more lasting form of self-
transformation. As Gordon recalls,

> In the early 1970s, just as the antiwar movement and the student rebellions
> in the West were exhausting themselves, Rajneesh was fresh. He wanted . . .
> to create a community, to start his own movement. The Westerners who
> were drawn to him were discovering the limits and limitations of leftist poli-
> tics, the sexual revolution, psychotherapy, feminism and psychedelic drugs.
> They felt the need to take a journey into themselves that would definitely
> alter the fearful or selfish . . . ways they had been relating to their friends and
> families, their political goals and sexual experiences.[70]

The movement in these days was thus an odd mixture of well-to-do
Indian businessmen and long-haired, shabbily dressed American and
European hippies: "The Indian crowd was mainly of affluent upper
class India," Ma Anand Sheela later reflected on those early days, "The
western crowd was . . . mainly hippy and new age group. The westerners dressed in . . . Indian kurtas and lunghis, not very neat with long
unkempt hair. . . . The westerners' appearance was scruffy, dirty and
always had the feel of a traveler."[71] Rajneesh's teachings during this
period also began to increasingly mix elements of Indian philosophy
with ideas drawn from European psychology, such as post-Freudian
psychoanalysis, bioenergetics, and Gurdjieff's eclectic mysticism.[72]

By 1971, Rajneesh had adopted yet another new identity—that of
Bhagwan Shree Rajneesh; he would use the new name for the next fifteen
years. Derived from the Sanskrit term *bhagavat*, Bhagwan means "holy,
glorious, venerable, or divine," and is also a traditional name of God.[73]
Shree is essentially an honorific title, meaning literally "light" or "radi-
ance," but also signifying high rank, power dignity, or auspiciousness. As
Rajneesh later put it, his adoption of this new title was a deliberate
attempt to provoke conventional religious believers. By assuming a traditional name for God, he was at once radically transforming its meaning
and also suggesting that we are all, in fact, already blessed ones or "gods":

I have been calling myself bhagwan just as a challenge—to the Christians, to the Mohammedans, to the Hindus. They have condemned me. . . . I have tried in my own way to transform the word, but the stupid Hindus won't allow it. I have tried to give it a new name, a new meaning, a new significance. I have said that it means the blessed one, a man with a blessed being.[74]

With Laxmi's shrewd organizational skills, the movement also began to move in a much more visibly "religious" direction, and Rajneesh made more explicit references to religious themes in his public talks. As we will see in chapter 2, he would also institute his own tradition of initiation and a new form of religious life called *neo-sannyasin*. This "religious turn" indeed seemed an ironic move for a man who had cultivated a national reputation as an iconoclast who mocked all organized religious institutions and infuriated religious leaders. After all, this was the same teacher who once said, "My effort is to take away all traditions, orthodoxies, superstitions, and beliefs from your mind, so that you can attain a state of no-mind, the ultimate state of silence, where not even a thought moves."[75] However, even his idea of religion was itself a uniquely "anti-religious" one—one he called a "religionless religion," which might ironically use the trappings of a traditional faith but employ them to liberate rather than bind the individual to any kind of dogmatic system or institution:

> My whole effort is to create a religionless religion. . . . Now my effort is . . . to dissolve religion also. Leave only meditation. . . . There is no God and there is no religion. By religion I mean an organized doctrine, creed, ritual, priesthood.
> For the first time, I want religion to be absolutely individual. Because all organized religions, whether with God or without God, have misled humanity. . . . Organization is really a political phenomenon, it is not religious. It is another way of power. . . .
> My effort is to destroy the priesthood completely.[76]

Rajneesh was also quite up-front about the fact that what he was doing with this religionless religion was very much a fiction. Like a good myth, it was a fictional but useful *story* that might help others to make the difficult step from the "lie" of conventional life to the "truth" of self-realization and enlightenment. Thus, when asked about his "way of religion" by a disciple in 1976, he replied:

> I am creating a fiction here: the fiction of the Master and the disciple, the fiction of the god and the devotee. It is really a myth, but very alive. And there is no way to come to the truth unless you pass through a great

mythology. Man is lost in lies. From lies there is no direct way to truth. Myth is a bridge between the lie and the truth. . . .

This is a tremendous Poona fiction story. Whatsoever is happening here is very fictitious—these people in orange, and so many crazing things going on . . .

Man lives in lies, God lives in the truth; but how to bridge both? . . . Myth is the way—fiction, yes, a spiritual fiction. All the religions are fictitious, all the mythologies are fictitious, but they are of tremendous help.[77]

It is also impossible not to compare Rajneesh's religionless religion with what Jeffrey Kripal has called the "religion of no religion" that emerged at the Esalen Institute in California during the 1960s. Like Rajneesh's early movement in India, Esalen was experimenting with new combinations of Eastern meditation and Western psychology, developing a powerful new form of alternative spirituality that drew from traditional religions, yet refusing to be bound by any orthodoxies (though we will see in chapter 3 that Esalen's cofounder, Dick Price, had a far more ambivalent reaction when he visited Pune in 1978).[78] Even today, the Osho community in Pune calls itself "the Esalen of the East."

MEETING THE BHAGWAN: THE "DEATH OF THE SUBJECT" IN THE EYES OF THE MASTER

Virtually everyone who describes meeting Rajneesh in those early days—even ex-followers who became disillusioned and left the movement—recalls the encounter as a profound and transformative experience. "Osho had a *Presence*," Joshi said in an interview in 2013. "I found him not just a person but a phenomenon, which one could feel, love, celebrate, but could not measure in any qualitative or quantitative terms."[79] Practically every narrative contains the same tropes: the sense of being lost in his eyes, the feeling that he had always known the individual, a sense of trance or hypnosis through his soothing voice, an experience like falling in love, and a sense of complete dissolution of the ego in his sublime depths. For example, Sheela Silverman (Ma Anand Sheela) had first met Rajneesh briefly in 1968 and then encountered him again with his first disciple, Ma Anand Laxmi, in 1972. As she recalled that second encounter, it was like an intense combination of falling passionately in love, of rapturous possession, and of mystical loss of self in the divine:

> That moment all disappeared. All that existed was me and Bhagwan. Everything in me melted. I had never experienced such feelings in my life as

these. . . . I felt elated. There was a certain glow in my face for days which I could not explain. . . . After this meeting all I could do was breathe for Bhagwan, eat for Bhagwan, sleep for Bhagwan, be for Bhagwan . . . I was possessed by the passion for Bhagwan.

What happened between me and Bhagwan was . . . passion. I had never felt it before, yet it was so intense I did not care to define it. All I wanted to do was to drown in it and indulge.[80]

Rajneesh's former editor and press officer, Jack Allanach (Swami Krishna Prem), described a similar first encounter in Bombay in 1973. As he recalls, when he first walked into his luxury apartment in the affluent Malabar Hill section of the city, he found Rajneesh reading none other than *Zorba the Greek*. This was not anything like the sort of stereotypical, otherwordly Indian guru he had expected to meet. Indeed, Allanach made particular note of Rajneesh's fair-skinned "European" complexion and strong virile physique, in contrast to the frail, skinny yogi he had imagined that he would meet: "He doesn't appear Indian at all. His complexion is pale, almost European, as if he never sees the sun. . . . This is not the frail ascetic I'd expected. This man's body is stocky, compact. It gives the impression of power, of virility, of strength."[81] Allanach recounts that he was struck by Rajneesh's spiritual power from his first look into his eyes, experiencing a kind of ecstatic inner explosion and a glimpse into the "superhuman" possibilities that this master had discovered and that also lay within his own soul:

The second our eyes met I'd exploded inside, my ears filling with an all-consuming roar. And then, like a far off sound cutting through the crashing waves of emotion, a distant voice had repeated a single word over and over again: Superman! Superman! Superman!

As the storm abates I realize with a new clarity that I am sitting in front of a being unlike any I have ever encountered before. . . .

"I couldn't believe anyone like you existed."

He chuckles, a deep rumble that seems to bubble up from his very toes, "What I am, you are also," he says quietly, leaning toward me, his eyes holding mine. "The only difference between you and me is that I have recognized it. If you allow me, I will help you recognize it too."[82]

Even Hugh Milne—Bhagwan's former bodyguard who later left the movement in disgust—recalled his first encounter with the master as an overwhelming and incredible spiritual experience. Though he eventually concluded that Rajneesh was a charlatan, he still recounted his first meeting with the master as a tremendous experience of awe and compassion:

From the minute I made my initial nervous steps into his . . . beautifully furnished room, I had the overwhelming sensation that I had come home. Here was my spiritual father, a man who understood everything, someone who would be able to convey sense and meaning into my life. It was a truly magical feeling. I was overawed, transported, and felt instantly that Bhagwan was inside my mind as no one else had ever been. . . . He radiated a palpable sense of unconditional love, which was simply electrifying. I was swept off my feet, enchanted, afloat in a sea of compassion emanating from this wholly original, unique being.[83]

In sum, these narratives of the encounter with Rajneesh follow a similar pattern, which in many ways mirror the narratives of Bhagwan's own enlightenment experience: the individual undergoes a radical dissolution of the ego and a loss of self within the sublime depths of the infinite, like a drop of water merged with the ocean—again, a "death of the subject." The recurring metaphors in these accounts are those of "drowning," "possession," "becoming lost," "floating in the sea." Yet always this narrative of ego loss is accompanied by a narrative of love, passion, and intense—at times quite erotic—intimacy.

CONCLUSIONS: MAKING SENSE OF RAJNEESH— A POSTMODERN GURU FOR POST-INDEPENDENCE INDIA

Given his ironic, playful, and self-contradictory personality, it is not surprising that there have been many conflicting attempts to make sense of Rajneesh. To his many admirers, Rajneesh was an enlightened master with a profoundly new message that was largely misunderstood by an ignorant society; yet to his many critics, he was a charlatan and con man, deceiving his naïve followers and concocting a superficial mishmash of Indian mysticism and Western psychology. At one end of the spectrum, there are more sympathetic authors such as Vasant Joshi, the early biographer of Rajneesh and still today a strong supporter and active teacher. In Joshi's view, Osho-Rajneesh was such a radically iconoclastic figure that he could only have been demonized by mainstream society; and it is perhaps only with time, once the initial controversies and scandals have died down, that we will really appreciate the true genius and originality of his message:

Osho describes himself as "one man against the whole history of humanity," and as it follows fairly naturally that he has been the most misunderstood. The misunderstanding arises mainly because most people see only one snapshot of what is really an adventure movie. They see a pool rather than a river of consciousness. . . .

As time goes by and our understanding of the full implications of that river increases, his unique contribution to humanity will continue to gain worldwide recognition. What is most striking in his contribution is the *process*—the process of self-transformation.[84]

Many ex-*sannyasins*, such as Rajneesh's former bodyguard Hugh Milne, have a more mixed and complex perspective on the Bhagwan. In Milne's view, Rajneesh was indeed a man of incredible intelligence, insight, and charisma; but he was also a man driven by the need for power and adoration, whose own egotism and greed would eventually lead to the disastrous collapse of his commune: "Rajneesh is not a simple man. The commune that arose around him reflected his complex and macabre personality. He undoubtedly possessed remarkable gifts, but at the same time he was in the grip of a need for power and wealth that was nothing short of megalomaniacal."[85]

My own view is that Rajneesh is best understood neither as a pure, enlightened master nor as a megalomaniacal manipulator. Rather, he is in many ways a kind of embodiment and even microcosm of the time and place in which he emerged: India in the first decades after independence. In a profound sense, Rajneesh was as successful as he was because he came along at "the right time and right place."[86] Despite his iconoclasm, his finger was always very much on the pulse of this newly developing nation as it struggled to find its identity amid the sometimes violent conflicts between Hindus, Muslims, and other religious communities, and as it navigated its relationship with America and Europe in a Cold War landscape "dominated by the United States and the Soviet Union."[87] Rajneesh's message as "India's most dangerous guru" was clearly crafted as a response to the dominant political and religious ideologies of postindependence India. Rejecting all dominant political systems and mounting a scathing attack on all religious orthodoxies, Rajneesh articulated a vision of a "religionless religion" that made a direct appeal not just to India's new business classes but also to a growing audience of American and European young people.

Yet perhaps reflecting the incredible diversity and rapidly shifting nature of India itself in these decades, Rajneesh was also a remarkably protean and fluid sort of guru. Already by the 1970s, the complex character of Rajneesh had undergone a number of identity changes, evolving from Chandra Mohan Jain to Acharya Rajneesh to Bhagwan. Yet this was entirely in keeping with his own ideal of the "new man." According to Rajneesh, the new man would be a "liquid human being" who would reject all orthodoxies and fixed identities, living perpetually in a fluid, ever-shifting present. Such a being would perpetually re-create her/himself at every moment. As he put it,

> The new consciousness is going to be counter to all orthodoxies. Any kind of orthodoxy, Catholic or communist, Hindu or Jain . . . is a kind of paralysis of the mind. . . . You stop living. . . . An alive person has to be flowing; he has to respond to the changing situations. And situations are constantly changing. How can you remain fixed in your attitudes when life itself is not fixed?
> The new man will be creative. Each moment he will find his religion, each moment he will find his philosophy. And everything will remain growing. He will not be obedient to the past . . . he will be obedient to the present.[88]

While Rajneesh does not explicitly use the term "postmodern" or "poststructural" to describe this ideal of the new consciousness, his ideas do very closely parallel those of European theorists who were writing at almost exactly the same time. For example, in 1972, just one year after Rajneesh took the title Bhagwan, French authors such as Gilles Deleuze and Félix Guattari would likewise reject the idea of a unified, self-identical ego or "sovereign subject," instead celebrating a kind of "perpetually renewed 'nomadic' subject always different from itself, a kind of 'permanent revolution' of psychic life."[89]

As we will see in chapter 2, Rajneesh's iconoclastic teachings were also closely tied to his larger social and economic views, which were soon put into practice in his early spiritual community during the 1970s. Not only did he launch a bold attack on Gandhian asceticism and Nehruvian socialism, calling instead for an embrace of American-style capitalism; he also put his "religionless religion" into living practice through the establishment of a wholly new kind of spiritual life, the neo-sannyasin, and then through his unique social experiment, the first ashram in Pune.

CHAPTER 2

"Beware of Socialism!"

The "Anti-Gandhi" and the Early Rajneesh
Community in the 1970s

To me, Adolf Hitler is less dangerous than Mahatma Gandhi.
Adolf Hitler is less violent than Mahatma Gandhi.
—Rajneesh, *The Wisdom of the Sands*

Indeed, it is the right time for India to take a decision and
resolve that . . . we will create capitalism and become
capitalist.
—Rajneesh, *Beware of Socialism*

Rajneesh's significance as a modern global guru was by no means limited to his spiritual teachings. His tremendous influence was as much
tied to his controversial social, political, and economic views as it was
to his spiritual message. In his later career as a global figure in the
United States in the 1980s, Rajneesh would become famous as the
"guru of the rich" and the "Rolls-Royce guru." However, he had
already articulated his views on economics, capitalism, and wealth a
decade earlier in the 1970s in India, where he was one of the most outspoken critics of Indian politics and an early advocate of American-style
capitalism. Indeed, Rajneesh presented himself as a kind of "anti-
Gandhi," who rejected the asceticism, simplicity, and nationalism of the
Mahatma in favor of global capitalism, materialism, and prosperity.[1]

In this sense, Rajneesh was remarkably prescient, foreseeing a larger
shift away from Nehru-style socialism and a growing embrace of global
capitalism, which swept India in the 1980s and 1990s. His intense
and often shocking critique of Indian politics was in many ways quite

"cutting edge," coming right at the cusp of a broader transition from the relatively closed and state-dominated economy of the 1960s toward the more open, transnational, and volatile economy that would emerge in the 1980s and 1990s. As Manfred Steger and Ravi Roy put it, India during these decades moved from the "socialist era" (1947–84) to the period of "liberalization by stealth" (1984–91) to the age of "reform by storm" (1991–present).[2]

By no means an isolated figure, Rajneesh was part of a wave of modern Indian gurus who emerged during these decades and whose rise to international stature went hand in hand with India's own rise to prominence in the global economy. As Lise McKean notes, "The activities of many gurus and their organizations during the 1980s and 1990s are related to the simultaneous expansion of transnational capitalism in India and growing support for Hinduism in India and abroad."[3] Yet unlike many other global gurus, such as his contemporary Sathya Sai Baba (1926–2011), Rajneesh was never an advocate of Hindu nationalism. Rather, his embrace of international capitalism was accompanied by a severe critique of any form of narrow religious orthodoxy and any appeal to national identity.

Rajneesh's economic philosophy was always intimately related to his larger spiritual outlook. Just as he attacked the asceticism, simplicity, and provincialism of Gandhi's spirituality, so too he advocated a new kind of embodied and sensuous spirituality that would embrace sexuality and physical pleasure along with modern technology and Western capitalism. Thus his rejection of socialism and his embrace of capitalism were also closely tied to his critique of all world-rejecting forms of religion—indeed of all existing religions—and his call for a new, this-worldly, sensual, materialist, and embodied "religionless" spirituality for a new global era.

This "anti-Gandhian" vision was began to be realized after Rajneesh's move from the chaotic metropolis of Bombay (Mumbai) to the cooler, quieter, and smaller city of Poona (Pune) in 1974. Here, with the help of his early financial backers in the business community, he established his first ashram or spiritual retreat and developed many of his key meditative techniques. However, just as he presented himself as a kind of anti-Gandhi with a "religionless religion," so too, his ashram was a kind of anti-commune and in fact an increasingly "capitalist commune" that attracted huge numbers of American and European young people during the 1970s. And his followers—dubbed *neo-sannyasins*—were in many ways the very opposite of the traditional ideal of the Indian *sannyasin* or "renunciant." Rather than rejecting the world through ascetic discipline, they embraced the world with full enjoyment of the senses, bodily experience, and material pleasure. Likewise, the techniques of meditation developed by Rajneesh during this period were also in many ways "anti-meditations," based not on silent withdrawal from the world but rather on chaotic, ecstatic practices such as his trademark "dynamic meditation," and various elements drawn from Western psychology, New Age therapy, and encounter groups popular in the 1970s. As a crucial global node or hyphal knot, the early Pune ashram thus really brought together Indian spirituality with pop psychology, transnational tourism, and the new forms of ad hoc, impromptu, "disorganized" capitalism that emerged in Asia during this fertile period.

THE PURSUIT OF LAKSHMI: RAJNEESH AND THE INDIAN ECONOMY IN THE 1970S

Rajneesh's emergence as a refreshingly new and iconoclastic spiritual teacher occurred almost simultaneously with much broader shifts in Indian culture, politics, and economic life. Up until the 1970s, as Lloyd and Susanne Rudolph note in their classic work on Indian political economy, Western-style capitalism was still viewed quite negatively by both the state and the majority of the Indian populace as a rapacious, greedy, and exploitative system: "Until the mid-seventies, modern capitalists in India had to contend with preindustrial cultural prejudices and postindustrial ideological doctrines that picture them, on the one hand, as heartless moneylenders or greedy merchants and, on the other, as antisocial profiteers or powerful exploiters."[4] The Indian economy in turn remained largely under the regulation of the state, which generally fostered small-scale, local businesses over large monopolistic corporations. A large part of the ideology underlying this economic ideal, they suggest, was Gandhi's emphasis on *swadeshi* or local Indian-based businesses and small-scale human modes of production rather than mass-scale machines:

> In addition to direct measures to limit and control private capital via licensing and the control of monopoly . . . the state under Congress and Janata governments has used indirect measures that have the effect of marginalizing private capitalism in class politics and making it dependent on the state. . . . The ideological justifications of these policies include Mohandas Gandhi's preference for human-scale, labor-intensive craft and commodity production

by self-employed workers, the belief that small-scale enterprises generate more employment per unit than large, and the socialist goal of increasing industrial production without increasing private economic power.[5]

From the mid-1970s to the 1980s, however, the Indian economy changed dramatically, shifting from a largely state-controlled, protectionist, and socialist system toward one that was increasingly friendly to private capital and to the influence of transnational corporations. As Achin Vanaik notes, the ideology of Nehruvian socialism had begun to seem increasingly out of sync with the realities of a global economy by the mid-1970s, leading many politicians, economists, and businessmen to look for other paradigms: "In the middle or late seventies, the age of ideological innocence began to draw to a close. The ideology of the mixed economy and of a socialist pattern of society became increasingly meaningless, out of kilter with the basic dynamic of the economy. . . . But the ideological vacuum created by the demise of Nehruvian socialism has yet to be properly filled."[6] In turn, the state during these decades also began to turn away from its older socialist roots and to open the economy to larger global markets and private investment. As McKean writes in her study of modern Indian gurus,

> During the 1970s and particularly during the 1980s, the private economic sector consisting of Indian and transnational corporations as well as medium and small-scale industries and services expanded rapidly. The Indian state justified changes in policy with explanations based on economic rationalism. At the same time it reduced its reliance on socialism as a populist ideology. . . . Pressured by coalitions of ruling-class groups, who wanted to more effectively compete in international markets as well as to expand their opportunities to invest capital in potentially profitable enterprises within India, the state formulated economic policies to support these goals.[7]

By the early to mid-1980s, India had begun to experience a new kind of capitalist transformation and consumer revolution. As the nation under Rajiv Gandhi moved farther away from Nehru's socialism toward a more liberal economic position open to the global free market, mainstream Indian publications such as *India Today* celebrated the transformation of the economy with articles such as "The New Millionaires and How They Made It."[8] As the Indian magazine *Sunday* put it, New Delhi was entering "the era of yuppie-style politics where style is all and austerity is yesterday's news."[9]

Rajneesh, we will see, was in many ways well ahead of the curve in this transition from socialism toward an embrace of global capitalism and private investment. His critique of socialism and his call for an infusion of American-style capitalism into the Indian economy was already articulated in the late 1960s and was well received by a small but growing class of entrepreneurial businessmen in the 1970s. Thus he could be said to have foreseen the economic trends of the 1980s by at least a decade or more.

THE ANTI-GANDHI: RAJNEESH'S ATTACK ON GANDHIAN IDEOLOGY AND ASCETICISM

As we saw in the previous chapter, by the mid-1960s Rajneesh already had a national reputation as India's most controversial guru, infuriating religious leaders and politicians alike with his deliberately provocative rhetoric. However, he would achieve a new height of both celebrity and infamy during the Gandhi Centenary Year of 1968–69, when he launched a personal and ideological assault on India's greatest national hero.[10] As all of India was celebrating the Mahatma, Rajneesh undertook an irreverent, satirical, and deeply serious critique of Gandhian ideology and its effects on the Indian economy that he would reiterate throughout his career. As he reflected later, in 1983, "For twenty years I have criticized Mahatma Gandhi and his philosophy."[11]

Rajneesh's assault on Gandhi was at least threefold. First, he regarded Gandhi's views of Indian society and its problems as "primitive and unscientific," rooted in a regressive appeal to tradition and utterly impractical in the late twentieth century.[12] While Gandhi advocated the spinning wheel and other traditional, low-tech means of production, Rajneesh argued that India needed to embrace modern technology and join the developing world. The politicians, Rajneesh believed, all knew this to be true but they went on worshipping Gandhi simply because he was popular with the voting masses who supported them:

> Gandhi is against technology. He was against the railway, he was against the post office, he was against electricity, he was against machines of all kinds. They know this is stupid . . . and they go on paying homage to Mahatma Gandhi because they have to get the votes from the people. . . . Mahatma Gandhi fits with the India mob. The Indian mob worships him. The politician has to follow the mob.[13]

[handwritten margin note: hatred for politics]

In Rajneesh's opinion, Gandhi's antitechnology policies were a recipe for economic and human disaster. As India's population had grown ever faster in the 1950s and 1960s, it had far outpaced any traditional means of production, so that only the embrace of modern technologies could help India avoid mass starvation and complete economic collapse:

> Gandhiji always wanted that the country should be rich, prosperous and spiritual but all his methods were conducive to poverty and distress. If Gandhiji had been successful, India would have been doomed to remain a poor country forever. The truth is, that if today the country decides to follow Gandhiji's teachings, of the fifty crores of our population, at least half the number will immediately become extinct. . . . One concept of Gandhiji, if put into practice, could kill more people than the massacres of Genghis, Hitler, Stalin and Mao put together. Why? Because when Gandhiji talked, he drew his inspiration from the society which existed in the feudal ages before the Industrial Revolution. He talks of the tools of that age—the spinning wheel, which has long outlived its utility. The machinery of which Gandhiji talked cannot keep alive so large a population. . . . We need technical means for mass production of commodities to keep the masses alive; but Gandhiji talks of Rama Rajya when the population of the world was so small that a feudal system could make do for survival.[14]

It is worth noting that similar criticisms have been made more recently regarding contemporary Indian advocates of traditional means of production, such as eco-feminist Vandana Shiva. While Shiva also calls for a return to traditional small-scale forms of labor and agriculture, many critics such as Meera Nanda argue that such a romantic ideal is utterly impractical in the twenty-first century, amidst India's massive population and ever-growing need for food and resources.[15]

Second, Rajneesh saw Gandhi as a figure who praised, honored, and therefore reinforced poverty. With his emphasis on respect for the poor, simple, honest Indian, Gandhi was attaching a kind of spiritual virtue to poverty, when, in fact, poverty is something that should be hated and combated. Rather than praising the poor as *daridra Narayan* (the poor God), Rajneesh called for the destruction of poverty altogether by embracing technology and modern economic ideas. Gandhi's rejection of birth control was equally idiotic, in Rajneesh's opinion, because it only further mired India in the problems of overpopulation and insurmountable poverty. In short, "to follow Gandhi is to put a seal on permanent poverty."[16]

> Gandhi worshiped poverty. Now if you worship poverty you will remain poor. Poverty has to be hated. . . . I don't see any religious quality in just being poor. But Gandhi talked much about poverty and its beauty. . . . Poverty is ugly and poverty has to be destroyed. And to destroy poverty, technology has to be brought in. Mahatma Gandhi was against birth control. Now if you are against birth control . . . India will become every day poorer and poorer.[17]

Finally, Rajneesh mounted a scathing critique of Gandhi's asceti-cism, calling him a body-hating masochist who turned the destruction of the body and physical pleasure into a spiritual virtue. In Rajneesh's eyes, Gandhi was more a pervert than a saint, a man who refused to make love to his own wife even as he brought naked girls to his bed to "prove" his chastity.[18] Rather than a path to the divine, asceticism is in Rajneesh's opinion the path to the madhouse, the expression of a patho-logical mind that has turned against its own body. In a critique that is reminiscent of Friedrich Nietzsche's critique of Christian morality, Rajneesh describes the ascetic denial of the body as a perverse form of power—a sick power that comes from violence toward oneself:

> It is an expression of an ill mind, it is an expression of a violent mind. Ordi-narily the violence is directed toward others, but the violence can be directed to oneself, too. . . . So to me, Adolf Hitler is less dangerous than Mahatma Gandhi. Adolf Hitler is less violent than Mahatma Gandhi. . . . This has been happening down the ages: the people who are masochistic have declared themselves religious. Religion is an excuse to be a masochist. There is a joy that comes out of torturing oneself: it consists of the feeling of power.[19]

As we will see in chapter 3, this attack on Gandhian asceticism would also be a key part of Rajneesh's attitudes toward sexuality, sensual pleasure, and his larger "Zorba the Buddha" ideal.

THE ANTI-SOCIALIST: RAJNEESH'S CRITIQUE OF INDIAN ECONOMIC POLICY

Rajneesh's assault on Gandhi was accompanied by an equally fierce cri-tique of socialism and Indian economic policies up to the 1960s. As his biographer Vasant Joshi recounts, Rajneesh had actually been seriously interested in socialism through his high school years and then became increasingly disillusioned with it as an economic system. "In fact," Joshi reports, "around 1950 . . . he began criticizing eminent elders of the Indian Socialist Party such as Jaya Prakash Narayan."[20]

By the late 1960s, however, Rajneesh's skepticism of socialism had evolved into a far more serious critique of its intellectual foundations and its social, economic, and ethical implications for modern India. His most comprehensive critique of socialism can be found in his book *Beware of Socialism,* but similar views run throughout his lectures from the late 1960s until his death. Anticipating right-wing attacks on social-ism in America and England by a good decade or two, Rajneesh denounced socialism as an ideology based primarily on jealousy—the jealousy of the poor have-nots toward the prosperous and hard-working individuals who have struggled and succeeded in accumulating wealth by their own means: "Jealousy is at the root of the influence that socialism has in the world. Jealousy is its very foundation."[21]

> The hold of socialism is not because it believes in equality between man and man. . . . The basic cause of its hold is the innate jealousy of man. He is jealous of those who have succeeded, who have prospered. . . . A major part of mankind has always lived in inertia; they have never produced wealth or power or knowledge. . . . And for sure, the jealousy of the masses, of millions of masses, can be aroused and whetted . . . And the talk of socialism in India also stems from this very source.[22]

At the same time, Rajneesh argued that socialism was an ideology that simply turns over more power to the state, transferring rights, freedoms, and power from the individual to a faceless and incompetent government. Such an abdication of individual rights for state control, Rajneesh argued—foreshadowing modern libertarians—would only turn over more and more power to an increasingly domineering but ineffectual state: "When we think of establishing Socialism, we are in fact taking a decision towards handing over the very basis of the production of wealth to the State. This is nothing less than suicide. It is dangerous. Those who hold the reins of the government are, as it is, mad with power."[23] Particularly in India of the 1960s—amid massive poverty and limited resources—socialism was simply illogical and absurd. It is impossible, Rajneesh argued, to distribute wealth when there *is* no wealth; in a nation of massive poverty, all one can distribute is more poverty: "Today Indiraji and her ignorant co-workers—the naïve Delhi politicians—are shouting themselves hoarse over the establishment of Socialism, of distribution of capital. . . . Today the country has no capital—what then are we going to distribute? For if there is anything that is in abundance, it is poverty."[24]

Finally, Rajneesh also presented a more deeply philosophical critique of socialism: it undermined and devalued the significance of the individual human self. Socialism, in his view, rests upon an "unscientific and anti-psychological" idea of equality, the false belief that all human beings are the same and equally deserving of the same rewards. "The fact that Socialism does not accept the inherent difference between one man and another can lead to fatal consequences. Every man is born different. Every single human being is rare—incomparable—unique. . . . We are never born equal."[25] In place of socialism's false ideal of equality, we should celebrate human difference, encouraging strong individuals to reject a conformist social order: "Man should have the full free-dom in an atmosphere congenial enough to allow him to be different, to say no, to rebel, to stand against the prevailing systems of thought and practice."[26] Here we see the real intersection between Rajneesh's spirit-ual teachings and his economic views: each individual is inherently divine, and the greatest task of spiritual work is to free the individual from the conditioning and conformity of mainstream social, religious, and political institutions.[27]

THE FIRST "CAPITALIST" GURU

If socialism is based on an "unnatural" attempt to distribute wealth to the poor, capitalism is, in Rajneesh's view, a far more "natural" ideol-ogy that simply accepts human differences and allows capital to grow on its own, without the intervention of meddling states or incompetent bureaucrats: "In capitalism, wealth is produced in a very natural man-ner. Capitalism does not use a stick, a gun, or force of any kind. It pro-vides incentive to work, to produce."[28] Capitalism creates a space in which "wealth will rain like water," laying the groundwork for "the coming of immense affluence, for abundance of wealth."[29] The primary obstacle that prevented India from rejecting socialism and embracing capitalism, in Rajneesh's view, was simply the political establishment. Again anticipating Reagan by over decade, Rajneesh declared that *gov-ernment is the problem* and that politicians are nothing more than a bunch of bungling "nincompoops" who are standing in the way of eco-nomic growth:

> Capitalism is an instrument for converting labor into wealth. And if capital-ism is allowed to grow unimpeded it can find ways to convert the entire labor of the country into wealth. But socialists say that they will hand over everything—the means of production and labor—to the state. The irony is that the politicians are and have always been the most inefficient and worth-less class of people in the world.[30]

Ultimately, for Rajneesh (as for Reagan), capitalism is about free-dom; and the squelching or stifling of capitalism by government and politicians is the death of the very freedom that makes us unique indi-viduals: "Capitalism is a humanistic system which gives full freedom to all kinds of people, and in all directions of life, to grow and be them-selves. . . . The death knell of capitalism may turn out to be the death knell of man himself."[31] For it is the rare individuals—the visionaries and entrepreneurs—who are able to bring about the innovations that generate wealth and then spread it to the rest of the nation. The creation of real prosperity is not the result of the ordinary masses, but rather of the elite few who know how to invest, how to develop new enterprises, and how to extend that to the less fortunate poor: "All the people of the world have not created wealth. Creation of wealth is the task of genius, and out of a few individuals, only one can rise to be a Rockefeller, a Morgan, or a Rothschild or a Tata, Birla or Sahu. Indeed if we take the big names out of the American industry, America will seem to be as poor as India."[32]

Ironically, then, it is ultimately the rich capitalist entrepreneurs—the Rockefellers and the Birlas—who will bring about true and lasting "socialism." By first generating wealth by capitalist means, they will then be able to disseminate it to the rest of the populace and create a society that is genuinely more "equitable":

charity

> No one will perhaps be aware that true Socialism will be ushered in by a Birla, a Tata or a Sahu. But in a true sense, it is these people . . . who are the real harbingers of Socialism. They are the ones who are producing the capital and ultimately this capital will make for greater distribution of wealth and Socialism will be established as a natural result.[33]

trickle down

Thus, in his characteristically paradoxical and contrarian logic, Rajneesh called upon his fellow countrymen to reject socialism and politicians alike in order to usher in the capitalism that would ultimately bring about a new kind of socialism. But again, he was also foreshadowing the "trickle-down" and "supply-side" economic theory that would become dominant in the United States during the Reagan era fifteen years later.

DYNAMIC MEDITATION: MATERIALIZING THE "RELIGIONLESS RELIGION"

Even as Rajneesh set himself up as a kind of anti-Gandhi with an anti-Nehruvian economic message, he also began to create a radical new kind of social and religious movement—or rather, as we saw in the previous chapter, a kind of religionless religion. Central to this religionless religion were new forms of meditation and new forms of spiritual life that, in many ways, turned traditional Indian ideas on their heads.

In Bombay in April 1970, Rajneesh introduced a striking new form of meditative practice that combined aspects of Indian meditation with

FIGURE 6. *Sannyasins* during meditation. Max Gutierrez photo, Oregon Historical Society, bb 011956.

elements drawn from "crazy wisdom" teachers such as Gurdjieff, post-Freudian psychoanalysis, encounter groups, and New Age spirituality. Known as "Dynamic Meditation" or simply "Dynamic," this technique remains the core practice of the movement to this day and is really Rajneesh's signature innovation (figs. 6, 7). In many ways a "microcosm" of Rajneesh's whole philosophy and method, Dynamic Meditation was a blend of Indian and European techniques explicitly designed to shock us out of our habitual patterns of thought and behavior.[34]

As it is still practiced today at the Pune center and around the world, Dynamic Meditation lasts an hour and consists of five stages. The first is a ten-minute period of fast, chaotic breathing, in which one intentionally avoids any particular pattern of inhalation and exhalation (in other

FIGURE 7. "Rajneesh disciples dance." *The Oregonian.*

words, the very opposite of traditional yogic techniques of *pranayama*).[35] This stage is designed to awaken the energy within. Second, there is a ten-minute period of intense catharsis, in which one releases all psychological, emotional, and physical suppressions through screaming, crying, shouting, and laughing. "Let the emphasis be on catharsis and total letting go," Rajneesh explained. "Just let whatever is happening happen. Do not suppress anything. If you feel like weeping, weep; if you feel like dancing, dance. Laugh, shout, scream, jump, shake—whatever you feel to do, *do it!*"[36] This stage is similar in many ways to primal scream therapy, which, not insignificantly, began to be widely popularized that same year (1970) after the publication of Arthur Janov's book *The Primal Scream.*[37] Third, there is a period of jumping up and down and landing the balls of one's feet while repeating the Sufi word *Hoo* (meaning "Him," one of the names of God in Islam). Landing hard on the balls of the feet is also supposed to stimulate the sexual center in the body and move that energy upward.[38] Fourth, there is a ten-minute period of silence, in which one freezes in whatever position one happens to be. And here—in a rare moment of crediting another teacher— Rajneesh himself acknowledged that this technique was inspired by Gurdjieff, who had also used a "stop exercise" in his radical "shock-tactic" style of meditation.[39] Finally, there is a fifteen-minute period of free form dance, in which one celebrates and expresses the "bliss that has been felt in the fourth stage."[40] In this sense, Dynamic Meditation is an explicit attempt to put Rajneesh's ideal of "conscious insanity" into practice, to acknowledge and then to purge the deep-seated psychological problems that we all carry with us: "My technique of Dynamic

Meditation accepts your neurosis as it is and tries to release it. The technique basically starts with a catharsis. Whatever is hidden must be released. . . . Unless you become 'consciously insane' you can never become sane."[41]

Both Indian and foreign observers initially regarded Dynamic Meditation as not simply iconoclastic but downright bizarre. As Joshi recalls, "The day he introduced Dynamic Meditation, everyone was taken aback and fascinated at the same time. The Indian press expressed its shock at watching the participants scream, take off their clothes—the whole scene appeared weird and was certainly intense."[42] Hugh Milne recalls a similar experience with his first performance of Dynamic Meditation on Bombay's Chowpatty Beach at 5 a.m. He later recalled how bizarre he and his fellow Western hippies must have looked in the eyes of the local Indian community, who watched in astonishment as long-haired young white people dressed in the robes of Hindu renunciants leaped and flailed wildly on the sand in the dark:

> We panted and cavorted and shadowboxed and released all our inhibitions and pent up anxieties through cathartic movements. The natives of Bombay, fishermen and the few coolies out at the time looked at us in complete astonishment. Here we were, a bunch of Westerners insulting Indian tradition by being so scantily dressed that the shapes of our bodies were all too clearly visible, wearing the holy saffron of the renunciant to take part in orgies.[43]

For many young people just beginning to follow the guru, Dynamic Meditation was literally a radical leap into the unknown—a wild, seemingly ridiculous but incredibly exhilarating plunge into a completely different kind of physical, emotional, and spiritual experience. American follower Jack Allanach described his first encounter with Dynamic Meditation in 1973 as the craziest, most absurd thing he had ever seen. But once he gave into its madness, he found it to be a liberating, life-changing practice:

> Suddenly the beach is alive with gyrating bodies, filled with the rasping sound of breathing—in and out through the nose, in and out, in and out, like a thousand saws felling a forest. *This is insane,* I tell myself. *What am I doing here on this filthy Bombay beach in the middle of the night with a bunch of loonies in orange robes? They're all quite crazy.* . . . "Aw what the hell!" I shout into the faintly reddening sky. And, donning my blindfold with the rest of them, I dive into the madness too.[44]

Allanach's sudden "what the hell" plunge into the seemingly absurd only to find it deeply meaningful is perhaps characteristic of the early

Rajneesh movement as a whole. For many young people who knew little about India or meditation, the movement as a whole was a seemingly crazy leap into unknown and unpredictable territory, but one that was also exciting, radically liberating, and often transformative.

I have personally practiced Dynamic Meditation during my own visits to the Pune center. Leaving aside whatever spiritual, psychological, and emotional benefits that have been claimed for the technique (which I would not dismiss), there is one fact about the practice that is undeniable: it is a tremendous physical workout. The initial phase of chaotic breathing alone is physically very demanding, and when combined with the "freak out" stage, jumping up and down and then holding a frozen position for ten minutes (possibly the hardest part of all), it is actually a very rigorous aerobic and muscular workout. This is also surely part of its appeal to health-conscious Americans and Europeans, who not only tend to lack the attention span for seated meditation but also want to use their leisure time for physical conditioning rather than navel gazing. Dynamic Meditation would also become one of the primary inspirations for the many other methods that began to become globally popular in the 1980s and 1990s, such as "Power Yoga," "Dynamic Yoga," "Hot Yoga," "Hot Fusion," and other extremely active techniques that combine elements of traditional Indian practice with an intense physical workout.

Moreover, while Dynamic Meditation may have seemed bizarre to many Indian observers at the time—and even to many still today—it actually makes much more sense when we place it in the context of these early encounters between Indian spirituality and the new waves of Western tourists, seekers, and ideas since the 1960s. While in some ways rooted in Indian techniques, Dynamic Meditation was also quite different from seated, silent yogic meditation and clearly indebted to Western psychological techniques such as primal scream and Reichian therapy (see chapter 3). In this sense, it is also a product of a late capitalist global context, in which ideas from "East" and "West" are increasingly melding together and often intersecting in the physical body itself. As Arjun Appadurai notes,

> In the context of the flexibility demanded by contemporary global capitalism, there has been a great deal of compression of time and space, and the body comes to be seen as a chaotic, hyperflexible site, ridden with contradictions and warfare. . . . This situation can also be looked at from the point of view of the logic of consumption in a highly globalized, unruly, late capitalism. From this perspective, the aesthetic of ephemerality becomes the . . . counterpart of flexible accumulation.[45]

Rajneesh's "chaotic" and intensely physical techniques, drawn from East and West in a world in which space itself is becoming smaller and smaller, were perhaps ideally suited to an increasingly chaotic late capitalist context. In many ways, this idea of the body as a site "ridden with contradictions and warfare" is epitomized in Rajneesh's dynamic methods, which use screaming, catharsis, and physical rage as key methods of spiritual release and self-realization.

THE FIRST *NEO-SANNYASINS:* THE BIRTH OF THE RAJNEESH COMMUNITY

In September 1970, while at a meditation camp in the north Indian town of Manali in the Himalayas, Rajneesh began to formally initiate followers into his new religionless religion, calling them *sannyasins* or *neo-sannyasins.* Now adopting the more obvious trappings of religious devotion, *sannyasins* began wearing orange robes and a necklace with a locket containing Rajneesh's picture.[46]

Traditionally in South Asian religions, a *sannyasin* is a renunciant or ascetic, one who has abandoned the worldly life of society, family, and employment in order to devote her- or himself full-time to the spiritual life. Derived from the Sanskrit term *sam-nyasa* or *sannyasa,* meaning "throwing aside," "resignation," or "abandonment," *sannyasin* refers to one who has voluntarily stepped out of the class system and conventional obligations in order to pursue a life of austerity and strict discipline. According to the traditional Hindu way of life, *sannyasa* is the fourth and final stage of life, after one has fulfilled the stages of being a celibate student (*brahmacharya*), a householder (*grihastha*), and a forest dweller or retired (*vanaprastha*). Throughout India today, one can see thousands of *sannyasins* leading the spiritual life either in *ashrams* (hermitages) or as independent wandering holy men (*sadhus*), typically wearing the clothing and markings of their particular sectarian tradition, and often with long dreadlocks and beards.[47]

Like his radical technique of Dynamic Meditation, however, Rajneesh's ideal of the *neo-sannyasin* was an extreme departure from the traditional ideal of *sannyasa,* in many ways turning it completely on its head. Rather than life denying, ascetic, and otherworldly, the *neo-sannyasin* would be very much life affirming and *this- worldly.* Rajneesh himself explicitly contrasted his ideal of *neo-sannyas* with that of the traditional Hindu model, arguing that the true holy man is not one who hates the world and retreats from it but rather one who loves life and embraces it: "My *sannyas* is life-affirmative. Nothing like that has ever flowered on the earth. It is a totally new phenomenon. All the old ideas of *sannyas* were based on escapism, renunciation. My *sannyas* has nothing to do with escape. . . . You have to live as totally as possible, as intensely as possible, as passionately as possible if you want to know God."[48] In an interview with the U.S. Immigration and Naturalization Service (INS), Rajneesh explained this ideal as a totally new kind of religion based on life and living rather than death and the afterlife:

> *Sannyas* to me means a life lived moment to moment, just the moment, sincerely without any idea of why. All the old religions are motivating people that you will get rewards either in this life or in another life or in after life. To me this is just exploiting their greed. This is not religious. This is pure business. . . . There is no need for you to believe in God. I don't teach belief. . . . *Sannyas* is a totally new kind of religion. Religion in the sense that it does not bother at all about God. . . . Its whole insistence is to know this consciousness that you already have, use this consciousness lovingly in whatsoever you are doing.[49]

The only thing that the *neo-sannyasin* is really "renouncing," Rajneesh suggests, is dependence on any form of dogmatic institution, whether it be politics, social class, or religion. It is a rejection of everything imposed on the individual from outside, and a full affirmation of the inner self, which is radically free and divine:

> The ancient meaning of *sannyas* is renouncing the world. I am against it. But I have still used the word *sannyas* because I can see another meaning far more significant that the old one. I mean renouncing the conditions that the world has given to you—your religion, your caste, your Brahminism, your Jainism, your Christianity, your God, your holy book. To me, *sannyas* means a commitment that "I am going to clean myself completely of all those things that have been imposed upon me, and I will start living on my own—fresh, young, pure, unpolluted."[50]

At the same time, this ideal of the *neo-sannyasin* is itself a kind of "postmodern" view of the individual that reflects Rajneesh's own uniquely postmodern character. The true *neo-sannyasin* will be radically free of any kind of fixed identity or stable self, instead celebrating the flexible, fluid, and ever-changing nature of life in the eternal present: "My *sannyas* is not a discipline. My *sannyas* is freedom, freedom from all control—even from self-control. A controlled man is a dead man. . . . My *sannyas* is spontaneity, living moment to moment without any prefabricated discipline."[51] He is, in short, a wholly "new man," who refuses to be fixed into any established pattern or identity: "The new

person will be a spontaneous person, unpredictable, willing to risk new-
ness, often willing to risk saying or doing the wild, the far-out thing. He
will believe that everything is possible and anything can be tried. He
will not cling to the known."[52]

Not surprisingly, Rajneesh's ideal of the *neo-sannyasin* took off
quickly, particularly among the new waves of American and European
tourists flooding into India in the early 1970s. From an initial six *sannyasins* he already had 400 by 1971.[53] Like Rajneesh himself, however,
the *sannyasins* typically had a sense of humor and irony about themselves, recognizing that what they were doing was something kind of
weird and radical even within the tradition of Indian spirituality. As
Aneesha Dillon recalls from her early days as a *sannyasin*, the spectacle
of these troops of young American and European hippies wearing
orange robes and *malas* (prayer beads), together with their long hair
and often open sensuality, was something both jarring and yet playfully
entertaining in the context of 1970s India: "*Sannyasins* are just—at
least used to be and still are, I guess, in many ways—quite ridiculous.
There is a certain quality that is actually quite annoying to the outside
world and still is—with the orange and the *malas* and the hair and the
beards."[54] And yet, that was also precisely the aim of Rajneesh's crazy
wisdom message—a message at once self-consciously ridiculous and
deliberately annoying to the surrounding society.

"AN INTENSE, REVOLUTIONARY, HIGHLY
CONTROVERSIAL EXPERIMENT":
THE EARLY PUNE ASHRAM

Until 1974, Rajneesh gave most of his talks from an apartment in Bombay, the rent for which was paid by a rich, local *sannyasin* who owned
a biscuit company.[55] But the number of *sannyasins* grew much too
quickly for an apartment to contain. Moreover, Rajneesh had long suf-
fered poor health, and by the early 1970s had developed asthma, allergies, and diabetes, all exacerbated by the heat, humidity, and pollution
of the rapidly growing metropolis. Ishverlal Shah and other members of
the Jivan Jagruti Andolan group of investors found the site for an ashram
in the affluent, green, and residential neighborhood of Koregaon Park,
nestled in the quieter and cooler city of Pune. Now named the Rajneesh
Foundation, the movement quickly took off, drawing far more American and European than Indian followers and blossoming into a truly
global spiritual community. Very quickly the Pune center became one of

the most popular ashrams in all of India, attracting hundreds and then thousands of spiritual seekers from all over the world—and particularly from the United States, the United Kingdom, and Europe. "As if pulled by a powerful magnet," Joshi recalled in an interview in 2013, " the young, energetic, educated men and women were drawn to [Rajneesh], creating an unparalleled assembly of seekers thirsty to find a new way of life, a new direction, a new source of energy. The place consisted of . . . a vibrant Commune—in an environment of festivity and creativity."[56]

Aneesha Dillon was one such young American pulled to Pune in these early days, and she fondly recalls the powerful mix of spiritual, emotional, and sexual vibrancy that filled the ashram when she first visited in 1976. For an American coming to India for the first time, the ashram was an incredibly exotic and mysterious place, filled with giant banyan trees and tropical birds: "There were many things that were magical about it. First of all just being in India. . . . There were parrots in the trees. . . . Inside the ashram it was like this little wonderland. It was like everybody was in love—either in love with Osho or in love with life or in love with meditation or in love with each other."[57] By the mid-1970s, the Pune center had become a remarkable global epicenter of spiritual searching, experimentation, and tourism: "His small ashram became . . . an intense pressure cooker of exploration in which hundreds, then thousands of people participated. It was an intense, explosive, revolutionary, highly controversial experiment that caught the media's attention, worried India's politicians, and attracted courageous seekers and adventurers from all over the world."[58]

Above all, Dillon recalls, the Pune ashram was not like any other ashram she had ever heard of. Rather than a quiet, otherworldly monastic retreat, the Pune ashram was remarkable in the way that it combined spiritual discipline with an ideal of joy, celebration, dance, and fun.[59] This would become the basis of Rajneesh's "Zorba the Buddha" ideal itself—the wedding of spirituality and pleasure, otherworldly transcendence and this-worldly enjoyment that has been the trademark of the movement ever since:

> The Pune ashram, as I kept discovering, wasn't a normal kind of ashram. Meditation was the backbone of what was happening, but celebration came a close second. In Osho's vision of life, meditation without celebration is too dry, while celebration without meditation lacks depth. A synthesis is needed, so the ashram's daily program offered many opportunities for singing and dancing . . . Every night there was singing and dancing in the Buddha Hall. . . . If someone were to ask me what I got out of those early years in

Pune I'd have to say that the lifestyle, as a whole, was far more important than any single experience or point of understanding. Osho called this collective phenomenon a "buddafield" where a group of seekers enhance each other's growth process simply by being together with an enlightened master in the same energy field.[60]

In a sense, the troops of young people visiting the ashram were willing subjects in a great and wondrous experiment—an experiment they did not necessarily understand but were too excited to worry about trying to make sense of at the time: "Everybody was there because we were in love with what we were feeling, with what we were experiencing, with Osho as a master, as a teacher. . . . It was like an organism of willing experimenters. It was Osho's experiment, and he didn't know where we were going necessarily. It was this vision, and we said, 'Yeah let's go!'"[61]

Early on, the ashram added therapy sessions modeled on European and American practices such Wilhelm Reich's techniques and other forms of psychotherapy, as the movement evolved into a complex hybrid of Indian and "Western" practices. Several visiting therapists from the human potential movement were brought in to set up therapy groups, including Paul Lowe, the founder of Europe's first growth center, Quaesitor; Michael Barnett, author of *People not Psychiatry;* and Leonard Zunin, a California psychologist. "By 1979 sixty different therapies were offered as well as Eastern meditations such as yoga, vipassana, Sufi dancing and tai chi."[62] As Dillon recalls, the ashram became a center for creative experimentation in an array of increasingly unconventional meditation sessions and encounter groups, which were famous for their tremendous physical, spiritual, and sexual energy. Combining spiritual, psychological and sexual experiments, that energy radiated far beyond the confines of the sessions themselves and helped to create a kind of ecstatic community:

> These groups were wild, intense non-limit structures in which all of the repressed emotional and sexual energy that people had been sitting on their whole lives was encouraged to be expressed. . . . It proved to be a potent cocktail that blew away our collective veneer of social morality and polite behavior. In these groups, I fought, kicked, screamed, wept, made love, and was generally forced by the extremity of many situations to make an inner quantum leap that left the person I thought I was far behind. In doing so, I discovered energy resources and raw animal emotions I never imagined I possessed. . . . Life in Pune was one long group. The ever-changing flux of love affairs, sexual encounters and relationships among the growing international community of *sannyasins* ensured that experience of such intense feelings continued, almost day and night.[63]

Very quickly, the Pune ashram began to be praised as the Indian counterpart of the famous New Age spiritual center in California, the Esalen Institute, which had also forged a popular hybrid of Eastern spirituality and Western psychology and modern science: "The Shree Rajneesh Ashram earned a reputation as the 'Esalen of the East,' drawing the attention of some big names in the emerging human potential movement that had its beginnings at the Esalen Institute in Big Sur."[64] In many ways, however, the Pune ashram went much further than its Esalen counterpart in pushing the envelope of every imaginable spiritual and psychological limit. (Moreover, as we will see below, there were also some fundamental differences between the two communities, and Esalen's own cofounder would become quite critical of the Pune ashram.[65]) A wide array of meditative, therapeutic, and encounter groups proliferated—though not always with much supervision or oversight, as "every conceivable boundary was confronted and challenged, wherever boundaries could be found. Anything was acceptable—you could fight, rage, cry, scream, fuck, sit in silence."[66] As one *sannysin*, Ma Satya Bharti, put it,

> The ashram is crazy, it's chaotic. It is the exact kind of ashram Bhagwan should have, and the kind of ashram that no other Master but he could have. It's a funhouse and a madhouse. A bawdyhouse and a temple.[67]

Later, in 1978–79, Rajneesh introduced yet another powerful and intensive hybrid practice called "energy *darshans*." Traditionally in South Asian religions, *darshan* refers to a "seeing" of the divine in the form of a statue, image, or human guru. Again, however, Rajneesh "updated" the traditional idea of *darshan* by combining it with wild music, ecstatic movement, and a kind of "collective effervescence" with up to 200 people dancing and swaying in an atmosphere reminiscent of a rock concert. In the midst of this effervescent fervor, Rajneesh would transmit his energy to *sannyasins* by pressing his hand to their "third eye" in the middle of the forehead. Meanwhile, a group of close female *sannyasins* were selected to serve as "mediums," who would then transmit his energy even more widely throughout the group. *Sannyasin* Ma Prem Shunyo described the energy *darshans* held in the ashram's Chuang Tzu auditorium:

> Music began—crazy music—and everyone present in the auditorium would be swaying and allowing any feeling that came across to move through their bodies. . . . Osho would touch the energy center on the forehead (known as the third eye) of a medium and with his other hand the third eye of the per-

son who had come for *darshan*. An energy transmission would happen that
. . . might look as though people were being charged with high voltage elec-
tricity. . . . Lights went on as the music reached a crescendo, and bodies
danced and swayed, screams and laughter filled the air.[68]

Thus the ashram quickly gained a reputation as far more than simply
a spiritual retreat but as a major global node in the expanding networks
of tourism, commerce, and entertainment during the 1970s. It was, in
many ways, a real "scene," where young people came to socialize, hang
out, and hook up as much as to experiment with new spiritual and
therapeutic ideas. "It was *wild*!" as one long-time *sannyasin* from the
Netherlands described the early days in Pune, looking back fondly on
an era of radical experimentation, sexual liberation, and the incredible
sense of freedom that many Europeans felt when set loose in India during the 1970s.[69] The Koregaon Park neighborhood grew into a "a huge
multinational camp of seekers," with orange-clothed *sannyasins* wandering everywhere.[70] By the late 1970s, there were at least 6,000 *sannyasins* living in the Pune area, though only about 600 actually lived on
the ashram's grounds. Meanwhile, some 25,000 to 35,000 visitors came
each year, filling the meditation halls, therapy sessions, and local restaurants—a seemingly endless flood of enthusiastic, orange-clad young
people.[71] Those who could not find space in the ashram itself found
lodging wherever they could, in guesthouses, hotels, or any free space,
spending as long as they could afford to live in India before going back
home to make more money to return. As Tim Guest recalls, the atmosphere in those days was intense, joyous, and chaotic. In a raucous mix
of spiritual experimentation, free love, and dysentery, male and female
sannyasins (Mas and Swamis) mingled freely in ever-new spiritual, sensual, emotional, and sexual configurations:

> There were Mas and Swamis everywhere. Mas hanging out on veranda steps,
> swapping tips on money, smoking bidi [small Indian] cigarettes. Swamis
> flirting in the dinner queue, giving a smile, and a blow, palms pressed
> together, to a passing Ma who caught their eye. . . . Everywhere, both Mas
> and Swamis were falling ill or recovering from illness, stricken at the very
> least with the meditative runs.[72]

Not surprisingly, given the large number of young people hanging
around the ashram, and given the context of the early 1970s, not all of
the activities in those days were directed toward spiritual enlightenment. Most of the foreign *sannyasins*, Guest recalls, spent much of their
time angling for ways to make money in order stay longer in India;

some of the women ended up prostituting themselves to rich business-men in Bombay, while some of the men ran blocks of hashish in suit-cases back home to generate some quick cash.[73]

As it grew in popularity during the 1970s, the community also began to shift in its global demographics and appeal, drawing ever more West-erners and fewer Indians by the end of the decade. Most of the *sannya-sins* by this time were American, British, or European; and they were mostly very young, in their twenties and thirties. "I want to rely on youth," Rajneesh proclaimed. "They are coming by breaking all the barriers. Future is not created by old people, future is created by youth."[74] A very high proportion were also well educated and/or pro-fessionals, including doctors, psychologists, lawyers, engineers, authors, photographers, architects, and journalists.[75] Rajneesh himself was becoming increasingly world famous and was now attracting the likes of famous Japanese composer Kitaro and the German musician and composer Deuter.[76] As Guest recalls, Rajneesh had ceased lecturing in Hindi, switching entirely to English, and gearing his message ever more to his growing non–South Asian audience, who were more excited and less shocked by his controversial teachings: "In the early days Bhagwan had lectured one week in Hindi and one week in English. It was the Westerners, though, who loved his message—and Bhagwan courted them most of all. . . . He stopped lecturing in Hindi. By mid-1981 only a few hundred Indian *sannyasins* remained at the ashram."[77]

In sum, with this new kind of ashram—or rather, this sort of "non-ashram" for "*neo-sannyasins*" and "religionless religion"—Rajneesh had created a remarkably successful global religious movement catering in particular to the needs and desires of Americans and Europeans in the post-1960s era. The ashram was able to offer the comforts of mod-ern life, the ideals of a countercultural commune, and philosophy drawn from Buddhism and the Upanishads. Emerging at the perfect time and place, the early Pune ashram was for many the ideal wedding of West and East, of familiar material pleasures and exotic spirituality. James Gordon reflects on the early community:

> The multinational and multiracial community that Rajneesh created in Poona was at once the response to the isolation and needs of those who came as disciples and the fulfillment of the utopian dreams and universalist hopes that pervaded the culture of the 1960s. It united . . . all the best features of capitalist creature comforts with the selfless sharing, the limitless sexual experimentation and the re-creative playfulness of the ideal—or idealized anarchist commune.[78]

A SYMBIOTIC BUSINESS MERGER: THE PUNE
COMMUNE AS SPIRITUAL MARKETPLACE

At the same time that it began to attract ever more foreign visitors, the Pune community also became a thriving business enterprise, in many ways embodying the new Indian capitalist model that Rajneesh had called for in his lectures. As Lewis Carter put it, "Rajneesh's dream of blending Eastern mysticism with Western psychology resulted in a symbiotic business merger";[79] and this merger began to grow and prosper at a remarkable rate. In the late 1970s. Rajneesh himself was quite open about the fact that his new community was not in fact an "ashram" in the traditional Indian sense of an otherworldly, detached hermitage, but rather an explicitly capitalist and commercial sort of space. Here, buying, selling, and enjoyment of this-worldly life would exist side by side with meditation and otherworldly transcendence. And this meant *paying* for spiritual teachings, even though that might offend many audiences:

> This place is a marketplace. Can you find any other place that is more like the market? I could have made the ashram somewhere in the Himalayas. . . . I want to remain part of the marketplace. And this ashram is run almost as part of the marketplace. That's why Indians are very annoyed—they cannot understand. They have known ashrams for centuries, but this ashram is beyond their comprehension. They cannot think that you have to pay to listen to a religious discourse. They have always listened free of charge. . . . Here you have to pay. . . . I want it to be absolutely part of the marketplace because I want my *sannyasins* not to move into the monasteries. They have to remain in the world. . . . My whole effort here is to create a miniature world where money is absolutely accepted, where women and men live together in joy, in celebration.[80]

Well known for collecting watches, cuff links, and other visible signs of wealth, Rajneesh also used these displays of "conspicuous consumption" as a part of his anti-Gandhian philosophy and as a means of challenging conventional ideas of spirituality.[81] He himself later recalled how he deliberately used a strategy of "conspicuous consumption" in order to attract more followers and solicit money from lenders. This was the inspiration for the purchase of his first Rolls-Royce, which he proudly displayed in order to persuade bankers to offer loans to the ashram, and in turn generate national media attention:

> I told my secretary Laxmi to purchase the most costly car possible in the country. . . . It worked—it was a device. Laxmi was knocking on the doors of the banks to get money for the new commune. We need much money;

near-about a million dollars will be needed. Who is going to lend that much money to me? The day she purchased the car, seeing that we have the money, banks started coming to her office, offering: "Take as much money as you want." . . . Now they are all interested. The news of the car has been published all over the country, in all the newspapers, in all the languages.[82]

The strategy apparently worked quite well, as the Pune ashram began to grow and prosper even more rapidly than Rajneesh or Laxmi had imagined. In the early days, Sheela herself ran an informal "bank" for the ashram, exchanging foreign currency from a tin box. Meanwhile, money began to pour in from seekers eager to enroll in classes at the new Rajneesh International University, which claimed to be "the largest and most innovative growth center in the world," offering over fifty different group offerings by 1977 and attracting some 1,000 to 2,000 people a week.[83] At the same time, the ashram added a publishing house, a press office, a clothing boutique, a carpentry shop that made musical instruments, a bakery, and studios for making jewelry and pottery and for weaving, essentially becoming its own small city with a thriving bazaar. In the words of Shobha Kilachand, a reporter who visited the ashram in early 1981, the boutique selling Rajneesh memorabilia reminded her of the "Elvis Presley Shop."[84]

By the end of the first Pune period, the Rajneesh Foundation had amassed some $1.2 million in four banks and $116,246 in cash at the ashram itself. According to financial documents filed with Maharashtra state charity officials, the university was the foundation's major source of income ($606,281), followed by donations ($586,583), and therapy groups ($188,253). "The ashram *is* big business," the Indian magazine *Sunday* reported in 1981. "And it is growing bigger, as the official figures show."[85] To help protect this growing wealth from as much taxation and scrutiny as possible, Sheela reportedly opened a Credit Suisse bank account in Zurich in 1980.[86]

In his typically ironic and playful style, however, Rajneesh not only acknowledged but even embraced the growing wealth of the movement and his own growing notoriety as the "guru of the rich." "All the religions have commanded and praised poverty, and I condemn all those religions," he would later explain to the INS, " . . . I am a materialist spiritualist."[87] Wealth is not only compatible with spirituality but is in fact *necessary*, since we first need to satisfy our material needs before we can think about things like meditation or spiritual development.

I am a rich man's guru. Absolutely it is so. . . . Religion is a luxury—the ultimate luxury I call it, because it is the highest value. . . . When a man is happy with his body, has enough to eat, has a good house to live in, he starts

have to have a base before anything spiritual

becoming interested in music, poetry, literature, painting, art. Now a hunger arises. . . . When your bodily needs are fulfilled, psychological needs arise. When your psychological needs are also fulfilled, then your spiritual needs arise.[88]

Here we should note that Rajneesh appears to be ironically referencing and playing upon Karl Marx and Friedrich Engels's core idea that "mankind must first of all eat." As Engels famously put it in his speech at Marx's graveside in 1883,

Mankind must first of all eat, drink, have shelter and clothing, before it can pursue politics, science, art, religion, etc.; that therefore the production of the immediate material means of subsistence and consequently the degree of economic development attained by a given people or during a given epoch form the foundation upon which the state institutions, the legal conceptions, art, and even the ideas on religion, of the people concerned have been evolved.[89]

Of course, Rajneesh is also deliberately turning Marx and Engels completely on their heads. For Bhagwan, religion is not simply an "opiate" that masks and mystifies our real material needs; rather, it is the necessary *spiritual complement* and *fulfillment* of our material needs, which can be perfectly harmonized in the "Zorba the Buddha" ideal. Taking a direct jab at Marx, Rajneesh even dismisses communism as a shelter for the poor, while declaring religion to be the luxury of the rich: "Religion is the last luxury. The poor man cannot afford it. He cannot afford food, he cannot afford even shelter. . . . How can he understand Mozart, Leonardo da Vinci, Tolstoy, or Dostoyevsky? . . . Only the rich can afford religion. The poor can afford communism. For the poor, communism is religion, and for the rich man even Christianity, Judaism, Hinduism, Buddhism are not satisfying because they are all old, rotten. He needs something up to date—and that's what I am offering."[90]

CONCLUSIONS: THE EARLY RAJNEESH MOVEMENT AS POSTNATIONAL SODALITY

The early Rajneesh movement in India, I would argue, was ultimately something far more interesting and more complicated than simply a bunch of American and European hippies gathering around an exotic Indian guru. Rather, it was an emerging global movement that was at the cutting edge of much larger social, political, and economic trends during the 1970s. In many ways, this was one of the first truly "postnational movements" in Appadurai's sense of a new kind of sodality that is increasingly independent of national boundaries and state regulations. As Appadurai suggests, a wide array of postnational sodalities have emerged even within and between the structures of late capitalism, including communities based on politics or sports, fan clubs and other groups formed through mass media, and "sodalities of worship and charisma," such as the following of the Hindu goddess Santoshi Ma, who became a nationwide sensation after appearing in a Bollywood film.[91]

With its broad international audience, its wild mixture of spiritual and psychological methods from across the globe, and its general disregard for local governmental regulations, the Rajneesh ashram was just about as postnational as a community could be during the 1970s, particularly in India. While he did not use the specific term "postnational" himself, Rajneesh was very self-consciously imagining that this would be an entirely new kind of movement that would transcend all existing national boundaries, creating a new kind of global "buddhafield" of interconnected communes spread in many countries like proliferating nodes in a complex spiritual web. As he put it in 1979, borrowing language from Christianity, wherever his *sannyasins* gathered in small communities, his presence would be among them:

> My effort is not only to create the buddhafield here but to create small oases all over the world. I would not like to confine this tremendous possibility to this small commune only. This commune will be the source, but it will have branches all over the world. It will be the root, but it is going to become a big tree. It is going to reach every country, it is going to reach every potential person. We will create small oases; we have started creating small communes, centers, all over the world. And wherever my sannyasins are together, I am there. Wherever they will sit in meditation, my presence will be felt.[92]

Here one is also reminded of Deleuze and Guattari's ideal of a "new earth" spreading through rhizomatic networks as a kind of "territory of permanent revolution—a nomadic territory freed from representation, cruelty, terror."[93]

What is perhaps most unique about the early Rajneesh movement, however, is that it was not simply a postnational community but one also rooted explicitly in both the theory and the practice of global capitalism. Not only did Rajneesh clearly articulate an incisive critique of Nehruvian socialism and Gandhian asceticism, but he also created a whole new kind of spiritual business that became itself the living embodiment of his economic vision. In many ways, this community was at the cutting edge of larger economic shifts in the Indian and global economies, as American-style capitalism spread to Asia in the 1970s, and above all in the 1980s and 1990s.

In some ways, the early Rajneesh community resembles the sort of "disorganized" form of capitalism that economists such as Scott Lash and John Urry believe was replacing early modern or "organized capitalism" during the 1960s and 1970s. The modern or organized forms of capitalism that were dominant until the mid-twentieth century, they argue, were characterized primarily by the concentration and centralization of industrial banking and commercial capital in regulated national markets; conversely, postmodern or disorganized forms of capitalism are characterized more by the deconcentration of rapidly increasing corporate power away from national markets, the internationalization of capital, the increasing independence of large monopolies from state regulation, and the rapid spread of capitalist development to new markets such as Asia.[94] It is not difficult to see most of these trends reflected in the Pune ashram of the 1970s, which had indeed emerged as a kind of chaotic, ad hoc, and "disorganized" global business enterprise that operated largely independently of any state government.

However, as David Harvey argues, the emerging form of global capitalism since the 1970s is perhaps best understood not simply as "disorganized"; rather, it has in many ways become *more* organized, precisely through its more fluid global circulation in more and more markets around the world: "Capitalism is becoming ever more tightly organized *through* dispersal, geographical mobility, and flexible responses in labour markets, labour processes and consumer markets."[95] As we will see in chapter 4, when we turn to the commune in Oregon, this increasing trend toward organization appears to be largely what the Rajneesh movement experienced. In the course of its rapid growth and success, the Rajneesh movement reflected an increasing tension and seeming contradiction: a tension between the noble ideal of a postnational community or "buddhafield" and the more utilitarian business of a multinational corporation enmeshed in the larger networks of global capitalism.

CHAPTER 3

"From Sex To Superconsciousness"

Sexuality, Tantra, and Liberation in 1970s India

The days of Tantra are coming. Sooner or later Tantra is going to explode for the first time on the masses, because for the first time the time is ripe—ripe to take sex naturally. It is possible that explosion may come from the West, because Freud, Jung, Reich, they have prepared the background. . . . They have made the basic ground for Tantra to evolve. Western psychology has come to a conclusion that the basic human disease is somewhere around sex, the basic insanity of man is sex-oriented. So unless this sex orientation is dissolved, man cannot be natural, normal.

—Osho, *The Book of Secrets*

The idea of sexual liberation as integral to larger social and political liberation was an underlying theme in radical and romantic theories since the early nineteenth century and became central to both the counterculture and New Left movements of the 1970s.

—Dennis Altman, *Global Sex*

Most people who remember Rajneesh today probably remember him primarily as the "sex guru." Even *Lonely Planet* —the most widely used guidebook for travel in India—still has a special insert in the chapter on Pune devoted to the "Guru of Sex" and his sensuous compound in the upscale neighborhood of Koregaon Park.[1] Rajneesh was also a primary inspiration for John Updike's 1988 novel *S.*, Mike Myers's 2008 film, "The Love Guru," and various other fictional accounts of dubious mystics and philandering gurus.[2]

Rajneesh himself would later complain that this focus on the sexual content of his teachings was exaggerated and that he had only really published one book on the topic (*From Sex to Superconsciousness,* based on lectures from 1968).[3] However, while it is partly true that the emphasis on the sexual nature of Rajneesh's teachings is exaggerated, it is also true that sexual themes run throughout his lectures from the late 1960s onward. They have also been consistently repackaged and reprinted by the current Osho presses in books and DVDs such as *Sex Matters* (2003), *The Science of Tantra* (2010), *Tantra: The Way of Acceptance* (2011), and *Tantric Transformation: When Love Meets Meditation* (2012).[4] Following Freud and post-Freudians such as Wilhelm Reich—one of his favorite authors—Rajneesh stated repeatedly that sexuality is "the most powerful human instinct,"[5] the most driving force in human nature, and the source of both our worst neuroses and our most sublime spiritual experiences: "Sex is so important, because the whole nature insists on it; otherwise man could not continue to be. If it were voluntary there would be no one left on earth. Sex is so obsessive, so compelling, the sex drive is so intense, because the whole of nature is for it."[6] In many ways, Rajneesh's teachings on sexuality are a hybrid of older Indian views of *kama* (desire, pleasure, sensuality) and post-Freudian psychoanalysis.

Even more importantly, Rajneesh was arguably the most significant figure in the modern transformation of the Asian tradition of Tantra in the twentieth and twenty-first centuries. An extremely complex body of texts and traditions that spread throughout the Hindu and Buddhist communities from roughly the sixth century onward, Tantra does involve the use of sexual symbolism and in some cases sexual practices as a means to spiritual liberation and worldly empowerment. However, in its traditional forms, these sexual elements are neither central nor even particularly "sexy"—at least not in the contemporary sense of sensual pleasure or optimal orgasm.[7] And yet, since the 1960s, and particularly in the United States, Tantra has come to be defined primarily as "spiritual sex," or the use of sexual orgasm as a form of both intense physical fulfillment and spiritual transcendence.[8]

With his popular new ideal of "Neo-Tantra" and his growing audience of American and European *sannyasins,* Rajneesh was one of the most important figures in this transformation. As one contemporary

Neo-Tantric author, Nik Douglas, put it, "Rajneesh offered everything Westerners imagined Tantra to be: a free love cult promising enlightenment, an exciting radical community, and the opportunity to rise up in the hierarchy. . . . Rajneesh slipped comfortably into the role of 'Tantra Messiah.' . . . Largely because of Rajneesh, Tantra reemerged as a New Age Cult in the 1970s and 1980s."[9] Just as Rajneesh had given completely new meanings to the words "*sannyasin*," "meditation," "ashram," and even "religion" itself, so too, he transformed the South Asian concept of Tantra into the path of "spiritual sexualogy" that has become so widely popularized in America today. In the wake of Rajneesh's teachings, virtually all forms of "Western Tantra" have identified Tantra with its (originally limited) sexual component and defined it as a kind of "nookie nirvana," as *Cosmopolitan* magazine described it.[10] As such, Tantra has become one of the most striking examples of our ongoing fascination with the "exotic Orient" and our continuing tendency to imagine India as the realm of otherworldly mysticism, unrestrained eroticism, and radical otherness.[11]

In this sense, Rajneesh and his early movement in Pune were a key reflection and profound embodiment of the larger cultural, political, and sexual changes taking place in the late 1960s and early 1970s. Emerging at the height of the sexual revolution and attracting huge numbers of foreign devotees, the early Rajneesh movement was a crucial node both in the importation of the Western counterculture to India and in the exportation of Indian spirituality to all points west. Rajneesh's open attitudes toward sexuality meshed perfectly with the sexual revolution in the United States, United Kingdom, and Europe, and in turn, American and European ideas of free love radically transformed the perception of Indian traditions such as Tantra. Rajneesh's hybrid teaching of "Neo-Tantra" has been praised by admirers as the best of both worlds and denounced by critics as the worst of both worlds, but no one can deny that it dramatically changed the popular perception of Tantra in the late twentieth and early twenty-first centuries.

Finally, this unique brand, Neo-Tantra, was also a central part of the larger Rajneesh community as it grew and thrived during the 1970s in India and even more so as it spread to the United States in the 1980s. For Rajneesh, Tantra really embodied his paradoxical ideal of a "religionless religion," or a spiritual path based on the rejection of all established institutions and aimed at the realization of divinity in and through the body itself. As he understood it, "Tantra is the religion of the body."[12] As such, Rajneesh's version of Neo-Tantra would have a huge and lasting influence on virtually all forms of New Age spirituality and American popular culture, particularly what Jeffrey Kripal calls the "American religion of no religion."[13] However, we will see that the new community that Rajneesh created in Pune also contained its own internal tensions and contradictions; side by side with the ideals of total sexual liberation and social freedom were seemingly quite "un-liberatory" practices, such as a growing authoritarianism, paranoia, disciplinary control, and violence.

THE "SEXUAL REVOLUTION": FROM GERMANY TO AMERICA TO INDIA, AND BACK AGAIN

The phrase "sexual revolution" was first used in Germany in the 1920s by the renegade disciple of Sigmund Freud, Wilhelm Reich (1897–1957)—a figure who, we will see, had a lasting influence on many New Age authors and modern Indian gurus, including Rajneesh. As David Allyn notes in his study of the sexual revolution, Reich "hoped to liberate Europeans from centuries of social, political and psychological enslavement," and was thus a key influence on much of the counterculture of the 1960s and 1970s.[14] Reich first met Freud in 1919 and worked closely with him in the 1920s. Reich agreed with Freud that sexuality is the most fundamental and powerful force in human existence, being "the center around which the life of society as a whole as well as the inner intellectual life of the individual revolves."[15] A key figure in the sex reform movements that swept Germany in the 1920s, Reich established clinics throughout Europe to help disseminate information about birth control and abortion.

Yet Reich also soon developed a more radical theory of sexuality that went well beyond the boundaries of standard Freudian psychoanalysis. In the mid-1920s Reich began to publish articles and books on his theory of the "orgastic potency," or the possibility of releasing emotions bound up in the muscles and even of experiencing a sublime loss of ego in a purely uninhibited orgasm: "It is not just to fuck," he wrote, " . . . not the embrace in itself, not the intercourse. It is the real emotional experience of the loss of your ego, of your whole spiritual self."[16] With the rise of the Nazi Party, Reich fled Germany for the United States and began to explore his key idea of "orgone" energy (derived from "orgasm" and "organism"). Imagined as a kind of cosmic vital energy—not unlike *ch'i* in Chinese thought or *prana* (breath) and *shakti* (power) in Indian thought—orgone energy is believed to pervade the entire cosmos and the human body: "The orgasm formula thus emerges as the life formula itself. . . . The sexual process is the productive biological process per se, in procreation, work, joyful living, intellectual productivity, etc."[17] Eventually, Reich even developed his own unique device called the "Orgone Accumulator," a special closet-sized box designed to help intensify and concentrate the orgone energy flowing through the environment.

Reich was particularly influential in combining sexuality and politics, wedding Freud and Marx in an analysis of the links between sexual repression and social-political repression. If this vital orgone energy circulates through the entire body and nature, it can also be repressed and blocked in various destructive ways, and above all through repressive political movements such as fascism and Nazism. Conversely, Reich maintained, the key to social and political freedom also lies in sexual freedom—an idea that became a central tenet of the 1960s and 1970s counterculture.[18] Hence Reich's ideal of sexual revolution had both personal and social-political dimensions, and this linkage would be picked up and developed by a wide array of other authors in the United States, United Kingdom, and Europe during the 1960s and 1970s:

> Reich had been one of Freud's leading disciples during the early years of psychoanalysis; unlike Freud, however, Reich was a socialist who thought it imperative to combine political activism and sexual theory. Sexual repression, Reich argued, was the cornerstone of totalitarianism, so in order to liberate people politically it was necessary to liberate them sexually first.[19]

Although Reich's dream of a sexually liberated society never materialized as he had imagined, the first half of the twentieth century did see rapid changes in attitudes toward sex in both Europe and the United States. Reich's phrase "sexual revolution" was used by a wide range of sources in many different contexts throughout the twentieth century, first to refer to sexually suggestive advertising and sexually titillating magazine images, then to the impact of birth control, and later to the repudiation of literary censorship by the U.S. Supreme Court, and finally in the late 1960s to refer to the new candor in American culture, particularly the acceptance of nudity in film. By the 1970s, when Rajneesh began developing his own new interpretation of Tantra, the idea of "sexual revolution" had paradoxically become a mainstream part of consumer culture and the larger commodification of everyday life in late capitalist America.[20] As Philip Jenkins describes this decade in the United States, "The story of American culture in the early 1970s can be seen as the mainstreaming of sixties values, the point at which the countercultural ideas reached a mass audience. . . . So rapid were the changes and so widespread their acceptance that for a while it looked as if the sixties cultural revolution was becoming institutionalized."[21]

Despite the different ways in which the phrase itself was interpreted, these various uses of "sexual revolution" did signal a real shift in at least the *discourse* surrounding sex in the United States and Europe, and this shift was quickly exported to developing nations such as India, above all through the new networks of tourism and transnational capitalism. As Dennis Altman notes, the discourse of sexual revolution and the attempt by Reich and others to link sexual freedom with social-political freedom helped form the "the dominant script by which westerners have interpreted sexuality" for the last hundred years.[22] By the end of the twentieth century, not only the discourse of sexual revolution but also the very real shifts in gender relations accompanied by that discourse had also begun to spread well beyond the bounds of "the West" and had come to impact the rest of the globe in complex and multiple ways:

> It is impossible to divorce the "sexual revolution" from the very major shifts in gender order over the past century which continue to change fundamentally the ways in which women and men understand themselves. . . . Part of the process of globalization is the rapid dispersion of these shifts.[23]

Rajneesh, we will see, would become one of the key figures in the importation of Reich's "sexual revolution" to India; and the early Rajneesh community in Pune would become a kind of global epicenter of counterculture idealism, in which sexual liberation and social, political, and spiritual liberation were intertwined.

RAJNEESH, FREUD, REICH, AND THE TRANSMUTATION OF DESIRE

As we saw in the previous chapters, Rajneesh had already become a hugely controversial and polarizing figure in India by the mid-1960s. One of the most infamous moments in his early teaching career was a 1968 lecture series in Bombay. The talks began with a five-part discussion of "love" in the prestigious Bharatiya Vidya Bhavan Auditorium in August and then finished with a speech to a very large audience at the Gowalia Tank Maiden in September. "If you want to know the elemental truth about love," Rajneesh told his (often shocked and infuriated) audience, "the first requisite is to accept the sacredness of sex, to accept the divinity of sex in the same way as you accept God's existence—with an open heart."[24] Published under the Hindi title *Sambhog se samadhi ki aur* and the English title *From Sex to Superconsciousness,* the lectures scandalized many Hindu leaders and earned Rajneesh the title "Sex Guru" in the popular media.

The basic theme running through these lectures is that sex is the most powerful driving force in human life. It cannot be suppressed or denied without creating all manner of psychological problems; but if it can be accepted and redirected in a positive direction, it becomes the most powerful means of achieving superconsciousness, or the transcendent loving awareness of an enlightened being:

> Man cannot be separated from sex. Sex is his primary point: he is born of it. God has accepted the energy of sex as the starting of creation. . . . If God considers sex as sin there is no greater sinner than God. . . . Man is engaged in fighting against his prime energy and so he has become weak, gross and coarse, devoid of love and full of nothingness. . . . Not enmity but friendship is to be made with sex. The spring of sex should be elevated to purer heights. . . . Only the sex energy can flower into a love-force.[25]

Unfortunately, Rajneesh argued, all the great religions and philosophies of the past—including not only Christianity, but even Hinduism and Buddhism—had taught human beings to deny, suppress, and fight their sexual nature rather than embracing it: "Only the energy of sex can flower into love, but everybody, including the great thinkers of Man, is against it. . . . Man is taught to fight against the sex energy, to oppose the sex tendencies."[26] That is why Rajneesh's philosophy was so radically new: it was the first to tell us not to reject our sexuality but instead to affirm, celebrate, and transform it into a vehicle to higher awareness—in short, to transmute carnal lust into spiritual love: "The lust which is inside us may become a ladder with which to reach the temple of love! The sex which is inside everyone of us may become a channel to reach the superconsciousness."[27] Indeed, sexual union is a surer means of approaching God than attending any religious service or establishment, because sexual union is the divine power of creation that comes from the Creator himself: "At the time of coitus, we are nearer to God: God is in the act of creation there, gives birth to a new life, and hence the mental attitude ought to be that of a man going to a temple or a church. At the climax we are nearest to the supreme. . . . In coitus we are nearest to the Creator himself."[28]

Clearly, we can see in Rajneesh's description of the tremendous power of sex the strong influence of Freudian and post-Freudian psychoanalysis. Even in these early lectures, Rajneesh both acknowledges and then goes on to critique Freud's view of sexuality. Freud, in his view, was correct about the tremendous importance and power of sex, but he was mistaken in only limiting sex to the psychological level and primarily to its deviant or unhealthy forms. Thus Freud was unable to grasp the higher spiritual levels of sexuality or the possibility of transforming sexual desire into superconsciousness:

> Freud knows nothing about what I am telling you here. Freud could never rise above the mental level. He has no idea even in his imagination of the existence of spiritual sex. Freud's whole work, his whole information, is on sick sex: hysterical behavior, homosexuality, masturbation; it is a research in all this. It is a research into sick and perverted sex, it is with the pathological. . . . The studies he made on people—in the West—are of people on the mental level of sex. He doesn't have a single case study, a single case history of what can be called spiritual sex.[29]

Yet despite his critique of Freud, Rajneesh still makes extensive use of clearly "Freudian" language—the language of the conscious and unconscious minds, the language of repression, psychic conflict, and neurosis. Perhaps the most important difference is that Freud believed in the inevitability of repression in order for humans to live in civilized society, whereas Rajneesh argues that repression must be left behind by the enlightened being who is brave enough to transcend mainstream social norms and experience true physical and spiritual integration. As he put it in one of his early letters, collected in the volume *A Cup of Tea,*

> Don't be afraid of sexual desire
> because fear is the beginning of defeat.
> Accept it,
> it is and it has to be.
> Of course, you must know it and recognize it,
> be aware of it,
> bring it out of the unconscious into the conscious mind.
> You cannot do this if you condemn it
> because condemnation leads to repression
> and it is repression that pushes desires and emotions
> into the unconscious.
> Really, it is because of repression
> that the mind is divided into conscious and unconscious,
> and this division is at the root of all conflict,
> and it is this division that prevents man from being total—
> and without integration
> there is no way to peace, bliss and freedom.[30]

In this sense, Rajneesh's understanding of sexuality has less in common with standard Freudian psychoanalysis than with the ideas of Freud's eccentric renegade disciple, Reich. Indeed, Rajneesh cites Reich frequently—and very positively—in his early lectures, even declaring his "love" for Reich.[31] Many of these Reichian ideas appear quite explicitly in Rajneesh's lectures of this period, such as *Meditation: The Art of Ecstasy* and *Yoga: The Alpha and the Omega*, where he discusses not only Reich's philosophy but also his life and imprisonment. At several points following his lectures, Rajneesh was asked directly by followers about the similarities between Reich's philosophy and his own. Rajneesh readily acknowledged the importance of Reich's ideas of orgone energy, sexual repression, and sexual liberation, and he noted that the primary reason Reich was persecuted was for speaking the truth about sex:

> And you ask about Wilhelm Reich's use of sexual energy to release body blocks that coincide with neurosis: I am wholly in agreement with Wilhelm Reich's approach. Really, sex is the problem; all other problems are byproducts. And unless man comes to a deep understanding of sex energy it is impossible to help him. . . .
> Sex is the most natural thing because it is the source of life. You are born of sex. Your every body cell is a sex cell, all your energy is sex energy. So if religions teach that sex is bad, sex is a sin, they have condemned you completely. . . . You are divided; you start fighting with yourself. And the more this guilt can be created in you—over the concept that sex is something unholy—the more neurotic you will become
> So Reich was right, absolutely right, that sex is the problem and all other problems are just byproducts of it, branches of it. . . . This is my understanding too. . . .
> So Wilhelm Reich was attacked in every way. It was forcibly declared that he was mad. They put him into prison.[32]

As we will see below, Reich's fundamental linkage between sexual and social-political repression became a key idea running through Rajneesh's teachings from the 1970s onward.

Not only did Reich's work find its way into Rajneesh's lectures, but many followers also found their way to Rajneesh through their interest in Reich. Aneesha Dillon, for example, is a contemporary teacher of Osho's Neo-Tantric methods, who had first taught Reichian therapy at the Esalen institute in the early 1970s. As she recalls, it was primarily her interest in sexuality—combined with the larger countercultural context of the 1960s and 1970s—that drew her to Reich's work: "I got my first book, *the Selected Writings of Wilhelm Reich,* and immediately there was this recognition that what he is saying is true; there is something about sexual energy and life energy. . . . There was a longing in me that was becoming a fire, this very permissive quality that was coming through of course also in the 60s and 70s. It was really my interest in sexual freedom and sexual aliveness that attracted me to Reich."[33] A few years later, when Dillon encountered Rajneesh's practices, such as Dynamic Meditation, she immediately recognized their affinity with Reich's work: "What struck me about this Dynamic Meditation technique was that it contained the same essential ingredients as Reich's orgasm formula, beginning with vigorous build up of an energy charge in the body, followed by discharge and relaxation."[34] After traveling to Pune in 1976, Dillon began offering her own workshops, which combined Rajneesh's and Reich's ideas of sexual energy—a practice that she continues to this day.

Another *sannyasin* who joined the movement in the early Pune days was Robert Raines, who also came to Rajneesh's teachings after first reading Reich. Raines was naturally drawn to Reich's central idea that "there was a possibility for transcendence in sexuality," having experienced a kind of annihilation of thought and a loss of self in orgasm.[35] After exploring other gurus such as Sri Chinmoy, Muktananda, and Maharishi Mahesh Yogi, Raines decided he wanted a teacher "who understood the creative power of sexuality as well as the necessity of abolition of character and the loss of ego; someone who saw the connection between personal goals and political change."[36] After writing to Rajneesh, he went to Pune and became a *sannyasin*.

This deep linkage between Rajneesh and Reich, particularly in their views of sexuality, was one of the key features of the early Pune community as a kind of global node, and one of the main attractions for many Western seekers during the 1970s. With its own history of fusing Indian meditation with Reichian therapy, the Esalen center in California would become both a model for and a global counterpart of the Pune ashram, which soon began to be known as the "Esalen of the East."

NEO-TANTRA AND SEXUAL REVOLUTION

At roughly the same time that Rajneesh began to deliver his controversial lectures on sex and superconsciousness, he also began to speak frequently on the equally controversial topic of Tantra. Indeed, Rajneesh would become perhaps the single most important figure in the modern reimagining of Tantra as it was progressively transformed from a highly esoteric and extremely diverse tradition into one that was both marketed to a mass public audience and increasingly identified with sexuality.

As most modern scholars agree, the term Tantra (or "Tantrism" or "Tantricism") does not refer to a singular, monolithic, or neatly defined category. Rather, it is an extremely messy and ambiguous term that is used to refer to a "bewilderingly diverse array of esoteric precepts and practices attested across much of South, Inner and East Asia from the sixth century down to the present day."[37] It covers a huge range of diverse texts and traditions that spread through the Hindu, Buddhist, and Jain communities of India, China, Japan, Tibet, Mongolia, and parts of southeast Asia; and it is reflected in a wide array of different sects and schools, such as the Kapalika, Kaula, Krama, Pancharatra, Pashupata, Shakta, Sahajiya, Shrividya, Trika, Vajrayana, and many others. Derived from the root *tan,* "to spread" or "stretch," the term *tantra* has been used since Vedic times in many different ways, signifying everything from a loom or weaving machine to a system of philosophy to a drug or remedy. Most commonly, *tantra* simply refers to a kind of text—but one that may or may not contain the sort of tantalizing and titillating things we normally associate with "Tantra" today.[38]

As André Padoux and others have argued, the abstract category of "Tantrism"—as a singular, unified "ism"—is itself a relatively recent invention and in large part the creation of European scholars and colonial administrators writing in the nineteenth century: "Tantrism is, to a large extent, a 'category of the West' and not, strictly speaking, an Indian one."[39] Initially the terms "Tantra" and "Tantrism" were used by British Orientalist scholars and Christian missionaries to refer to a large body of texts and traditions that fell outside of brahmanical Hinduism—and particularly those they found to be morally repugnant: "It so happened that it was in texts known as *tantras* that Western scholars first described doctrines and practices different from those of Brahmanism . . . so Western experts first adopted the word Tantrism for that particular, and for them, repulsive aspect of Indian religion."[40] In the nineteenth century, many Hindu reformers such as Rammohun Roy and Swami Vivekananda likewise began to use the term to refer to those aspects of Hinduism that they found most embarrassing and in need of either radical reform or expunging from the tradition.[41]

However, in the second half of the twentieth century—and above all in the United States during the 1960s—Tantra was reappropriated and transformed by a new generation of spiritual seekers who turned the Orientalist denigration of Tantra completely on its head. Rather than a depraved path of perversion, Tantra was now celebrated as a much-needed affirmation of the human body and sensual pleasure. As we see in works such as Omar Garrison's *Tantra: The Yoga of Sex* (1964) and Philip Rawson's *Tantra: The Indian Cult of Ecstasy* (1973), Tantra was now imagined as a liberatory path of sexual ecstasy and thus as a necessary antidote to the repressive attitudes of the modern West.[42] As Garrison wrote in his 1964 book, "Through the principles of Tantra Yoga, man can achieve the sexual potency which enables him to extend the ecstasy crowning sexual union for an hour or more, rather than for the brief seconds he now knows."[43] Thus the rediscovery of Tantra in the 1960s and 1970s fit perfectly with the larger counterculture, adding the exotic allure of the "mystical Orient" to the broader mix of sex, drugs, and rock 'n' roll. In 1968, Mick Jagger would even produce a film called *Tantra*, a psychedelic journey through Tantric practice, culminating in a rite of sexual union.[44]

In the course of its complex "journey to the West," then, Tantra was progressively transformed from a highly esoteric path focused on the pursuit of spiritual liberation and the acquisition of supernatural power into a popular path identified almost entirely with sexual pleasure.[45] As David Gordon White has persuasively shown in his historical study of Tantric sex, many of the oldest Tantric rituals do involve sexual practices; yet these are really not particularly "sexy" by modern standards. Rather than a matter of sexual pleasure, these rites are more concerned with unleashing the tremendous power (*shakti*) believed to flow through the universe and to use that power for both spiritual and worldly purposes. According to the earliest Tantric texts that describe sexual rituals, White argues, the primary aim is not pleasure at all but really the emission of the sexual fluids, which are considered to be tremendous power substances and are consumed as part of a sacramental meal.[46]

Conversely, in virtually all forms of modern or Neo-Tantra, sexuality is the central and often only concern, with a primary emphasis on sensual pleasure and optimal orgasm. Today, countless books as well as videos and websites focus on Tantric practices, including *Urban Tantra: Sacred Sex for the Twenty-First Century, Tantric Orgasm for Women,* and, of course, *The Complete Idiot's Guide to Tantric Sex.* Virtually all of these reduce Tantra to sexual pleasure, usually confused with the *Kama Sutra* and typically with a healthy dose of the *Joy of Sex* mixed in.[47]

Rajneesh was at the forefront of this redefinition of Tantra during the late 1960s and 1970s, both in India and in the English-speaking world. While he only really cites one actual *tantra* in all of his lectures—the *Vijnana Bhairava Tantra,* and even in that case with only loose reference to the text[48]—he helped radically alter the modern understanding of Tantra. As Dillon herself acknowledges, Osho's Neo-Tantra might not be particularly accurate from a historical perspective, but it has been tremendously successful as a reimagining of Tantra for a contemporary audience: "Osho explained the Tantra vision, its implications and its importance as a spiritual path, but neither was he much interested in historic details. His whole effort was to make Tantra a contemporary, living force that we could experience immediately and directly, in our own bodies. And in this he was dramatically successful."[49]

Significantly, Rajneesh himself drew direct connections between Tantra and the work of Western psychoanalysts such as Reich, even going so far as to suggest that Reich was himself a kind of "modern tantrika."[50] Rajneesh repeatedly praised Reich in his lectures collected as *Sermons in Stones* in 1987:

> I will call Wilhelm Reich a modern Tantra master, although he was not aware of it. Perhaps in his past lives he may have known the secrets of Tantra—because his work contained the secrets of Tantra.[51]
> [Reich] had no idea of Tantra, he had never been to the East. But the exercises that he found are ten thousand years old.[52]
> Reich will have a revival because what he was doing was absolutely scientific. . . . I have so many sannyasins educated in psychology, psychoanalysis, in analytical psychology. . . . He belongs to us. I give him posthumous *sannyas*.[53]

Rajneesh also notes how sad it is that Reich's important work remained unfinished after his imprisonment and death, offering the hope that his own followers might later develop his research on sexuality, above all by combining it with South Asian Tantra: "It is strange that after his death his work has remained where he left it. It has immense potentiality. It needs to be developed and it needs to be developed in collaboration with Tantra."[54]

Tantra would be a recurring theme throughout Rajneesh's lectures from the 1970s onward, published in book form in texts such as *Tantra, Spirituality, and Sex*. Here Tantra is presented as perhaps the only truly "Rajneeshian" religious path, because it is the only path that teaches, accepts, and integrates sexuality rather than rejecting it and repressing it, as all other mainstream religions have done for millennia:

> All the religions are against sex, afraid of it, because it is such a great energy. Once you are in it you are no more, and the current will take you anywhere; that's why they fear it. So: "Create a barrier so that you and the current become two . . . be master of it!" Only Tantra says "mastery is going to be false, diseased, pathological, because you cannot be divided from this

current. You are it!" . . . Tantra says "try to melt . . . and become one with the river."[55]

Here we can see that Rajneesh is clearly redefining Tantra primarily in terms of its sexual aspect. As he put it in a later lecture entitled "Tantra: The Science of Tantra,"

> Tantra is basically a spiritual sexualogy. . . . Tantra is the only science which teaches you expression of sex but not as indulgence but as a spiritual discipline. This is a transformation of a biological phenomenon into a spirituality.[56]

Rajneesh appears to have been aware that what he was doing had little in common with traditional, historical South Asian forms of Tantra but was instead a contemporary reimagining. A radically different kind of practice, Neo-Tantra explicitly rejects all traditional, ritualistic trappings and aims to bring about a completely spontaneous experience of liberation:

> What I am saying is absolutely alive, new, fresh, young. . . . It is not traditional at all. Hence I call my Tantra, Neo-Tantra. It is a totally different phenomenon. . . . We have to free Tantra from all ritualistic patterns. We have to make it more poetic, more spontaneous, less patterned, less structured.[57]

Ultimately, Rajneesh suggests, Tantra uses the power of orgasm itself as the supreme means to spiritual experience. In the fullest union of two partners in sexual orgasm, one has the possibility of dissolving the individual ego and experiencing the infinite abyss of the divine. It is the kind of "COSMIC ORGASM" or radical experience of ecstasy that all the world's mystics have been talking about.[58] According to Rajneesh, this is what the Tantric Buddhists mean by the concept of *mahamudra*, literally "great gesture," which is typically depicted in Tantric art by the union of a Buddha and female consort. As Rajneesh put it in *Tantra: The Supreme Understanding*, a text based on lectures from February 1975,

> In deep love people are afraid of becoming mad, or going to die—of what will happen. The abyss opens its mouth, the whole existence yawns, and you are suddenly there and you can fall into it. . . . In love you are not, the other is also not: then only, suddenly, the two disappear. The same happens in Mahamudra. Mahamudra is a total orgasm with the whole existence. That's why in Tantra . . . deep intercourse, orgasmic intercourse, between lovers is also called Mahamudra, and two lovers in a deep orgasmic state are pictured in tantric temples, in tantric books. That has become a symbol of the final orgasm.[59]

In many ways, Rajneesh's Neo-Tantric understanding of sexual orgasm is the most extreme articulation of the postmodern "death of the subject," which, as we have already seen, runs through his work from the 1960s onward. In the moment of Tantric orgasm, the illusion of a unified, coherent ego dissolves, and the fictional self is revealed to be a playful flow of vital energies and desires: "In sex, for the first time you lose your ego; you become egoless. . . . You are not, nor is there any other."[60] Sex, he explained, "is such a great energy. Once you are in it you are no more, and the current will take you anywhere."[61] Lines like these could easily have been written by French poststructuralist authors of the 1960s and 1970s such as Gilles Deleuze and Félix Guatarri, who likewise mounted a scathing critique of Freud and celebrated the polymorphous play of desire in place of a unified, singular "sovereign subject."[62]

TANTRA AS SEXUAL, SPIRITUAL, AND SOCIAL REVOLUTION

—we are all Gods/Buddhas...

However, Tantra in Rajneesh's view represents not simply the path to a full bodily and spiritual integration, and not simply the means to a kind of final or cosmic orgasm; rather, it is also a potentially revolutionary spiritual path, one that offers the vision of a religion without institutional hierarchies or established authorities, a religion based solely on the supreme divinity of each individual human being: "The Tantra vision is one of the greatest visions ever dreamt by humanity: a religion without a priest, a religion without a temple, a religion without an organization, a religion that does not destroy the individual but respects individuality tremendously."[63] Because sex is the deepest and most intense drive in human nature, it is the one that priests, politicians, and rulers have most often tried to suppress. Therefore Tantra—as the one spiritual path that accepts and liberates sexual desire—is also the most liberating of spiritual paths, offering such a profound kind of individual freedom that it cannot be subjected to any religious or political domination:

> Sex is the most powerful human instinct. The politician and the priest have understood from the very beginning that sex is the most driving human energy. It has to be curtailed, it has to be cut. If people are allowed total freedom in sex, then there will be no possibility of dominating them; making slaves out of them will be impossible.[64]
>
> Listen to the Tantra message. . . . It is a great revolutionary message. It is against all priests and politicians. It is against all those poisoners who have

killed all joy on the earth just so that people can be reduced to slaves. Reclaim your freedom.[65]

Here again Rajneesh is clearly echoing Wilhelm Reich and other post-Freudian theorists such as Herbert Marcuse (though we will see below that Marcuse would later rethink this position in the light of the rampant commercialization of sexuality in the 1960s).[66] With Reich and the early Marcuse, Rajneesh sees sexual repression and political domination as being intimately connected, and therefore sexual freedom and political liberation likewise going hand in hand.

It is not difficult to see how this "revolutionary" interpretation of Tantra as a path of individualism and personal freedom would also have fit in very well with the counterculture of the late 1960s and 1970s. In many ways, Rajneesh's Neo-Tantric message—with its mixture of Reichian antifascism and an exoticized interpretation of Indian mysticism—could have served as the mantra of the counterculture and the sexual revolution itself. "Look at the Tantra approach to everything," he concludes. "Taste God in every taste. Flow totally into your touch, because whatsoever you touch is divine. It is a total reversal of the ascetic, so-called religions. It is a radical revolution—from the very roots."[67]

Not only was Tantra a key expression of Rajneesh's early philosophy, it was also closely tied to his economic and political views, which we discussed in the previous chapter. Like his fiercely antisocialist and procapitalist economic ideals, Rajneesh's version of Tantra is based on a kind of fierce individualism, nonconformity, and "selfishness." Because we are all inherently divine beings, we must first "be absolutely selfish" and accept ourselves before we can think about trying to help others: "Tantra says that unless YOU are filled with light, how can you help others to be Enlightened? Be selfish; only then can you be altruistic."[68] Whereas other religions split human beings into good and bad, virtue and sin, Tantra is the path of total acceptance, which embraces and absorbs even the greed, anger, and desire of the personality:

> Tantra acceptance is total; it doesn't split you. All the religions of the world, except Tantra, have created split personalities. All the religions of the world, except Tantra, have created schizophrenia. They split you. They make something bad in you and something good. And they say . . . the Devil has to be denied and God accepted. . . . Anger is there, sex is there, greed is there; you have not created them; they are given facts of life. . . .
>
> Tantra says a transformation is possible, but destruction, no! And a transformation comes when you accept your total being . . . then anger is also absorbed, then greed is absorbed.[69]

Ultimately, the goal of Rajneesh's Neo-Tantra is to allow us to become fully realized, liberated, and "godlike" beings, while still enjoying the food, wine, and sensual pleasures of the worldly marketplace: "This is the ultimate for Tantra, to become gods and yet be part of this world. When you can come back to the marketplace with a wine bottle in your hand, the ultimate is achieved."[70] It is not difficult to see the fit or "elective affinity" between this Neo-Tantric ideal of absolute selfishness and Rajneesh's broader attack on Gandhian asceticism and his embrace of American-style capitalism.

THE COMPLEX QUESTION OF RAJNEESH'S OWN SEXUALITY

Given Rajneesh's highly affirmative public teachings regarding sexuality, his very sexualized reinterpretation of South Asian Tantra, and his belief that sex could lead to superconsciousness, surely a fair question would be, What was Rajneesh's own sexuality like? Did he practice his own form of Tantric sex? Had he used sexual techniques to achieve his own enlightened state? Or had he transcended sexuality altogether in his own sort of uniquely Rajneeshian superconsciousness? Certainly, already by the early 1970s, Rajneesh had acquired a reputation throughout the Indian media as not only a sex-friendly guru but also a dangerous sexual predator or even a "Rasputin." Ma Anand Sheela recalled in her unpublished memoir:

> I remember one of my aunts clearly warning me against Bhagwan's habits of sexuality and how many young women Bhagwan had managed to destroy with hypnosis. My aunt compared him to Rasputin. . . . It wasn't just my aunt who was negative towards Bhagwan but the majority of the population. . . . His teachings were to go beyond all established dogma, creed and religion. He condemned orthodoxy and criticized all social and moral mores. He took your day-to-day gods and bibles and gave them a new meaning. . . . He took tabooed sex and made it a ladder to reach to consciousness.[71]

Despite his extensive autobiographical statements, Rajneesh himself never addressed this question publicly. And not surprisingly, the opinions of his many disciples over the years have varied tremendously and offered many conflicting portraits of Bhagwan's sexual life. As Gordon recalls from his time in the first Pune era of the 1970s, some *sannyasins* believed that Rajneesh had simply "dropped sex" at age twenty-one, when he became enlightened, leaving that particular human desire behind when he moved on to a suprahuman condition. Others offered the more pragmatic view that Rajneesh no longer had intercourse, only blow jobs, because of his asthma, allergies, diabetes, and bad back. Still others said that he had two or more women every night.[72] And some recall that women disciples were periodically called into "special *darshans*" with Bhagwan, a ritual that was considered "a great honour by the women he chose (although they were asked by Laxmi to keep these *darshans* a secret)."[73]

Although they were told not to talk about their private *darshans* with Rajneesh, many women did, and, again, had conflicting tales to tell. Some recalled that Rajneesh was really not much of a lover, but rather was more interested in voyeurism and spent just a couple of minutes on top before it was over. One woman who had been his lover in Bombay said that he liked to "look and touch," but that she had never had an orgasm with him, and another recalled that he seemed simply distant and detached but not really sexual. And a few more cynical partners concluded that Bhagwan's sexual relations were primarily "a form of control, a means Rajneesh was coldly using to bind her and his other disciples to him."[74]

Some women, however, claimed that Rajneesh was working on a more profound sexual, emotional, and spiritual level during intercourse. One of his former partners told Gordon that Rajneesh had been in fact "rewiring her circuits" during their lovemaking: "He was moving energy in the lower center, and I was trying hard to raise, to transform it. I could feel he was charging me, making me a magnet so I could communicate his energy to large numbers of people. . . . I began to feel my own powers, to see past lives."[75]

Of course, many *sannyasins* would also say it doesn't really matter what Rajneesh's own sexuality was like; even if he had an active and promiscuous sex life, that would in no way contradict his own Zorba the Buddha and Neo-Tantric philosophy, which would make a sexually active guru not scandalous but really only logical. As William Foster put it, "He had immense amounts of sex with disciples. But I don't have trouble with that."[76]

These contradictory and conflicting views of Rajneesh's own sexuality are, of course, in perfect keeping with the paradoxical, often contradictory nature of his teachings and his larger "religionless religion." It would actually be more surprising to discover that Rajneesh had been consistent in his sexual practice than to see that he was consistently inconsistent, as he put it.

A NEW VISION OF WOMEN'S LIBERATION: CREATING
A NEO-TANTRIC COMMUNITY IN PUNE

Although it was by no means the only or most important reason why many young people came to the Pune ashram in the 1970s, Rajneesh's ideal of Neo-Tantra was surely part of the attraction. As Tim Guest recalls his mother's involvement in the ashram, the idea of a liberated and sexually affirming community was definitely appealing to many young people who grew up in strict Christian families: "For people like my mother, brought up in a strict Catholic family, Bhagwan's permissive mysticism was a revelation. . . . She could have her path to enlightenment, with sex, drugs and rock and roll along the way."[77] For many early *sannyasins,* Rajneesh was the first guru they had ever encountered who taught that sensuality and spirituality were not in fact at odds, but rather that the body and all its pleasures could become part of the spiritual life. "Here was somebody who was saying, with great authority, don't be ascetic, don't deny yourself," Hugh Milne recalls. "The path to enlightenment is through indulgence and gratification of sensual pleasures, so long as it is done with conscious awareness."[78] More than just sex, Rajneesh's commune also encouraged "conscious indulgence" in an array of other sensual activities, ranging from music and massage to eating ripe mangoes from between women's legs:

> Bhagwan encouraged our complete sexual freedom. He also . . . encouraged frequent changes of partner among ashram members. This, plus our own inclinations, engendered an atmosphere of frank promiscuity, a promiscuity for which the ashram was already becoming famous in the outside world. . . . It is no exaggeration to say that we had a feast of fucking, the likes of which had probably not been seen since the days of the Roman bacchanalia. Never had people's carnal needs been so well catered for.[79]

Later, in 1981, when Rajneesh was interviewed by the INS in Portland, the officer interrogated him about the role of sexuality in the encounter groups at Pune. Rajneesh responded in his characteristically frank and unapologetic manner, throwing in a playful jab at Christianity along the way: "Nothing was prevented. A question of allowing is not important—nothing was prevented. People do the encounter group only to bring whatsoever they have repressed in themselves. If they are sexually repressed, then naturally that repression will come out, and for that I am not responsible. For that, the Pope is responsible."[80]

Of course, the liberated and promiscuous atmosphere of the ashram was definitely a bit at odds with the surrounding Indian society in Pune of the 1970s, which was far more conservative and certainly not used to seeing scantily clad and physically demonstrative young people roaming around. As Dillon recalls, the early Rajneesh movement was in many ways accepted as an ashram or spiritual community in the traditional Indian sense, but it also clearly made many locals uncomfortable with its open display of bodies and sexuality:

> In India the ashram is very built into the culture, and they are very accepting of the guru–disciple thing. So they have a lot of built-in respect for that, and we were often quite supported. But at the same time there were also the skimpier blouses and all that western stuff that eventually has permeated India. . . . And we were all quite nubile and juicy, with straps hanging over our shoulders, and hugging and shmoozling each other all over the place. We were pretty threatening, I think, to Indian culture. . . . There was always an undercurrent of that kind of "you guys are going to ruin our culture, here." And eventually we did.[81]

As we will see in chapter 4, this tension with the surrounding Indian society would be one of several reasons why Rajneesh made the decision to leave India for the United States in 1981. While the idea of Neo-Tantra and the path from sex to superconsciousness was perhaps a bit ahead of its time in India of the 1970s, it seemed quite well adapted to America of the 1980s.

Finally, in addition to its appeal as a sexually liberated Neo-Tantric community, much of the draw of the early Pune ashram was also its emphasis on the power, potential, and authority of women. Even as new forms of feminism such as "second wave" and "radical feminism" were developing in the United States and Europe, Rajneesh was articulating his own "new vision of women's liberation." And many of the women who joined the ashram in the 1970s found this vision immensely appealing. In Rajneesh's view, women are in many ways inherently superior to men because they are naturally in possession of greater sexual energy (*shakti,* or feminine power, in traditional Indian yogic and Tantric philosophy); this is evidenced by the fact that "women are capable of multiple orgasms, man is not."[82] Yet precisely because of their fear of female power, men have for millennia oppressed and dominated women.

Now, in Rajneesh's view, the age of women is dawning, and the time is ripe for female power, sexual energy, and spiritual authority to be liberated after thousands of years of repression. This is not the "stupid" and simplistic freedom imagined by the feminists and women's liberation advocates in America, according to Rajneesh, but rather a deeper spiritual freedom that will unlock her inherent capacity for love as her path to Buddha-hood:

> My own vision is that the coming age will be the age of woman. Man has tried for five thousand years and failed. It is enough! Now feminine energies have to be released. . . . The freedom of women cannot come through stupid movements like women's liberation. . . . If we can create a few woman buddhas in the world then woman will be freed from all chains and fetters. . . . Love is going to be her meditation. . . . That is going to be her path towards light, towards godliness.[83]

Demographically and in terms of leadership roles, the Rajneesh movement was in fact predominantly "female." Based on various estimates, women outnumbered men at different times in the movement's early history by ratios that ranged from 3:1 to 3:2.[84] And as we have seen in the roles played by powerful women such as Laxmi, Sheela, and others, women were given an unusual degree of spiritual authority in the movement. As sociologist Susan J. Palmer noted, "He is urging women to join his commune, where they can throw off their shackles, discover their true strength, indulge their polyandrous tendencies, and as the 'pillars of his temple' assume positions of leadership to usher in the New Age of Woman."[85] As we will see in chapter 4, moreover, the Rajneeshpuram community in Oregon was run almost entirely by women—at least visibly—as Rajneesh himself retreated into a vow of silence and allowed Sheela and her female associates serve as the public voice of the movement.

CONCLUSIONS: THE CULTURAL CONTRADICTIONS OF THE SEXUAL REVOLUTION

If Rajneesh's early Neo-Tantric community was in many ways an embodiment of the sexual revolution as it became globalized and exported to parts of the developing world, it also embodied the deep ambivalence of that revolution. As Allyn notes, the sexual revolution of the 1960s and 1970s was far from a homogenous or internally consistent movement; rather, it was deeply fissured by a range of contradictions: "It was spiritual yet secular, idealistic yet commercial, driven by science yet colored by a romantic view of nature." And it was also increasingly torn between a utopian ideal of social and political freedom and a co-option of sexuality as another commodity in the consumer marketplace: "In some respects the permissiveness of the era was just the logical extension of the commercial free market to include sexual goods and commodities."[86] Perhaps nowhere is this tension between idealism and commercialism more evident than in the Pune community of the 1970s. Indeed, Rajneesh's ideal of radical freedom and complete self-acceptance through Tantra sat side by side with the growing wealth and commodification of the ashram, which by the late 1970s had begun to generate millions of dollars from eager seekers coming from all parts of the world.

Moreover, despite his repeated declaration that Tantra is about "unconditional freedom" and a revolutionary liberation of sexuality, Rajneesh was not always accepting of all forms of sexuality. In particular, he was quite vocally opposed to homosexuality, which he described in no uncertain terms as an unnatural perversion and the by-product of religious repression: "I call homosexuality a perversion. . . . There is no biological program in you for homosexuality. The biological program in your sperms is heterosexual. I am simply stating a fact that homosexuality has arisen under ugly pressures in the monasteries of the religions where it is forced in the name of the purity of celibacy."[87]

Many of the seeming contradictions in the early Pune community were even further highlighted with the release of the film *Ashram* by a former German *sannyasin* named Wolfgang Dobrowolny in 1978. The film included a fifteen-minute sequence that showed explicit violence during a seven-day nude encounter group held in a padded room. Soon major newspapers in the United States, such as the *Los Angeles Times*, reported that the path to enlightenment at the ashram involved not simply Neo-Tantric sexual freedom but also "broken bones, black eyes, bloody noses, and shattered egos."[88]

Already by the end of the first Pune experiment, moreover, critics of the movement were beginning to describe an increasingly authoritarian structure within the ashram. As former German *sannyasin* Eckart Flöther claimed in an affidavit for the INS, "The hierarchy of the ashram is highly authoritarian. . . . Rajneesh is directing the movement according to his desires and inspirations. They are inconsistent, contradictory, and irrational, like his teachings."[89] A similar authoritarian vibe was described by Indian journalist Shobha Kilachand, who noted the strange juxtaposition of wild freedom and "delightfully irreverent practices" combined with the tight security and an almost "Gestapo air" during her visit in 1979.[90] Many critics commented on the rather odd fact that Rajneesh had employed official "sniffers," whose task was to sniff all visitors before they entered his lecture hall to make sure they didn't carry any trace of smoke, perfume, or other odors that might offend

Bhagwan. As Kate Strelley recalls, the official reasoning was that this would protect Rajneesh from allergens, given his fragile health; but she also wondered whether the sniff tests weren't simply used as a tool to weed out undesirable or subversive members from the community:

> The official reason for the existence of the "sniffers" was the fact that Bhagwan was allergic to perfume, scented shampoos, cigarette smoke, and anything with a strong fragrance. . . . But the main importance, I think, was that it provided an ideal tool for manipulation. Once the darshan list left Geeta, it would pass by Sheela, Laxmi, Shradda, Asha, and myself for any final stars or comments.[91]

This growing authoritarianism and violence within the Pune community was even noted by Dick Price himself, the cofounder of the hugely influential Esalen center (of which the Rajneesh community in Pune claimed to be the Eastern counterpart). Price had been a tremendous admirer of Rajneesh's work, even announcing to his friends and colleagues that he had become a devotee of the charismatic guru, with his unique synthesis of Tantric yoga and Western psychology. Price received a new name from Rajneesh ("Geet Govind"), and an article from 1978 suggested that, just as Pune (Poona) had become the "Esalen of the East," Esalen would become "Poona West."[92] Price's enthusiasm for Rajneesh, however, was short-lived. After about two weeks in Pune, he expressed his concern, shock, and horror at the violence taking place at the ashram, where he witnessed broken bones and other trauma during encounter sessions. He also stated his intense dislike of the authoritarian atmosphere of the ashram, whose unquestioning reverence for the guru contrasted strongly with Esalen's commitment to democracy and antiauthoritarian leadership:

> Rajneesh is well worth reading. . . . He can speak brilliantly of the transformative possibility of human life. His "meditations" are worth practicing. However, the ashram "encounter" group is an abomination—authoritarian, intimidating, violent—used to enforce conformity to an emerging new orange order rather than to facilitate growth. Broken bones are common, bruises and abrasions beyond counting. As such it owes more to the S.S. than to Esalen.[93]

Rajneesh was asked directly about this seeming lack of freedom and apparent condoning of violence at the ashram by a *sannyasin,* and the exchange was published in the group's *Sannyas* magazine in 1978. In this exchange—entitled "This Is Not a Democracy"—Rajneesh is quite explicit that the ashram is by no means a democratic affair but a quite *autocratic* one. He also argues that the violence and sexual experimentation of some of these groups are necessary for the radical breaking of all boundaries that leads to total spiritual liberation:

> This is not going to be a democracy. You are not to be asked what should be done and what should not be done. . . . This should be remembered from the very beginning—that this is not going to be a democracy. Your votes will never be taken. You become part of it with that knowledge—that whatsoever I decide is absolute. If you don't choose that way, you are perfectly happy to leave.
>
> The Encounter group that is going on here is the best in the world at this moment. Nowhere else is such absolute freedom allowed. . . . I only send people to the Encounter group when I see that now they understand that they have to go beyond all boundaries—boundaries of sex, boundaries of violence, anger, rage. They have to break all boundaries. . . . "Why do you allow such violence?" That is not your business. If you are not capable of going into it, you are not required to go into it. You can do some non-violent group.[94]

In this sense, Rajneesh's ideals of sexual freedom and Neo-Tantra reveal some of the deeper cultural contradictions in the larger ideals of the sexual revolution and counterculture during the 1960s and 1970s. As Altman notes, linking sexual freedom and social-political liberation became increasingly popular in the second half of the twentieth century, particularly among post-Freudian thinkers: "Suggestions that the sexual is political . . . became central for a number of twentieth century thinkers . . . like Wilhelm Reich and Herbert Marcuse"; and then it became a central article of faith for much of the counterculture.[95] Yet as we see in the proliferation of pornography and the use of sexually explicit imagery in advertising, the promise of "sexual liberation" also clearly became co-opted by consumerism and transformed into a lucrative sex industry within the new global economy: "The use of 'sexy bodies' . . . in advertising and mainstream newspapers . . . has become ubiquitous, and with it the creation of a homogeneity of desire through global advertising campaigns and interchangeable glossy magazines."[96] Even radical post-Freudians such as Marcuse himself realized this in 1966, when his ideal of sexual liberation had clearly begun to be co-opted and absorbed by the logic of consumer society and divested of most of its revolutionary potential. Sexuality, Marcuse concluded, had been subjected to a "repressive de-sublimation," in which the very rhetoric of freedom and liberation had been exploited to sell cars and cigarettes, to elect politicians and to provide citizens with an illusion of freedom within an increasingly oppressive capitalist system.[97]

As Altman suggests, sexual and social freedom are indeed linked in complex ways. After all, if there were no link between sexual and social justice, "then why is sexual repression so central to both organized religion and most authoritarian regimes?" However, sexual freedom does not *by itself* magically bring about social or political freedom. Rather, social, economic, and political freedoms provide the necessary context in which any sort of genuine sexual freedom can meaningfully exist: "Perhaps we should turn the precepts of the seventies around, and recognize not just that sexual freedom is connected to other struggles, but that it is meaningless in the absence of other forms of freedom and equality."[98]

In many ways, this was one of the central tensions within the early Rajneesh movement both in India and in America—namely, how to realize an ideal of individual and sexual liberation while creating a new kind of community that would foster genuine freedom rather than new forms of control. As we will see in the following chapters, the movement would struggle to achieve this ideal with greater and lesser degrees of success during the next several decades. In many ways, the apparent contradictions within the early Pune ashram would become even more evident in the Oregon community of the 1980s. While founded on these same radical ideals of freedom, self-discovery, and self-acceptance through the Neo-Tantric path, the Oregon community would quickly become not only incredibly wealthy but also increasingly controlled, regulated, and quite "un-free" by the time of its collapse in 1985.

CHAPTER 4

"The Messiah America Has Been Waiting For"

Rajneeshpuram in 1980s America

Q: Who is the better showman—in metaphysical
terms . . . —you or President Ronald Reagan?
A: Nobody can beat me! I am the best showman in the whole
history of man.
Q: If that is true, what kind of show do you enjoy? Is this
theater, or circus?
A: This is my circus, my carnival. And I enjoy it immensely!

—Rajneesh, interview by Jeff McMullen, *60 Minutes*, Australia

If, indeed, a postnational order is in the making, and
Americanness changes its meanings, the whole problem of
diversity in American life will have to be rethought.

—Arjun Appadurai, *Modernity at Large*

Surely the most astonishing, controversial, and at times quite surreal chapter in Osho-Rajneesh's global journey is the period in Oregon from 1981 to 1985. Within the first few years of its existence, the Rajneesh community attracted thousands of followers from across the globe, amassed millions of dollars in assets, and built a huge utopian commune—indeed, an entire city, called Rajneeshpuram—in the middle of the Oregon desert (fig. 8). At its height in the mid-1980s, Rajneeshpuram had become one of the largest—and certainly the most developed and wealthiest—communal religious experiments in American history.[1]

And yet, less that five years after its birth, this spiritual experiment collapsed in the most spectacular way, amid a stunning assortment of criminal charges, ranging from arson and wiretapping to attempted murder. What began as a remarkably progressive social experiment, complete with programs of water conservation, recycling, and organic farming,[2] deteriorated into a highly controlled—and quite paranoid—community, enmeshed in guerrilla warfare with the local town government. From one of the largest communal religious experiments in U.S. history, Rajneeshpuram quickly descended into the largest biological terrorism attack in U.S. history, the largest illegal wiretapping case ever uncovered, and the largest instance of immigration fraud ever conducted on U.S. soil.[3] As one former *sannyasin* recalls, "No 'Dallas' or 'Dynasty' scriptwriter could possibly imagine a more astonishing and sensational plot. Murders, the poisonings of entire cities, machine guns, sex orgies, midnight flights from the law—all this existed side by side with . . . a continual influx of millions of dollars in donations and six thousand beautiful people sitting in absolute silence every day to listen to a man of God."[4]

The Oregon community was remarkable for many reasons: for its sheer size and number of followers, for its meteoric success and rapid collapse, for the audacity of its vision and the outrageous acts committed in its latter days. But one of the most fascinating aspects of the Oregon experiment was its explicit wedding of spirituality and global capitalism. The union of the spiritual and material, we have seen, was an idea that Rajneesh had already articulated and realized to some degree in the Pune community. But the Oregon experiment was the most elaborate attempt to date to bring this ideal to fruition on a mass scale. As noted in the introduction, Sheela expressed this in an interview during the Oregon years, in her characteristically blunt style: "Our religion is probably the only religion which has synthesized capitalism and religion. . . . It's wonderful. It works. . . . And by the way, if you happen to be a Christian, and if you are a Christian, you have to look at Vatican and its business, too. They are very lousy business people, too."[5]

Yet if the Oregon experiment was a bold synthesis of religion and business, it also clearly reflected the shifting nature of global capitalism during the 1980s. As the movement quickly evolved into both a spiritual and a commercial enterprise, it developed an incredibly complex, interlocking corporate structure with a large number of ostensibly independent but ultimately interconnected corporate entities and a vast, fluid, and flexible network of religious and secular enterprises around the world.[6] In this sense, much as the early Rajneesh movement in Pune

FIGURE 8. "Thousands of tents fill fields at Rancho Rajneesh."
The Oregonian.

embodied a new challenge to Indian-style socialism and a turn toward American-style capitalism, the Oregon experiment was a striking embodiment of the new forms of "late" or "deterritorialized capitalism" spreading rapidly worldwide during the 1980s, which David Harvey has dubbed "flexible accumulation."[7]

Ironically, even as Rajneesh attacked Reagan as a "Hitler,"[8] and later presented himself as a victim of Reagan's America, he was in some ways a reflection of certain aspects of Reagan's policies during the 1980s. As Jeremy Carrette and Richard King observe, many religious movements that emerged during this period embodied the policies of neoliberalism that became dominant during the 1980s, with Reaganism in the United States and Thatcherism in the United Kingdom. Just as neoliberal economic policies under Reagan emphasized individual freedom, less government intervention, and unfettered market capitalism, many new spiritual movements likewise embraced an ideal of personal freedom, privatization, and a "marketplace" approach to spirituality.[9] Perhaps nowhere is this more apparent than in the rapidly growing Rajneesh empire of the 1980s. In certain respects, the Rajneesh community could even be seen as the ironic spiritual flip side or inverse mirror of the Reagan era and neoliberal policies in 1980s America. In the unique religious experiment of Rajneeshpuram, we see progressive and postnational utopian ideals paired with "conservative" commitments to free market capitalism and global business. And in its stunning collapse in 1985, we see a strange "spiritual parallel" to the collapse of other large multinational corporations during the economic crises of the late 1980s and early 1990s.

THE END OF THE FIRST PUNE ASHRAM AND
THE MOVE TO AMERICA

The reasons for Rajneesh's transplantation from India to the United States are multiple and complex. First, even before the move to America, the movement had already evolved into a huge and successful global network outside of India. "Buddhafields" were established widely abroad, in communes such as "Medina Rajneesh" in the countryside of Suffolk, England, where some 400 *sannyasins* gathered in the early 1980s. By 1981, there were 126 centers scattered across Europe, including twenty-two in the United Kingdom, forty-three in Germany, and one in Yugoslavia; and by the mid-1980s, there were some 200,000 disciples in 400 centers around the world.[10] Thus, expanding into the United States—the ultimate realm of "Zorba" to complement India's "Buddha"—was in many ways just the next logical move.

However, there were also more practical and financial reasons for the move. First, the Indian authorities had become increasingly uncomfortable with Rajneesh's iconoclastic teachings and frequent public attacks on Hinduism. Rajneesh even began receiving threats and angry assaults from conservative Hindus, such as one man who stood up at a morning lecture and shouted, "You are insulting our religion!" Others worried that Rajneesh might be put under house arrest for inciting religious unrest. At the same time, seeing the vast sums of money made by the community—around $80 million—the charity commissioners in Pune had begun to question the charitable status of the ashram, and launched an investigation into its financial affairs. Eventually, the government canceled the tax-exempt status of the ashram, which meant that it owed up to $5 million in current and back taxes.[11]

During this same period, there was a series of fire bombings of Rajneesh facilities in Pune, including the destruction of one of the main book depositories and an explosion outside the health center. While the Rajneesh community declared these acts to be "a clear case of fanatics trying to suppress a minority religion,"[12] the local police and Indian CID later concluded that these attacks were more likely "perpetrated from the inside" by Rajneesh followers themselves in order to create the picture that they were a persecuted community.[13] But whoever was behind them, these attacks helped put the final nail in the coffin of the early ashram and push it toward the move to America. And so in early 1981, the ashram's money was emptied into a Credit Suisse account in Zurich, and Rajneesh emigrated to the United States. A new corporation was formed—Rajneesh International—which would have no legally binding connection to the Pune ashram or its $5 million tax debt and other large debts to publishing houses, bookbinders, fabric manufacturers, and suppliers of raw materials to the ashram.[14]

Declaring himself "the messiah America has been waiting for," Rajneesh first moved into a late nineteenth-century mansion in Montclair, New Jersey. However, it quickly became apparent that the Montclair house would not be nearly big enough for the community's plans, which involved not simply the transplantation of a few *sannyasins* but rather the creation of an entire utopian society. Thus in the summer of 1981, Sheela used $5.75 million to purchase a 64,229-acre ranch named Big Muddy in central Oregon, a vast, sprawling, arid, and isolated tract of land that had been the location for several Hollywood Western films. Nineteen miles from the nearest town, tiny Antelope, Oregon, the ranch was imagined to be the site of Rajneesh's ideal of a *Homo novis* or Zorba the Buddha. According to a booklet printed for the new community entitled "Rajneeshpuram: A Blueprint for Man's Future," the ranch was intended to be a perfect society, a model of alternative living and the perfect integration of spirituality and materiality.[15] In Rajneesh's words, this was to be a bold communal experiment indeed: "I am experimenting. The new commune will be on a big scale—10,000 *sannyasins* living together as one body, one being. Nobody will possess anything, everybody will use, everybody will enjoy. Everybody is going to live as comfortably, as richly, as we can manage, but nobody will possess anything."[16]

Ironically, Rajneesh himself had entered into a period of voluntary silence during this chapter in the movement's complex global journey, and he would refrain from speaking publicly from April 1981 until December 1984. As we will see, this would leave others—mainly Sheela and her close associates—to serve as the public voice of the communal experiment (fig. 9).

"A COMMUNE FOR AMERICA": AN OASIS IN THE DESERT

Virtually everyone who witnessed the Oregon experiment in the early 1980s—including not only *sannyasins* who were there at the time, but also local journalists and critical observers—acknowledged that it was a remarkably successful social and religious experiment. As Rajneesh himself put it, they had set out to "transform a desert into an oasis,"[17] and, for a brief time at least, they did indeed create a thriving alternative

FIGURE 9. "Ma Anand Sheela in red." *The Oregonian.*

spiritual community that was well ahead of its time. "It is a commune for America," Rajneesh explained in an interview with an INS officer in 1982.[18] Most of the *sannyasins* who were involved in the early days of the ranch recall the tremendous energy, excitement, and enthusiasm that pervaded the community in its first years. As Aneesha Dillon remembers, the Oregon experiment was crazy and confusing in many ways, but community members were filled with an incredible sense of possibility and the potential to build something wonderfully new:

Sometimes when I look back on it I think, "What was that? What was I doing there?" It was very complex and multilayered. It's very hard to figure out even while being in it. I can say that it was, especially in the beginning, just full on positive, hopeful, "let's all do this together" energy. I got so excited about it that I wanted to quit group leading and simply work to build the commune. I worked in construction and in many different departments on the ranch. I was excited about this experiment. It was very cool after being so kind of light and floaty in "Pune I" and then coming to the ranch and having to get so in the earth. It was a wonderful happening there.[19]

Whatever else we think about the ranch, it was certainly an incredibly industrious and productive place. Milt Ritter was a cameraman for KGW television during the 1980s and spent most of his time in those years covering Rajneeshpuram. As he recalls, the Rajneeshees had bought a ranch that was basically a "run-down, over-grazed piece of desert that had no value"—which seemed like pure folly to most observers—and yet, "in a short time things actually started to change." The Rajneeshees quickly set up an array of new buildings and began a surprisingly innovative project of organic gardening, at a time "when nobody knew what organic gardening was"; it was "stuff nobody had done before."[20] By 1985, the Oregon community housed more than 5,000 residents, who had their own complex urban infrastructure, complete with fire departments, a police station, shopping malls, a water reservoir, a sewage disposal plant, a post office, a security force, a 1,300-meter airstrip, and one of the largest mass transportation systems in Oregon.[21] The community even had its own Chamber of Commerce, which advertised tours of the ranch as well luxury hotel accommodations, a beauty salon, a gambling casino ("the Omar Khayyam Lounge and Card Room"), a bank ("Rajneesh Financial Services Trust," which offered its own "currency card"), and the acclaimed "Zorba the Buddha" restaurant. As Ritter recalls, Rajneeshpuram offered by far the best food anywhere east of the Cascades, and the news crew would often stop by just to eat when they happened to be in the area.[22]

The farming side of the ranch, meanwhile, included some 60 acres of vegetables, 900 acres of dry land grain crops, 100 beehives, 2,800 chickens, 100 ducks, 20 geese, a flock of peacocks, and 2 emus. At its peak, the ranch was producing 3,000 gallons of milk and 1,500 eggs a day, roughly 90 percent of its own vegetables, and even included a vineyard that would produce some 20,000 bottles of wine.[23] Not only was all of the farming organic, but the community's sewage was biologically treated and purified for irrigation. Finally, 70 percent of everything used on the ranch was recycled. In 1980s America, all of this was well ahead of its time, as most Americans had never heard of organic food and almost no one recycled anything.[24] Still more impressive was the huge earthen dam built by the community, and called—appropriately enough—the "Gurdjieff Dam"; besides building 140 check dams, they reshaped streambeds and planted thousands of trees to stop flooding and erosion. "Then they built a dam," Ritter recalls, "and we said, 'what the hell?' They were changing the landscape!"[25]

In fact, for the first two years, the ranch was favorably reported by the media. With a kind of charmed wonder, early news reports described this band of red-clad young hippies who had turned a piece of desert wasteland into a thriving utopian communal experiment. Until late 1982, local Oregon TV broadcasters defended Rajneesh against what they saw as the bigotry and intolerance of the state and federal agencies.[26] Even the most skeptical government agents who visited the ranch, such as INS criminal investigator Thomas N. Casey, were impressed by the energy, productivity, and organization of the community.[27]

The high productivity and ingenuity of the ranch were perhaps not that surprising, considering the well-educated, skilled, and creative individuals from all over the world that Rajneeshpuram was now attracting. A survey of the people of Rajneeshpuram conducted in 1983 found that this was an unusually highly educated, affluent, and professional community. Almost all of the members were high school graduates, while 64 percent had graduated from college. In fact, a full quarter of them had MAs, 12 percent had PhDs, a third were professionals (doctors, lawyers, and professors), and at least half were "white collar."[28]

SPIRITUAL CHARISMA AND DISORGANIZED CAPITALISM: THE GLOBAL CORPORATE STRUCTURE OF THE RAJNEESH MOVEMENT

Not only was Rajneeshpuram a remarkably successful communal experiment—at least during its first few years—it also quickly expanded into a large, wealthy, and successful business empire. As the Oregon community grew, and as Rajneesh centers proliferated around the world, the movement developed an increasingly complex, interlocking corporate structure. In many ways, the complexity and confusing nature of this corporate structure was very similar to that of other new religious movements that also evolved into successful business empires. The Church of Scientology, for example, was also infamous for its bewildering, byzantine, and deliberately confusing corporate architecture.[29] The expansion of the Rajneesh movement into a global network had already begun toward the end of the first Pune period in the late 1970s, as the movement faced increased pressure from the Indian government and began developing other corporate entities in New York, New Jersey, London, and Zurich.[30] But it expanded rapidly in the 1980s with the remarkable growth of Rajneeshpuram as the center of its global network.

Much of the success of the Rajneesh movement as a business enterprise, I would suggest, was based on the same iconoclastic principles as Rajneesh's spiritual teachings—namely, a kind of radical pluralism, eclecticism, and fluidity, which allowed for a wide range of organizational structures and business experiments. "Sannyasins were encouraged to experiment with any business or organizational form which offers convenience," Lewis Carter notes. "Sannyasins required no justification for the enterprises save that they be profitable."[31] In this sense, the Rajneesh movement might be best understood not simply as a spiritual group or religion but rather as a kind of "charismatic variant of a multinational corporation."[32] The Rajneeshees themselves seem to have agreed with Carter's assessment, describing the proliferation of "Buddhafield businesses" based not just on dry economics but on the Rajneesh's ideals of fun, freedom, and flow: "Business decisions in the Buddhafield tend not to be taken solely in light of commercial, economic considerations. Intuition, risk-taking adventurousness and fun value are thrown in the decision making and into the way the businesses are run."[33]

With the help of some sophisticated legal and business management, the movement created an extremely complicated system of parent companies and subsidiaries that was incredibly confusing to virtually everyone except Rajneesh's lawyers (including government agencies, and perhaps intentionally so). Three separate but mutually reinforcing organizations were formed, which supported one another in an interlocking structure. The parent organization was the Rajneesh Foundation International (RFI), which was managed through the Rajneesh Investment Corporation (RIC) and the Rajneesh Neo-Sannyas International Commune (RNSIC). The RIC was a for-profit corporation to which ownership of the ranch was transferred and which then served as the depository for funds taken in from other centers around the world. The RNSIC or "commune," on the other hand, was established in 1981 as a nonprofit, tax-free "religious community" to provide subsistence for members who donated their labor to the construction of the ranch.[34] Through the interlocking of these three corporations, and through their skillful combination of religious (tax-exempt) and secular enterprises, the movement was able to maintain a remarkably fluid structure.[35] For example, when Rajneesh's appetite for Rolls-Royces began to exceed the needs that a religious leader might be expected to have, the solution was to create an entity separate from the church called the Rajneesh Modern Car Collection Trust to hold the titles. And so it went—"not according to a grand scheme, but in an adaptive, expedient and ad hoc fashion."[36] The complex interlocking of these different corporate entities allowed the Rajneesh movement to maintain—for a time, at least—the image of a separation of church and state while also paying as little tax as possible. As *The State of Oregon* reported in 1984, "The legal function of Rajneesh Foundation International, the center or head of this financial empire, is completely obvious: by virtue of its being a non-profit church, RFI does not have to pay any taxes whatsoever on its considerable income."[37]

Meanwhile, outside of the United States, in London, yet another entity was established called the Rajneesh Services International Limited (RSI). As journalist Win McCormack reported in 1984, the principal function of the RSI appears to have been "to transfer money from one component of the Rajneesh International financial empire to another."[38] By mortgaging all of their properties in the cities of Rajneeshpuram, Antelope, and Portland to this U.K.–based corporation, the RIC effectively made them "invulnerable to court judgments against them in America" and, as one Portland attorney put it, created a "nearly impregnable wall of protection for their assets."[39]

In a remarkably short time, a great deal of money began to flow into and through the Oregon commune. Some of this came from *sannyasins*, including many who were willing to sell their possessions to support the ranch (such as one who recalls selling his Porsche for $20,000 to donate to the cause).[40] A great deal of revenue also came from the many courses offered at the ranch, which ranged from the "Rajneesh Fresh Beginning Course" ($2,500) and "Rajneesh Movement Therapy" ($2,100) to the "Rajneesh DeHypnotherapy Basic Course" ($5,500) and "Rajneesh Rebalancing Course" ($7,500).[41] And finally, a huge amount of money flowed in during the annual World Festival, which began in the summer of 1982. Admission for the seven-day festival was $509 for a place in a four-person tent or $1,804 for a room in the hotel, while the cost of the therapy groups, food and drink in the restaurant, and souvenirs, was extra. During the 1984 festival, the 15,000 people attending spent over $10 million.[42] Overall, between 1981 and 1985, an estimated $130 million poured into the ranch. As Hugh Milne recalls, "Bhagwan said that in the new commune we would grow money on trees. . . . Bhagwan was quite open about the fact that the primary object was to make money."[43]

Yet as a charismatic multinational corporation, the operations of the Rajneesh movement were by no means limited to the United States. On the contrary, the Oregon community was very much interrelated with and dependent upon a vast global network of Rajneesh centers. These included not only meditation centers and spiritual institutions but also seemingly "secular" enterprises, such as discotheques and restaurants. In all, some twenty corporations were created worldwide with twenty-eight bank accounts, including twelve in Switzerland. As Carter suggests, this global network had a markedly fluid and flexible structure; rather than a fixed corporate organization with permanent structures, the Rajneesh movement adapted quickly to the needs of different contexts. The individual businesses within the Rajneesh Foundation served, in effect, as "empty forms" or fluid structures that might be a discotheque one week, a yoga center the next, or a health-food store the next, depending on the shifting needs of the market. "Corporate identities are used as disposable devices . . . created as a need of the moment arises and discarded. . . . Specialized corporations of limited life span can be created to provide vehicles for new activities or transfers of assets."[44]

Ironically, while Rajneesh presented a radically iconoclastic and rebellious message, and the surrounding American society saw the commune as a dangerous and deviant cult, Rajneeshpuram was also in some ways a striking embodiment of the global dynamics of late capitalism. As we saw in chapter 2, the early Rajneesh movement in Pune was a kind of spiritual reflection of the increasingly decentralized and shifting dynamics of "disorganized capitalism." Yet by the 1980s, the movement had evolved into a fluid multinational network of protean corporate structures that were perhaps uniquely suited to the dynamics of what Harvey calls "flexible accumulation." In the global marketplace of postmodernity, as Harvey suggests, funds can be transferred and exchanged instantaneously from any point on the planet, through a network of constantly shifting, increasingly flexible corporate structures, labor markets, and patterns of consumption:

> *Flexible accumulation* . . . rests on flexibility with respect to labour processes, labour markets, products and patterns of consumption. It is characterized by the emergence of entirely new sectors of production, new ways of providing financial services, new markets and, above all, greatly intensified rates of commercial, technological and organizational innovation.[45]

FIGURE 10. "Ma Anand Sheela walks along as Rajneesh drives."
The Oregonian.

As a kind of "charismatic" multinational corporation with a wide array of fluid, protean forms, the Rajneesh movement was in many ways not just a reflection but the epitome of flexible accumulation, which Harvey sees as the condition of postmodernity.

"GURU OF THE RICH"

Although he had entered into a vow of silence in 1981, Rajneesh was in many ways the fluid, protean center of this complex multinational corporation. Today, most Americans probably remember Rajneesh primarily as the "Rolls-Royce Guru," who made national headlines because of his massive fleet of expensive cars and his daily "drive-bys" in which he drove his Rolls slowly along a road of cheering red-clad *sannyasins* at the ranch (figs. 10 and 11). As we saw in chapter 2, Rajneesh had never made any secret of his procapitalist sentiments and his fondness for expensive objects of conspicuous consumption. As he explained in a 1982 interview with an INS officer who asked him about the importance of wealth, "All the religions have commanded and praised poverty, and I condemn all those religions. Because of their praise of poverty, poverty has persisted in the world. I don't condemn wealth. Wealth is a perfect means which can enhance people in every way. . . . So I am a materialist spiritualist."[46]

With the move from India to Oregon, however, Rajneesh's tastes had evolved from gold cuff links and jeweled watches to high-end automo-

FIGURE 11. "Disciples garland Rajneesh's Rolls-Royce." *The Oregonian.*

biles. His first two Rolls-Royces were a Corniche and Silver Shadow, which were shipped from the Pune ashram to the Oregon ranch; and these were soon joined by an expanding fleet of cars that would eventually number ninety-three. The cars became part of an almost surreal form of "drive-by *darshan*" or viewing of the guru, in which Rajneesh would slowly drive down the city's central avenue while thousands of red-clad *sannyasins* waved, cheered, and played instruments in throes of joy:

> Each day at 2 o'clock Bhagwan drove at walking pace along the Ranch's central street. Along each side of the length of the road, standing sometimes twenty deep, *sannyasins* gathered to sing and wave their arms. . . . People played trombones, banged drums, waved their arms, craning their necks to get a better look. . . . One by one *sannyasins* stepped forward to place long-stemmed pink and red roses, stripped of thorns, on the bonnet of his car. Occasionally Bhagwan took his hands off the wheel to press them together in reply.[47]

Bhagwan's fondness for Rolls-Royces and daily drive-bys even made its way into popular newspaper comic strips of the 1980s. In the comic strip *Bloom County*, the character Opus asks a *sannyasin*, "Say, brother . . . uh, how about refreshing me on this Rajneesh business?" The *sannyasin* replies: "Well, Rajneesh is the truth, and the truth is the light, which is life. Life's truth, light, and happiness. Which is wearing red pajamas and blowing kisses toward the Bhagwan's 72 Gold Rolls Royces."

Finally, Opus concludes, "Whoa! By golly . . . that *does* make a lot of sense."[48]

Rajneesh himself later described his own conspicuous display of wealth as a kind of joke. While many spiritual leaders of 1980s America were making vast amounts of money (we need only think of Christian preachers such as Jimmy Swaggart or new religions such as the Church of Scientology), Rajneesh was perhaps the only one to not only embrace and display his tremendous wealth but also make fun of it in the very same breath. This unapologetically commercial attitude was embodied in a famous bumper sticker sold at the Rajneeshpuram annual festival: "Jesus Saves, Moses Invests, Bhagwan Spends!"[49] In a way, this is pure Rajneesh: shrewd humor, self-parody, and outrageous embrace of consumerism all in one. Indeed, even his own habit of collecting Rolls-Royces could be an object of self-parody and an opportunity for a funny but oddly telling bit of satire:

> People are sad, jealous, and thinking that Rolls Royces don't fit with spirituality. I don't see that there is any contradiction. . . . In fact, sitting in a bullock cart it is very difficult to be meditative; a Rolls Royce is the best for spiritual growth.[50]

Beyond its function as a display of conspicuous consumption or parody, however, Rajneesh's fleet of cars appears to have served a more practical and serious purpose. As *The Oregonian* reported, the ownership of the cars was transferred from the Rajneesh Foundation International to the tax-exempt Rajneesh Modern Car Collection Trust in 1982. The trust served as a tax-exempt conduit for donations from wealthy *sannyasins* who "leased" the cars for as much as $6,000 a month; in 1982 alone, $498,784 flowed into the Rajneesh Investment Corporation through this convenient conduit.[51]

TROUBLE IN PARADISE: EARLY TENSIONS WITH THE LOCAL COMMUNITY

From the very outset, the ranch ran into serious problems in its negotiations with the local community and government. While Rajneesh had imagined building a utopian community or "Buddhafield" of thousands of *sannyasins,* it turned out that the ranch was zoned for agricultural purposes with a maximum of just six residents allowed to live there. Thus when a government inspector arrived for a visit, the group had to use the cover story that it was a farming cooperative, and the numerous other *sannyasins* hanging around were mere visiting farmworkers and not permanent residents. Yet within two months of its establishment, over 200 *sannyasins* were living on the ranch, which started arousing complaints from the locals.[52]

A watchdog group called the 1000 Friends of Oregon, dedicated to land-use laws, advised the Rajneeshees that the non-farm-related uses of the land should be located in an already existing urban area with a designated urban growth boundary. In response, the Rajneeshees turned to the nearest city, the small retirement town of Antelope, and started buying up as much property as they could—which was quite a lot, since as much as 50 percent of the property was for sale. "They bought up everything available, even the store," recalls Ritter.[53] Their rapid push into Antelope, however, quickly alarmed the local residents, who were mostly either longtime residents or retirees and saw the Rajneeshees as bizarre, un-Christian hippies with a strange-looking guru who was launching an "invasion" of their town. On April 15, 1982, the city council held an election to "dis-incorporate" the city of Antelope, with the aim of stopping the Rajneeshees from taking over and using the city to further their plans. However, with the new population of *sannyasins*, the vote failed. And not long after, *sannyasins* were elected to three of the six seats on the city council and also won the mayor's seat, with the write-in candidate Karuna. By 1984, now completely in charge of the city, the Rajneeshees voted to change its name from Antelope to Rajneesh, and even to change street names to those of famous philosophers and religious teachers, such as Gurdjieff Road, Ouspensky Road, Ramakrishna Street, and so on. They also took over the local school system—renamed the Rajneesh International Meditation University—as the Antelope schools became increasingly dominated by children of *sannyasins*.[54]

Initially, the Rajneeshees approached their new control of Antelope with a sense of humor and playfulness—for example, by passing a resolution that every city council meeting must include the telling of at least one joke.[55] And sometimes this playfulness had a certain bite to it—for example, when they placed their garbage dump, called the Adolf Hitler Dump, next to Antelope's community church.[56]

However, few of the locals found any of this very funny. On the contrary, all of it was met with growing fear, hostility, and often quite aggressive rhetoric from the town residents. When the Rajneeshees arrived in 1981, the town of Antelope had a population of just thirtynine people, most of whom were retirees and Christians. The sudden presence of hundreds of red-clad, long-haired young people from all over the world with a strange guru and seeking to buy up local property—

perhaps not surprisingly—made the residents extremely nervous and generated widespread fears of a "takeover" or worse. This was, after all, just a few years after the mass murder/suicide of Peoples Temple—another new religious movement with a utopian communal ideal—in Guyana in 1978, which created widespread fear that this could be yet another "cult crisis" in the making.[57] According to ranch foreman Robert Harvey, already in January 1982 rumors circulated in the area that "the Rajneeshees sacrifice children and that's why there are no kids down on the ranch. . . . The Rajneeshees have to steal kids from other people so that they can sacrifice them."[58] According to an open letter from a local resident addressed to "senators, congressmen, judges and the president," many in the community were deeply concerned about "the godlessness that goes on down there" at the ranch:

> That cult, with their ways of coming in and buying up the land, have destroyed the old ways of life here in Oregon . . . and who knows what next? They could multiply like rabbits and take over the whole state. And they are not even Christian. They have these strange ideas and beliefs that are not pure and native Oregonian.[59]

At least one Oregon senator did in fact respond to local residents' pleas for an investigation into the Rajneesh community. In June 1982, Senator Hatfield began to express his fears about the "cult," which was rumored to have to engaged in all manner of disturbing transgressions, including "group sex involving sadomasochistic elements" and perhaps even "violence and loss of life."[60]

Just as the ranch was beginning to mass-produce T-shirts, bumper stickers, *malas*, and other merchandise to promote the commune, so too the growing number of local critics of the movement began to produce anti-Rajneesh merchandise. The University of Oregon Library's Special Collections has preserved a number of fascinating artifacts from this period, including "Nuke the Guru" T-shirts, featuring Rajneesh's face superimposed on a mushroom cloud, anti-Rajneesh silver coins with the slogan "Bye Bye Bhagwan," and even a *mala* made of bullets and beads, designed to mock the necklaces worn by *sannyasins* (figs. 12 and 13).[61] The anti-Communist motto "Better dead than red" started to reappear on bumper stickers, and one could even buy customized versions of Rajneesh caps showing a picture of Bhagwan branded with rifle crosshairs on his forehead. Flyers circulated during this period encouraging hunters to "bag a Red Rat" (i.e., a Rajneeshee), warned that the Rajneeshees are

FIGURE 12. "Nuke the Guru" anti-Rajneesh T-shirt. Rajneesh
Artifacts and Ephemera Collection, 1981–2004, University of
Oregon Special Collections and University Archives, Coll. 275.
Photo by the author.

known carriers of many known and unknown diseases. The (D.E.Q.) has
ruled that the carcass can not be left where the animal has been bagged, as it
is a proven fact that the coyotes, vultures and carrion eaters will not touch
the filthy carcass. If not disposed of the stench would be an intolerable pol-
lutant. . . . These Red Rats are loaded with crotch crickets and are very trou-
blesome to remove from the carcass.[62]

Other flyers enthusiastically urged local hunters to "get your Guru tags
now" with the motto "Let's Bhang Wan Today!"[63] Meanwhile, gun
sales in Oregon reportedly doubled.[64] Not surprisingly, this helped fuel
the Rajneeshees' own growing paranoia and contributed to a kind of
escalating, feedback loop of fear, suspicion, and aggressive rhetoric
between Rajneeshpuram and the local community throughout the next
few years.

FIGURE 13. Anti-Rajneesh mock *mala* made of bullets. Rajneesh Artifacts and Ephemera Collection, 1981–2004, University of Oregon Special Collections and University Archives, Coll. 275. Photo by the author.

THE BIRTH OF THE "RELIGION" OF RAJNEESHISM

Another immediate problem facing the community was Rajneesh's own immigration status. In his initial visa application, Rajneesh had described his occupation as "religious teacher" and had first requested entry to the United States for a back operation in New Jersey.[65] After moving to Oregon and establishing the new commune, Rajneesh then petitioned to remain in the United States first for an additional six months and then permanently in order to carry out his professional duties as a religious leader. The INS conducted a lengthy interview with Rajneesh in Portland and sent officers to investigate the ranch, but their conclusions were skeptical, at best, and often downright hostile, at worst. Thus, despite his favorable impression of the productivity of the ranch, the INS investigator Thomas Casey also described Rajneesh himself as a fraud and his operation as a money-making scheme based on the sale of psychospiritual mumbo jumbo:

> In the opinion of writer SUBJECT and/or his closest associates are opportunistic charlatans deriving a handsome income from his "disciples." . . . . SUBJECT appears to absolve his followers from the restraints of personal responsibility in exchange for substantial amounts of money. . . . The hierarchy of the organization seems comprised of shrewd, dedicated persons with considerable funds at their disposal.[66]

In 1982 and 1983, the INS denied Rajneesh preferential status as a "religious worker" and refused to change his status from a visitor's visa to that of a permanent resident. In their estimation, Rajneesh's various medical conditions and his self-imposed silence rendered him incapable of fulfilling his role as leader of a religious organization.

This decision was repeatedly appealed by the community, who compiled vast amounts of evidence, testimonies, text, and photographs in an attempt to prove that Rajneesh was in fact "a religious teacher" and the leader of a vast international movement that should be understood as a legitimate "religion."[67] Many of these testimonials—for example, a letter from Swami Anand Santosh to the INS—explicitly invoked ideals of America as "a land of religious freedom" and tolerance, enshrined in the First Amendment.[68] Rajneesh's lawyer, Swami Prem Niren, likewise denounced the INS decision as an act of "harassment, prejudice . . . bigotry and intolerance" aimed at destroying a genuine "religion" simply because of the agency's "unreasoned fear of and hostility to the communal lifestyle and religion of the unfamiliar 'Eastern guru and cult.'"[69]

At the same time as the INS inquiry was taking place, various other politicians were also raising questions about its nonprofit and charitable (i.e., tax-exempt) status. Thus in May 1982, Senator Hatfield wrote a letter in which he described his own investigations into "the Rajneesh cult." He noted that he had "asked for the Internal Revenue Service to review the Ranch's non-profit charitable status"—although, of course, he wanted make sure that actions taken by his office were "consistent with constitutional rights of religious freedom."[70]

Throughout his early lectures, as we have seen in previous chapters, Rajneesh was intensely critical of mainstream religions and often of the very idea of "religion." As he put it, "It will not be possible to make a dogma out of my words. . . . Every institution is bound to be dead. . . . I am destroying your ideologies, creeds, cults, dogmas, and I am not replacing them with anything."[71] If anything, his new "religionless" philosophy was presented as one that would undermine and dismantle all existing belief systems, not create a new one in their place. Nonetheless, in 1983—in the midst of the disputes with the INS—Sheela announced the foundation of a new religion called "Rajneeshism," complete with its own sacred texts, rituals, prayers, holidays, and clergy.

In 1983 and 1984, the community published a number of texts that were primarily designed to assert the "religious" character of the Rajneesh movement in the United States. The first was a booklet entitled *Rajneeshism: An Introduction to Bhagwan Shree Rajneesh and His Religion,* and the second was a fat, two-volume compilation called *The Rajneesh Bible.* This attempt to assert the "religious" nature of controversial new movements is hardly a new phenomenon in the United States, of course. We can identify similar attempts to establish the religious legitimacy of new movements, from Joseph Smith's *Book of Mormon* to the Church of Scientology's elaborate, aggressive, and ultimately successful attempt to win recognition as a tax-exempt religion in the eyes of the IRS. It is probably not accidental that the Rajneesh community's effort to redescribe itself as a religion took place in the early 1980s, at the same time that Scientology was enmeshed in an intense legal battle with the IRS and other federal agencies over its own claims to religious status. Meanwhile, during this same period, many other new movements were attempting to defend themselves against the "cult" label and to show that they were not another Peoples Temple or a Manson Family waiting to commit mass suicide or murder.[72]

Rajneeshism was explicitly designed to present Rajneesh's philosophy as a bona fide religion, Rajneesh as a bona fide religious leader, and the Oregon commune as a bona fide religious organization. While other religions were formalized long after the founder's death, the text explains, Rajneeshism is the first religion to be created while the Master is still alive, and is therefore the only one that accurately reflects his true intention.[73] The text opens with the "Three Refuges" of Buddhism, which are part of the core articles of faith for Buddhist monks and laity worldwide: I take refuge in the Buddha; I take refuge in the *sangha* or community; I take refuge in the *dhamma* or teaching of the Buddha. Rajneeshism, however, substitutes Rajneesh for the "awakened one" or Buddha; Rajneesh is the "Master" whose magnetic force is a source of ultimate protection.[74] Likewise, the Rajneesh commune in Oregon is identified with the Buddhist *sangha,* and the *dhamma* is Rajneesh's own unique spiritual message.[75] The text also describes a hierarchy of religious members based on levels of spiritual awakening, using the Buddhist terms *acharyas, arihants,* and *siddhas.* Sheela, meanwhile, had also taken to wearing more explicitly "religious" garb during this period, such as a special red robe emblazoned with the logo of a golden dove, and a nun-like head covering. And the community's newspaper, the *Rajneesh Times,* also began to run a series of articles on religion, driving home the point that this was now a religious organization.[76]

Later, after the collapse of Rajneeshpuram, Bhagwan would claim that the creation of the "religion of Rajneeshism" was entirely Sheela's idea. She had, he argued, seized the opportunity of his long period of silence to turn the community into a full-blown religious organization, complete with its own "fascistic" hierarchies and bureaucracy: she had "created the whole idea that this is a religion. She collected few of my sentences from here and there . . . and managed to compile a small book: *Rajneeshism.* . . . Sheela managed to create it in a more organized, fascist fashion: a religion, a hierarchy."[77] However, this claim seems a bit disingenuous when we consider the fact that the very first talks Rajneesh gave after breaking his period of silence in late 1984 were entitled "The Rajneesh Bible" and were clearly designed to present something like a "scripture" for the movement. Advertised in *Bhagwan* magazine with the announcement "Bhagwan Shree Rajneesh Speaks Again! Series of Talks on His Religion," this was to be the Master's return to public speaking after his years of silence.[78] In the introduction, the editor, Swami Krishna Prem, describes the text as a unique example of an enlightened being writing his own Bible, and doing so while still alive and still on earth, unlike the world's other major scriptures, which were all written by disciples long after the founder's death: "THE RAJNEESH BIBLE is pure, direct communion. It is the living enlightened Master Bhagwan Shree Rajneesh speaking on His religion, on the vital, unfolding religion of Rajneeshism."[79] The text itself, meanwhile, declares Rajneeshism "the first and perhaps the last religion" insofar as it is the first based on acceptance and celebration rather than fear and repression.[80]

Interestingly, however, this Bible contains some of Rajneesh's more thoughtful discussion of the concept of religion itself, which he defines in terms of its (possible) etymological meaning of "re-uniting" or "re-integration."[81] By this he means the reuniting of body and soul, materialism and spirituality. As such, he defines it in explicitly religious and yet anti-institutional terms. That is, it is a form of "religiousness," or an inner spiritual attitude that is also strongly against "religion" in the sense of an established normative, doctrinal, and dogmatic institution:

Religion has nothing to do with God, the devil, heaven or hell. The word religion . . . means putting the parts together, so that the parts are no more parts but become the whole. . . . Each part, separate, is dead; joined together a new quality appears, the quality of the whole. And to bring that quality into your life is the purpose of religion. . . . But the way the religions have functioned in the world, they have changed its whole quality. . . . The religions of the world have helped humanity to forget even the meaning of the word. They are against the integrated man, because the integrated man does not need God, does not need the priest, does not need the church.[82]

The reasons for this shift in a more explicitly "religious" direction are many, complex, and not entirely easy to sort out. As James Gordon recalls, many of the *sannyasins* felt quite "baffled and betrayed" by this sudden turn to "religion." After all, Rajneesh had long inveighed against the hypocrisy and superficiality of organized religions, and many followers had been drawn to him precisely *because* of his bold and often hilarious iconoclasm.[83]

According to Rajneesh himself, when he reflected on this period after the collapse of the Oregon commune, the use of the term "religion" was initially simply a way to satisfy the INS, who were now threatening to deport him and his followers and needed a category in which to fit this unusual community. As he put it, the INS officials could only slot him into the category of "religion," and that was the only reason that he accepted the label:

> When I was talking to the INS, I insisted that I would like to call my philosophy a religiousness, but they said, "That is difficult because we don't have any category for religiousness. You can apply only under the category religion. We don't have any category for religiousness.
>
> I explained to them that there is a difference. A religion is a fixed dogma, a fixed belief system. A religiousness is just a quality like love. It is not an organized thing. It has no priests, no priestesses. It is rebellion against all that destroys human reason."
>
> But they said, "We cannot accept the application unless you use the word religion."
>
> It was just because of them. I said, "Okay. I will use the word religion just to fulfill your stupid categories."[84]

[margin handwritten note: have to conform in order to survive]

Another possible motive was simply tax exemption, a powerful financial motive that also inspired other new religious movements such as the Church of Scientology. Even as he denounced all organized "religions," Rajneesh still maintained that his movement should have the benefit of tax-exempt status as a spiritual and "religious"—albeit "religionless"—movement: "It is a way of being religious. It is not a religion. It is a way of being spiritual. It is not an organized religion. It has every right not to pay any taxes to anybody."[85]

But regardless of the original motivation of the turn to "religion," it did seem to pay off for the Rajneesh community. In the spring of 1984, after receiving thousands of supporting materials, including letters of recommendation from followers, psychologists, and academics, the INS finally granted Rajneesh preferential status as a "religious worker." It did not, however, rule on his residence application.[86] And it also did not prevent an escalating series of attacks from government officials, politicians, journalists, and local residents over the next two years.

FROM FREE LOVE UTOPIA TO APOCALYPTIC PARANOIA AND SEXUAL PANIC

The story of the Oregon ranch is in many ways the story of a utopian experiment that began with an ideal of radical freedom, experimentation, and self-expression, yet somehow ended in an increasingly controlled, regulated, and almost fascistic police state. As Dillon reflected in an interview in 2013, "It was a wonderful happening there. But as it built more and more, it also became more regulated and controlled in various ways." Like many who were there at the time, Dillon places most of the blame for the increasing regimentation of the community on Sheela and her small group of female associates (called the "Ma-archy" by some). With Rajneesh still in his period of silence and Laxmi forced to leave Oregon by the INS, Sheela was left to exert increasing control over the community. Ordinary *sannyasins* such as Dillon were faced with a choice between submitting to Sheela's growing authoritarian rule or leaving the community they had worked so hard to build:

> What started out as a very kind of free floating project got more and more regulated according to how Sheela wanted it. . . . So there started to be more and more of an undercurrent of discomfort. And yet we wanted to still be there. We wanted the thing to succeed. And if you didn't really fit in with the thing at least outwardly, you're going to get asked to leave, and nobody wanted to get asked to leave.[87]

Sheela was also known for her acerbic tongue, which she frequently let loose to attack any enemies of the ranch. Branding the Oregon locals "fascists and bigots," she also freely used colorful obscenities before the media. When she appeared on ABC's TV show *Nightline*, for example, she referred to fellow guest Wayne Fawbush, an Oregon state representative at the time, as "Mr. Fascist" and had to be "bleeped" when she told him, "You're full of —."[88] Reveling in her own outrageous and deliberately over-the-top, inflammatory rhetoric, Sheela announced: "This country is so fucking bigoted that it deserves to be taken over. You tell your governor, your attorney general . . . if one person on Rancho Rajneesh is harmed, I will have fifteen of their heads. I mean it. Even though I am a nonviolent person, I will do that."[89]

Sheela's hold over the ranch itself, meanwhile, became increasingly firm—and some would say quite totalitarian in its own way. Already by 1983, journalists were beginning to describe the ranch as "the closest thing to an Eastern Bloc experience available in the United States."[90] Among other things, Sheela established an incredibly elaborate wiretapping system throughout the community; not only were rooms and phones throughout the ranch bugged, but the conference room at the city hall was also bugged prior to a meeting with investigators from the attorney general. Later it was revealed that a bug had been placed on a table leg next to the favorite chair of Bhagwan himself, who was told that it was a "panic button."[91] Eventually, the community would spend $100,000 a month on surveillance equipment as it carried out the largest wiretapping conspiracy in U.S. history (at least prior to the more recent revelations about the NSA's secret wiretapping programs after 9/11).

One of the most jarring moments for many journalists who covered the ranch during this period, however, was the realization that members of the Rajneesh "Peace Force" were beginning to carry and openly display heavy weaponry (fig. 14). Not only did Peace Force members possess Uzis, Galil assault rifles, M1 riot shotguns, and some $25,000 worth of ammunition, but they also made a clear show of force by carrying these weapons openly and having themselves filmed at target practice. While this was intended to send a message to local opponents that they were not to be trifled with, it sent a much broader message to the national media that they might in fact be a dangerous "cult" and potentially even another Jonestown mass murder/suicide about to unfold.[92]

As the conflict with the local community and the state and county governments escalated, the rhetoric coming out of Rajneeshpuram also became increasingly apocalyptic. Indeed, the utopian ideal of a paradisiac oasis in the desert was often juxtaposed with imagery of impending global catastrophe. This apocalyptic trend was evident even in the 1983 publication of *Rajneeshism*, which included a lengthy warning about an imminent global crisis that would swallow up most major

FIGURE 14. "One of Rajneesh Security Force Members Holds
Automatic Weapon." Max Gutierrez photo, Oregon Historical
Society, bb 001285.

urban centers within the next fifteen years. The religion of Rajneeshism,
meanwhile, was presented as the "Noah's Ark" that alone could offer
an escape:

> Man is now living his most critical moment and it is a crisis of immense
> dimensions. Either he will die or a new man will be born. Rajneeshism
> accepts this challenge and is making the only worldwide effort to transform
> human consciousness so that man can die and a superman can be born out

of these ashes. . . . Unless human consciousness changes totally man cannot survive. . . . The period of this crisis will be between 1984 and 1999. During this period there will be every kind of destruction on earth including man-manufactured auto-suicidal efforts. . . . There will be floods which have never been known since the time of Noah, along with earthquakes, volcanic eruptions and everything else that is possible through nature. The earth cannot tolerate this type of mankind any longer. There will be wars, which are bound to end in nuclear explosions, hence no ordinary Noah's Arks are going to save humanity. Rajneeshism is creating a Noah's Ark of consciousness. . . . Tokyo, New York, San Francisco, Los Angeles, Bombay, etc.—all these cities are going to disappear and the holocaust is not going to be confined to certain places. It is going to be global so no escape will be possible. You can only escape within, and that's what I teach.[93]

This terrifying warning in *Rajneeshism* was widely repeated in other publications for the next two years. For example, several issues of the *Rajneesh Times* in 1984 featured a full-page ad headlined "The Center of the Cyclone," which showed Rajneesh's face amid a dozen newspaper headlines describing an array of catastrophic global events: the use of nerve gas in Iraq, volcanoes, tornadoes, storms, floods, forest depletion, and terrorism around the world. The ad repeated the warning of global holocaust, suggesting that Rajneesh was "the only hope in this destructive cyclone."[94] Ironically, however, Rajneesh also explains that the best possible response to this impending apocalypse is not dread or fear but rather *laughter and celebration*. Even as the human race is hurtling toward violent self-destruction, our greatest weapon in response is to create a new world of joy, bliss, and dance:

> Time is short—dance, sing. Be joyous. If there were no possibility of nuclear destruction, no threat, you could postpone. You could say, tomorrow we will dance. But now there may be no tomorrow; you cannot postpone. . . . The whole earth may disappear, may explode. . . . If we can start a new climate in the world—of rejoicing, of dancing, of singing, of meditation, of prayer—and if people become full of bliss, cheerfulness, laughter, if the world is full of laughter, there is every possibility we can avoid nuclear destruction. . . . If destruction has become global, we have to make laughter and dancing also global in the same proportion to counteract it.[95]

One of the most remarkable transformations in the Osho-Rajneesh movement was its shift from a promiscuous community of free love and sexual abandon to an increasingly puritanical and uptight community of sexual fear. Within a very short time, the commune that had been world-famous for having so much sex that it "blew the roof off" became obsessed with a new external and internal threat: AIDS. On March 5,

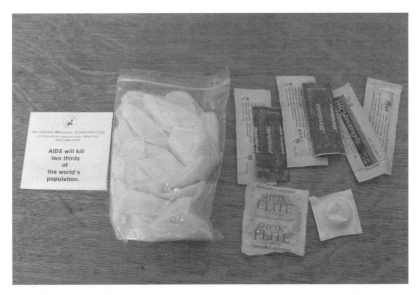

FIGURE 15. Rajneeshpuram AIDS kit. Rajneesh Artifacts and Ephemera Collection, 1981–2004, University of Oregon Special Collections and University Archives, Coll. 275. Photo by the author.

1984, Sheela made an announcement on behalf of Rajneesh that AIDS was indeed a threat—in fact, not merely a health threat but a plague of almost apocalyptic proportions, and even the "disease with no name" predicted by the sixteenth-century prophet Nostradamus. In a radical shift from the days of free love and sexual promiscuity, oral and anal sex were prohibited, and couples were advised to undergo scrupulous washing after any sexual exposure. Instead of encouragements to explore the road "from sex to superconsciousness" in any way imaginable, *sannyasins* were now issued kits containing condoms, packets of lubricating jelly, latex gloves, and a brochure entitled "AIDS Will Kill Two Thirds of the World's Population" (fig. 15).[96] Meanwhile, special waste bins for disposal of contaminated materials were made available in the kitchens, toilets, and dorms, alcoholic sprays were installed in every toilet, and everyone on the ranch was to be tested for AIDS. Thus, as Gordon recalls, in a very short time, "the feast of fucking was over. The time for fasting had come."[97]

In many ways, however, the Rajneesh community's response was a reflection—though perhaps an exaggerated and extreme one—of the larger response to AIDS in the United States and around the world. As

Dennis Altman notes, the sexual revolution had radically changed the way we understood and practiced sex through the widespread availability of contraception, making intercourse less directly related to the dangers of sexual disease and death. But the emergence of AIDS reversed much of that revolutionary shift, reintroducing the threat of danger and death in the sexual act:

> AIDS has transformed the ways in which we understand sex, linking it once again to concepts of danger, disease and death. . . . Only with the advent of relatively safe and effective contraception, and the ability to cure venereal diseases, could sex be decoupled from danger. This was the real meaning of the "sexual revolution" of the 1960s, and the advent of AIDS has undermined it.[98]

As a kind of extreme microcosm of this sudden shift, the Rajneesh movement had gone from free love utopia to paranoid police state in just a few short years.

hierarchy

THE RAPID DECLINE OF RAJNEESHPURAM: FROM CHARITY FOR THE HOMELESS TO BIOLOGICAL TERRORISM

This apocalyptic paranoia was followed by an array of increasingly bizarre and illegal activities. Among the many astonishing things that took place in the later years of the Rajneeshpuram experiment, the "Share a Home" program was surely one of most outrageous. Begun in late summer and early fall of 1984, Share a Home was promoted as a charitable program designed to help homeless people from around the country by bringing them to the ranch, feeding and housing them, and offering them work and a place in the commune. Buses were sent across the country, all the way to the East Coast, to find homeless people and to offer to give them a fresh start at Rajneeshpuram. By the time the program ended, nearly 4,000 people—mostly single males, many of them African American, and all of them over eighteen—were brought to the ranch. Suddenly, nearly half the ranch was black.[99] According to interviews with these men from the time, moreover, many of them enjoyed the program and appreciated the food, the housing, the beer, the nightly disco, and even in some cases the spiritual teachings.[100]

Yet to most observers, including many *sannyasins* at the time, this was a purely cynical and calculated attempt to sway a political election. In November 1984, the Wasco County elections were held, and it was clear to many both inside and outside the movement that Share a Home was essentially an attempt to get enough registered voters to outnumber the local voters in order to put *sannyasins* on the county council and then get their various plans approved. In the words of former *sannyasin* Will Foster, who worked in the Share a Home program, the scheme was simply "morally corrupt" and a transparent political maneuver.[101]

Moreover, keeping thousands of street people inside a commune for several months also proved to be a challenge, since not all of them were necessarily on board with the *sannyasin* experience. In one of the most shocking revelations to come out of the ranch, it turned out that these new residents were unknowingly being given serious drugs—heavy-duty tranquilizers and Valium—in their food and beer to keep them quiet. "Haldol in the chili," Ritter recalls.[102]

The Wasco election officials quickly grew suspicious of the Rajneeshees' plan to bring in thousands of new voters, and announced a blanket rejection of all the new registrations. Despite the Rajneeshees' intense protests that this was unconstitutional, undemocratic, and even fascistic, they had no chance in the election, which brought out record numbers of Wasco County voters. Shortly after the election, many of the street people were abruptly bused out of Rajneeshpuram and dropped off in nearby cities, such as Portland, where they were abandoned without any resources or contacts, often thousands of miles from their starting place.[103]

If Share a Home was outrageous for its pure Machiavellian politics, even more surreal events would soon unfold. From simple election fraud, things rapidly escalated to psychological and physical warfare. At first, this seemed limited to acts of harassment and disgusting jokes; for example, animal parts were dumped on the porches and in the driveways of local officials, letters alleging scandals were sent to Rajneesh opponents, and sexually explicit magazines, dildos, and condoms were sent to clerks at court houses.[104] Yet by the end of 1984, these sorts of pranks were followed by biological terrorism on a massive scale.

The now-infamous poisonings seemed to follow a plan of escalating breadth and ambition. This began in August 1984, when three county officials visited the ranch and were offered glasses of water by Sheela. Two of them, Jefferson County District Attorney Michael Sullivan and Wasco County Commissioner William Hulse, became seriously ill and later were found to have been poisoned.[105] This was followed by a massive poisoning of at least 751 people in the county seat of The Dalles, 45 of whom required hospitalization. Later, the poisonings were traced to eight salad bars in the area that had been contaminated with Salmonella bacteria. Using her credentials as head of the Rajneesh Medical Corporation, Ma Anand Puja had obtained Salmonella culture from the V.W.R. Scientific Company in Seattle and took it to a secret laboratory at a remote spot on the ranch. Another *sannyasin,* Ma Anand Avelos—dressed in blue rather than red to avoid suspicion—then carried the bacteria to The Dalles and contaminated not only salad bars but also restaurant coffee creamers and a grocery store produce department.[106] Later, it became evident that Sheela and her cohorts had used these early episodes as test runs for a far more incredible plan to poison the entire The Dalles water supply in order to reduce voter turnout for the upcoming elections. Even without this last hypothetical attack, the hundreds of poisonings in The Dalles area marked the largest act of bioterrorism in American history.[107]

In the months that followed, various other violent schemes came to light. In one scheme, Sheela and her associates purchased five guns and began staking out the home of Charles Turner, the U.S. attorney in Portland who was presenting the Rajneesh case to a grand jury. This action was apparently part of a plot to assassinate Turner as well as David Frohnmayer, state attorney general.[108] Back home on the ranch, Sheela also plotted to kill Rajneesh's own physician and close confidant, Devaraj (George Meredith, aka Swami Amrito), who was injected with poison yet survived the attack. And yet another still more outlandish plan under consideration was to fly a bomb-laden plane into the county courthouse in The Dalles.[109] Ironically, the same Rajneesh who had once claimed to be a "spiritual terrorist" wielding words instead of weapons had now become the head of a movement that engaged in very real physical terrorism, the spiritual aims of which were unclear.

- attempted murders

THE END OF THE DREAM

Once investigations into the bioterror attack began in early 1985, the Oregon experiment disintegrated very quickly. In September 1985, Sheela and a small group of her closest associates abruptly fled the country, and a week later Rajneeesh himself began to hold press conferences in which he publicly denounced his secretary and accused her of a range of crimes. Claiming that *Rajneeshism* had actually been written by Sheela and her "gang of fascists" using his name, Rajneesh called for 5,000 copies of the book to be burned along with Sheela's robes.[110]

The subsequent criminal investigations produced a staggering amount of evidence and a stunning array of charges. In all, some twenty-

FIGURE 16. "Federal marshals escort Bhagwan Shree Rajneesh to bail hearing." *The Oregonian.*

five individuals were charged with electronic eavesdropping conspiracy, thirteen with immigration conspiracy, eight with lying to federal officials, three with harboring a fugitive, and others with criminal conspiracy, burglary, racketeering, arson, assault, and attempted murder. Sheela herself was arrested in Germany on October 28, 1985, and extradited to the United States, where she was fined $400,000, ordered to pay $69,353 in restitution for arson, and given six consecutive sentences for attempted murder, second-degree assault, her role in the Salmonella poisoning, wiretapping, and immigration fraud—a total sentence of sixty-four years. However, she was later released after just two and a half years in prison and immediately left the country for Switzerland. Rajneesh himself abruptly left the ranch on a Leer jet headed for Bermuda, but he was tracked down and arrested at a stop in North Carolina. Although charged with one count of conspiracy and thirty-four counts of making false statements to federal officials, he reached a plea bargain agreement and was found guilty of just two counts, fined $400,000, and allowed to leave the country voluntarily (fig. 16).[111]

Meanwhile, Oregon Attorney General Frohnmayer concluded that the city of Rajneeshpuram—as a combined religious entity and city—violated both the Oregon state constitution and the U.S. Constitution because of its nonseparation of church and state. Rajneeshpuram, he argued, could not perform any of the normal functions of a city because of the "pervasive and unavoidable" intrusion of religion into city government.[112] The litigation over the legal standing of the city dragged on until 1987, leaving Rajneeshpuram essentially bankrupt and deserted.[113] Finally, in perhaps the most ironic twist of all, the ranch was eventually sold and transformed into a Christian youth camp called the Washington Family Ranch, which is run by the evangelical group Young Life. Once a utopian experiment based on Neo-Tantric sensuality and Dynamic Meditative ecstasy, the ranch is today a summer camp for Christian teens hoping to find a personal relationship with Jesus Christ.

CONCLUSIONS: MAKING SENSE OF RAJNEESHPURAM—UTOPIAN CAPITALISM IN REAGAN'S AMERICA

Even forty years later, it is difficult to make sense of the Rajneeshpuram experiment. How exactly did this movement change from a vibrant, progressive, and exciting utopian spiritual project to a criminal, terrorist, and authoritarian regime, in just five short years? Why did everything go so wrong, so fast, and in such bizarre ways?

Rajneesh's response—and the one condoned by most of his current supporters—was that the movement began with the noblest of intentions but was hijacked and perverted by Sheela and her minions. Rajneesh was quick to meet with the authorities and to hold press conferences after Sheela's departure, and he blamed more or less all of the wrongdoing on her pathological desire for power. It was Sheela, he claimed, who had deceived and manipulated him, taking advantage of his period of silence in order to create the false "religion of Rajneeshism," while turning "a meditation camp into a concentration camp."[114] Professing complete innocence, Rajneesh revealed all of Sheela's crimes to the federal and state authorities, along with numerous fanciful allegations. This remains the official line of the Osho community in Pune today. As Swami Amrito recounted to me in early 2013, the Oregon ranch started out as a remarkably progressive experimental community, but was hijacked and destroyed by Sheela's power-hungry machinations.[115] Another Rajneesh defender, Jack Allanach (aka Swami Krishna Prem), likewise placed the entirety of the blame on Sheela and her cohorts, who manipulated the vulnerable guru and destroyed a beautiful utopian vision out of sheer desire for power and domination: "I watched Sheela build it and I watched Sheela destroy it out of a lust for power laced with paranoia and a vision of herself as modern-day maharani of an empire. . . . Out of love for Osho, an amazing city was created, but since he was in silence and unavailable to us . . . it had no beating heart. Sheela ruled by fear and coercion, with a coterie of self-ish, hard-hearted power-hungry women enforcing a single rule: submit in silence or leave."[116] This also seems to be largely the narrative that was accepted by the authorities, given Rajneesh's relatively light charges and Sheela's very long list of criminal accusations.

Another possible interpretation is that Rajneesh himself was largely incapacitated during the Oregon period, and so not in much of a condition to control the machinations of Sheela and her crew. As Milne recalls, the guru was heavily dependent on drugs—mainly nitrous oxide and Valium—during this period and largely incapable of functioning as a religious leader, much less reining in the criminal activities that were taking place on the ranch: "I felt sorry for Bhagwan, trapped and manipulated by these powerful women, going out only on his monoto-nous daily drives around the ranch."[117]

Sheela, on the other hand, has written a memoir that portrays herself as the victim in this story. Published in 2012, her book, *Don't Kill Him,* describes Rajneesh as a brilliant, eloquent, and tremendously charismatic man who later succumbed to his own thirst for power and to a heavy addiction to drugs. As Sheela tells the story, Rajneesh changed dramati-cally after moving the United States, becoming increasingly attached to his wealth and largely forgetting his own spiritual vision: "His people, His commune, His vision, His dream, everything seemed to have been forgotten. . . . His leadership and guidance had become limited to only how He could get more money."[118] She then became the "fall-woman," offered up as a convenient scapegoat to the authorities and to the media so that he might escape without a long-term prison sentence.

Others, however, have concluded that Rajneesh and Sheela were probably equally to blame in this complex mess. "He was manipulating her, and she was manipulating him," one former *sannyasin* concluded.[119] Journalists such as Les Zaitz and Milt Ritter told me that they find it implausible that someone as shrewd as Rajneesh could not have known what was going on under his own nose on the ranch. He must, they think, have been more directly involved all along.[120] Likewise, as James Gordon concluded after interviewing Rajneesh and numerous others involved in the Oregon experiment, it seems likely that the guru was responsible for far more than he later admitted. In Gordon's opinion, Rajneesh must have known about Sheela's shocking activities and yet did little to obstruct them: "He was certainly responsible for the ranch's arrogant attitude, the consolidation and sclerosis of power, the paranoia. He had described the religion of Rajneeshism and the centralization of the communes . . . he knew Sheela was doing wiretapping . . . he knew that Sheela was turning a meditation camp into a concentration camp . . . but hadn't stopped her."[121] Even many of those who investigated the ranch, such as Attorney General Frohnmayer, believed that Rajneesh was guilty of many more crimes than those he was actually convicted of.[122]

My own view, however, is that the most interesting question is not whether Rajneesh or Sheela was primarily "to blame" for the collapse of the Oregon commune. Rather, the far more important question is, How and why did this amazing spiritual experiment emerge in the midst of Reagan's America and become such a successful but violently contested space? How can we make sense of the Rajneeshpuram phenomenon within the larger historical, social, political, and economic context of the United States during the 1980s?

In many ways, I would argue, Rajneeshpuram is best understood as both a product and a striking embodiment of Reagan's America. The remarkable yet tragic community that Rajneesh created highlights in many ways the promises and perils of neoliberalism, which emerged as a dominant economic and ideological paradigm during the Reagan and Thatcher eras.[123] On the one hand, this was—at least in its first few years—an incredibly innovative, creative, and successful community that was experimenting with new forms of agriculture, recycling, energy, land reclamation, tourism, and business. Much of what the commune accomplished in the early 1980s was far ahead of its time and embodied the best of the American entrepreneurial spirit. On the other hand, the community also quickly came to embody the least admirable aspects of neoliberalism and American capitalism. If, as Harvey suggests, neoliberalism can be characterized as the "commodification of everything,"[124] it would be difficult to think of a more extreme example of this neoliberal logic than Rajneesh's famous declaration "I *sell* contentment. I *sell* enlightenment." While Rajneesh rejected all other forms of blind faith and dogmatism, he did seem to accept the neoliberal blind faith in the market as the best means of conducting all human affairs. And yet, within a few short years, the Rajneeshpuram experiment went from generating millions of dollars in wealth to utter catastrophic collapse.

Ironically, despite his outspoken disdain for Reagan, Rajneesh could be described in some ways as the spiritual counterpart of Reagan and American capitalism during the 1980s. As historian Michael Schaller notes, "Reagan persuaded many Americans that . . . 'government is the problem,' while assuring them that the United States remained a unique community of rugged individualists."[125] At the same time, Reagan used his skills as a charismatic actor/politician to create a compelling sort of mythological narrative about America and capitalism that persuaded many Americans to embrace an ideal that did not always correspond to reality;

> Reagan succeeded, as few actors or politicians have, in persuading Americans to suspend their disbelief. It was an era when saying something made it so, when, as in a daydream, anything seemed possible. Deficits did not exist, were someone's else's fault, or did not matter; the poor caused their own plight or were impoverished because they received too much money from the government; the wealthy, on the other hand, had been abused by not being permitted to keep more of their income.[126]

However, as Garry Wills argues, Reagan's policies also embodied a series of tensions that in many ways reflected deeper tensions in American capitalism during the 1980s. Above all, Reagan helped reinforce the myth that capitalism is somehow a "conservative" thing and even identical with conservatism; yet in fact, Wills argues, capitalism is anything but conservative and is in many ways an inherently radical, destructive, and perpetually transformative economic system:

> Conservatism, in a minimal definition, wants to conserve; but capitalism is an instrument for change, for expansion, driven toward ever-new resources, products, markets. It reorders life drastically. . . . In this flow of products created by a growing surplus, 'capital has no home,' in the words of Bernard Shaw. It is a roving, restless, innovative force. . . . There is nothing less conservative than capitalism, so itchy for the new. It spends in order to expand, it razes to rebuild, it destroys to employ.[127]

All of these trends and tensions within Reagan's America can be seen reflected and in some cases epitomized in the Rajneesh community of the same decade. Not unlike Reagan, Rajneesh combined a fiercely pro-capitalist, antigovernment, and antiregulation ideology with the rhetoric of rugged individualism and personal freedom. But perhaps most striking was his own Reaganesque role as a larger-than-life charismatic leader whose mythic power often obscured lived realities of inequality and scandals occurring right under his nose. Both Rajneesh and Reagan enacted a highly choreographed and crafted stage presence that was tremendously persuasive while it lasted; yet both also left behind a series of scandals upon their respective departures from office (which occurred within two years of one another).

Finally, the uniquely hybrid spiritual-yet-capitalist community that Rajneesh created in Oregon also reveals the radical and often quite "un-conservative" nature of capitalism. We might even say that Rajneesh-ism is Reaganism and free-market neoliberalism but without the pretense of being "conservative." While embracing many of the same ideals of individualism, antiregulation, entrepreneurialism, and unquestioning faith in the market, it was also radically opposed to the conservative religious values of right-wing Republicans, celebrating sexual liberation (at least initially). And with its brief rise to success and rapid collapse, Rajneeshpuram also reflects the "roving, restless, innovative," and crea-tive-yet-destructive nature of global capitalism.

In many ways, the Rajneesh experiment in Oregon was an odd mir-ror image of the excesses and perils of neoliberal capitalism during the mid-1980s. While Rajneesh never used the exact phrase "Greed is good," his radically individualistic and procapitalist ideal of being "absolutely selfish" in many ways echoes that view of Gordon Gekko in the 1987 Oliver Stone film, *Wall Street*.[128] Inspired by the real-life Wall Street inside trader Ivan Boesky, and his famous claim that "greed is healthy," Gekko was a powerful metaphor for the excesses of unregu-lated capitalism in the 1980s.[129] Similarly, I would argue, Rajneesh serves as a powerful metaphor for the excesses of the corporate merger of spirituality and capitalism that took place at exactly the same time in Reagan's America. The Rajneeshees' takeover of the local town of Ante-lope was a kind of spiritual reflection of the hostile takeovers taking place in the United States, encouraged in large part by neoliberal poli-cies of deregulation, which "fueled a series of mergers, acquisitions, and leverage buyouts, involving some of the nation's largest corpora-tions."[130] Rajneeshpuram's rapid collapse in 1985 also mirrored the tra-jectory of many corporations that grew rapidly during the bubble of the 1980s and then collapsed during the "Black Monday" crash of 1987, followed by the savings and loan crisis a few years later, in 1991.[131]

As we will see in chapter 5, this unique blend of neoliberal economics and spiritual experimentation was reborn in yet another new form fol-lowing the collapse of the Oregon commune, as Rajneesh returned to India and created a new global spiritual center in Pune. And it was dogged by another wave of scandals, crises, and legal debates that have haunted the movement—as they have other big multinational corpora-tions—since the 1980s.

CHAPTER 5

"Osho"

The Apotheosis of a Fallen Guru
in 1990s India

I don't want to be called bhagwan again. Enough is enough.
The joke is over!

—Bhagwan Shree Rajneesh

Every year thousands of people visit this luxurious resort. . . .
The atmosphere is really like a fairy tale. A paradise where all
your emotional, bodily and spiritual needs are met.

—*Elle* magazine

While the Oregon experiment was surely the most outrageous and an
often surreal episode in Rajneesh's global journey, in some ways the
most surprising period was his return to India and rebirth in the new
Pune ashram. After being denied entry to every country to which he
applied, Rajneesh finally returned to his homeland and to the original
Pune ashram, where he dropped his title Bhagwan and finally assumed
the new title Osho in 1989. Amazingly, however, the new Osho movement in India reemerged as a kind of phoenix from the ashes, becoming
in many ways even more popular than before and transforming the
Pune center from a lively but rustic ashram into an upscale, five-
star international resort. Although Osho himself died in 1990, the
Pune center quickly expanded throughout the 1990s into an attractive
and popular destination for spiritual seekers and tourists from around
the world. As Aneesha Dillon recalls, "It was a huge creative explosion
in the early '90s of many different kinds of work,"[1] as the ashram
attracted a whole new generation of global seekers and added an

ever broader array of spiritual practices from around the world to its offerings.[2]

By the early 2000s, the Osho movement had evolved from a commune consisting of longtime residents to a complex, decentralized global network in which the Pune center is just one node in a much wider transnational web of travel, trade, tourism, and spiritual practice. Dropping the label "ashram," the center has been renamed the Osho International Meditation Resort and now boasts luxury international hotel accommodations, tennis courts, and a swimming pool, in addition to its vast array of spiritual and psychological offerings drawn from both East and West. While some *sannyasins* today lament this shift toward a high-end tourist resort,[3] others see it as simply the next logical step in the global spread of Osho's message to an ever broader and more mobile audience.[4]

It is no accident that the new Osho Meditation Resort began to flourish and attract global visitors in the 1990s, at exactly the same time that India itself was beginning to open up to a new influx of global capitalism, trade, development, and tourism. Up through the 1980s, it was still relatively difficult for Americans and Europeans to travel in India; international communications were poor; and India was still largely closed to goods such as Coke, Pepsi, and McDonalds. In the 1990s, this India's attitude toward the rest of the world shifted rapidly and dramatically, as India emerged as one of the world's fastest-growing economies, a global center of IT development, and a trading partner increasingly open to goods from and investment by transnational corporations. As Achin Vanaik notes, in the 1980s and 1990s India followed the lead of the United States and United Kingdom toward greater privatization and an openness to global markets, developing what he calls a kind of "Indian Thatcherism" in response to the failures of Nehruvian socialism.[5] Thus in the late 1980s publications such as *India Today* and the *Wall Street Journal* began to celebrate India's "new millionaires" and "a thriving middle class [that] is changing the face of India in a land of poverty."[6] In short, the neoliberal policies of Reagan and Thatcher had now spread globally, leading to a kind of "reform by storm" in India and other parts of Asia that some have called the "second wave of neoliberalism."[7] This was in many ways the "capitalist transformation and consumer revolution" that, as we saw in chapter 2, Rajneesh himself had called for over a decade earlier.[8]

The new Osho resort clearly reflects India's new attitude toward the global marketplace. The Pune center quickly became a vibrant New Age mecca for seekers not just from the United States, the United Kingdom, and Europe but also from Japan, Israel, Brazil, and other nations. As we will see in this chapter, the new global audience of the movement was also reflected in the increasingly eclectic and global spiritual teachings on offer, which now include every imaginable style of meditative, contemplative, and psychological technique. Describing itself as "the largest center in the world for meditation and personal growth processes," the resort claims to encompass "all the current western therapy approaches, the healing arts of East and West, esoteric sciences, creative arts, centering and martial arts, Tantra, Zen, Sufism, and Meditative Therapies."[9]

After retracing the development of the second community in Pune, I will suggest that the Osho International Meditation Resort represents a unique sort of sacred space—one well adapted to the contours of twenty-first-century global capitalism. At first glance, the Osho resort might not appear to be a "sacred space" in the classic sense, as described by scholars such as Mircea Eliade and his many students. As Eliade famously defined it, sacred space is a unique kind of space that is filled with being, power, and existence: it is "strong, significant"; it is the only *really* existing space, and it stands in fundamental contrast to profane ordinary space, which is "formless, amorphous, and without significance or ultimate reality."[10] In fact, the space of the Osho resort has many elements that would seem quite "profane" by Eliade's standards, such as a huge outdoor dance floor, a Jacuzzi, and luxury accommodations.

However, if we adopt a more nuanced and less rigid definition of sacred space, such as that of Jonathan Z. Smith, we can perhaps begin to make a bit more sense of the unique sort of space embodied in the Osho resort. As Smith describes it, sacred space is not so much a radically different kind of domain but rather simply a kind of "focusing lens." That is, it serves to frame and highlight what is most significant to a given religious community, while downplaying or minimizing what is secondary or accidental: "When one enters a temple, one enters a marked-off space in which, in principle, nothing is accidental: everything, at least potentially, is of significance. The temple serves as a *focusing lens*, marking and revealing significance."[11] In Smith's sense, then, the Osho resort is a very powerful kind of "sacred space"—an effective focusing lens that highlights the ideals most central to Osho's own Zorba the Buddha philosophy. Indeed, it casts in sharp relief this community's ideal of wedding body and spirit, its celebration of sensual pleasure and religious transcendence, and its unapologetic synthesis of spirituality with global tourism, big business, and consumerism.

THE AFTERMATH OF RAJNEESHPURAM: FROM FAILED
UTOPIA TO GLOBAL MOVEMENT

Following his abrupt departure from the United States, Rajneesh began
a new global journey that would eventually lead him back home again,
albeit by a ratherroundabout route. Barred from every country in which
he attempted to stay, Rajneesh was seized by the police in Greece and
expelled from the country; he was refused entry into Canada and West
Germany; and he spent only brief periods in Nepal and Uruguay.[12]
Finally, "after six months of waiting in airport detention rooms . . . and
being manhandled by police conducting midnight raids (as in Greece)
Bhagwan returned to India."[13]

During the post-Oregon period, moreover, various rumors and reports
began to circulate that Rajneesh had in fact been poisoned during his
brief period of imprisonment in the United States. Thus a book published
in 1988 entitled *Jesus Crucified Again: This Time in Ronald Reagan's
America* claimed to reveal evidence that Rajneesh had in fact been poisoned with thallium while in American custody. In feigned amazement,
the book wonders how "the government of the world's most powerful
country could be so frightened of a single man that they would literally
stop at nothing to silence him."[14] Other works of this period also tried to
link Rajneesh's poisoning to the machinations of Reagan's attorney general, Edwin Meese, whose aim all along, such works claimed, had been to
destroy the commune. Rajneesh's health deteriorated significantly after
his expulsion from the United States, which was taken as confirmation of
the secret poison attacks.[15] Of course, it is a bit ironic that the same group
found guilty of the largest act of bioterrorism on U.S. soil would now be
accusing the U.S. government of secret poisonings of its own guru.

Despite these rumors and his failing health, Rajneesh himself came
out with his own fresh critique of the United States and vowed to build
a new and better spiritual community. Thus in November 1985,
Rajneesh declared that the world must "put the monster America in its
place," for "either America must be hushed up or America will be the
end of the world."[16] Less than a year later, he was announcing that the
Oregon experiment had really just been the start of a much larger and
grander undertaking that extended not only to America but to the entire
world. Indeed, the fate of the world was itself at stake in this new communal movement:

> The commune in America was only the beginning—a beginning of many
> more communes to happen around the world. They will go on spreading,

because it is not only a question of orthodox religions and dirty politics. It is also a question of the future of humanity.[17]

While briefly in Crete, Rajneesh even declared that he was ready for a "public contest with Reagan," and then predicted that he and his followers would be "back with a commune in five years in the USA, but it won't be in a desert; it will be in Washington."[18] In his opinion, the Rajneesh community offered the perfect alternative to the Cold War binaries of the 1980s, the middle way between Reaganism and Communism, combining the American ideals of individualism and freedom with the Soviet ideals of order and communal solidarity. It would have worked, too, if the meddling politicians had not interfered:

> It was a dream come true. . . . We had created the answer to both Soviet communism which has destroyed individuality and freedom to become a huge concentration camp, and America's lack of philosophy. . . . Love was the only law. There were no rapes, no murders and no one went mad. . . . There were no rich and no poor in the commune because money meant nothing there. We had created a model for the whole world if the politicians hadn't gone mad.[19]

While Rajneesh's proposed public contest with Reagan never came about, his second Pune community did in fact emerge as a new kind of global node that helped tie together a wide array of spiritual, economic, and cultural strands in the twenty-first century.

FROM BHAGWAN TO BUDDHA TO MAITREYA TO OSHO

As we saw in chapter 1, Rajneesh was always a kind of postmodern spiritual figure, who both displayed and indeed embraced a shifting, plural, and fluid identity. From young Chandra Mohan Jain, he had morphed into Acharya Rajneesh and then into Bhagwan Shree Rajneesh. And in the wake of the Oregon collapse, he appears to have been playing with a new series of identities and experimenting with various titles. Initially, he and his followers briefly toyed with the title of the future Buddha, who was prophesied to come for the end of this cosmic era, and Rajneesh was recognized as such by a Japanese seeress named Katue Ishida. Announcing that "the joke is over," he dropped the title Bhagwan and briefly assumed the new name Gautama the Buddha.[20] Thus, the *Rajneesh Newspaper* from November 1986 presented a series of articles under the headline "Buddha Merges into Bhagwan."[21] As Rajneesh put it, "My message and Gautam Buddha's message are almost parallel—so parallel, so similar that it can be said that he was my vehicle or it can be said that I am his vehicle."[22] Shortly after that, however, he explained that he was not to be called Gautam the Buddha himself but rather Maitreya—that is, the "friend" prophesied by the Buddha as his future representative:

> I have to remind you of Gautam Buddha's prophecy twenty-five centuries ago: "When I come again I will not be able to be born through a woman's womb. I will have to take shelter in a man of similar consciousness. . . . I will be called 'The Friend.'" . . . Although he has taken shelter in men, I will not be called Gautam the Buddha. I will love to be called according to his prophecy: Maitreya the Buddha. *Maitreya* means "the friend."[23]

However, in keeping with his fluid, shifting, and protean nature, this was to be only "the first of four new names," which included Shree Rajneesh Zorba the Buddha, among others.[24] In February 1989, he took the name Osho-Rajneesh and then in September 1989 simply the title Osho. Three factors may help to explain the choice of the designation Osho. First, Osho is a traditional title for a Zen Buddhist priest, and during this period Rajneesh was devoting most of his discourses to Zen Buddhism (which was arguably always the closest analogue to his own iconoclastic teachings). Second, the name Osho resonates with the "oceanic feeling," a phrase used by both mystics to describe the experience of nirvana or dissolution into the infinite and Freudians to describe the early state of the fetus in the womb.

Finally, based on the Osho community's own legal statements, one has to think that the name was also chosen for its aesthetic, commercial, and marketing value. The Osho International Foundation clearly states on its trademark and copyright website, the change of names was very much a matter of "rebranding" the Master and all of the work, property, methods, and merchandise associated with him.[25] However, as we will see in chapter 6, this "rebranding" of Osho quickly led to a new series of disputes, this time over intellectual property and trademark issues in cyberspace.

FROM ASHRAM TO "MULTIVERSITY"

Even as Rajneesh was reborn successively as Maitreya, Zorba the Buddha, and Osho, so too the Pune ashram underwent a series of spiritual and commercial makeovers in the late 1980s and early 1990s. Moreover, the city of Pune itself was radically transformed from a sleepy, quiet, former British hill station to a large, bustling, and increasingly polluted metropolis that now has a population of over three million and is the ninth largest city in India. Even in the wealthy and secluded neighborhood of Koregaon Park, bicycles and bullock carts have largely been replaced by swarms of motor scooters, cars, and taxis, and simply crossing the street to the resort can be a life-threatening undertaking.

Already by early 1988, thousands of people from around the world were either returning or coming for the first time to Pune to participate in workshops; and this influx in turn required that the former "ashram" be expanded into a much larger and sophisticated facility to accommodate the new global audience. According to a "Rajneesh Ashram Update" from February 1988, there were 5,000 people attending Rajneesh's daily discourses and 1,000 participating in workshops, while the ashram itself was rapidly renovated to meet the new demand:

> The ashram quickly expanded its facilities to cope with the rush of foreigners. A 1600 square foot marble floor was laid in the ashram's meditation hall. New community dining areas were constructed. Sophisticated water filtration and health equipment was installed to create western hygiene standards.[26]

In June and July 1989, the new Pune community also established a "Multiversity," complete with its own series of schools and academies, each with their own courses and workshops.[27] Global and extremely ambitious in scope, the Multiversity included the "Osho Mystery School," the "Osho Academy of Creative Arts," the "Osho International Academy of Healing Arts," the "Osho Center for Transformation," the "Osho School for Centering," the "Osho School of Zen Martial Arts," and the "Osho Faculty for Liberation."[28] The courses offered by the various schools ranged widely and included techniques and ideas from every corner of the planet and every period of history, from Tibetan Pulse Healing to Past Life Hypnosis Training, from Vision Improvement to Alchemical Hypnotherapy and Tantra Training. Meanwhile, the "Osho School of Music" offered an array of workshops that combined Osho's methods with various musical traditions, such as "Osho Rhythm Roots and Tribal Song," "Osho Jazz and Keyboard Workshop," and "Osho Heart and Soul Singing."[29]

Meanwhile, the leadership of the community also underwent an important shift during these years. On April 6, 1989, Osho established a committee known as the "inner circle" that consisted of twenty-one disciples who would take care of the mundane, practical affairs of the commune. Foremost among the disciples were Jayesh (Michael O'Byrne) as chairman, Amrito (aka George Meredith, formerly known as Swami Devaraj) as vice chairman, and Anando as the secretary.[30] Some *sannyasins*, such as Ma Prem Shunyo, also suggest that there was an earlier "secret group" of thirteen that was formed eight months before the twenty-one-member committee. There appears to be only partial overlap between these two groups.[31] As we will see in chapter 6, many *sannyasins* today are intensely critical of the inner circle—particularly of Jayesh and Amrito—and charge them with turning Osho's legacy into a purely commercial business enterprise and of misappropriating the commune's wealth for personal gain.[32] *point of entire guru*

FROM ASHRAM TO INTERNATIONAL MEDITATION RESORT: A POSTMODERN AND GLOBAL SACRED SPACE

By the late 1990s, the Pune center had undergone a remarkable transformation, quickly expanding from a fairly rustic ashram with a commune atmosphere into a far more upscale and sophisticated "luxury resort for meditation and self-discovery."[33] With its new name, the Osho International Meditation Resort, it was now marketed not simply as a spiritual retreat with a global array of meditations and therapies but also as a world-class tourist destination with five-star accommodations. As Dillon recalls, the nature of the Pune community also underwent a significant transformation; no longer a "solid community of people that were living together over many years," the Pune center became a resort for short-term visitors, while the older *sannyasins* began drifting away to live and teach in other parts of the world.[34]

Despite the rapid growth of the Pune urban area in the last two decades, today the resort remains a kind of protected, quiet oasis amid the chaos of Indian city life. Tucked into the heart of Koregaon Park's green and wealthy residential neighborhood, surrounded by enormous banyan trees and towering stands of bamboo, the resort explicitly presents itself as a unique sort of global sacred space. All those who enter the walled and gated compound are required to pass an HIV test, to wear special maroon and white robes, and to observe specific rules of physical hygiene (such as no handling of paper currency). The focal points of the resort are a giant pyramid-shaped meditation hall—the space for morning and evening meditations—and a large open-air dance pavilion—the space for all variety of sacred and secular dance performances. Advertised as both a luxury hotel and a spiritual retreat, the resort is a striking example of the complex intersections between spirituality and transnational capitalism in the twenty-first century.

The new Osho resort is thus an explicit attempt to put the "Zorba the Buddha" ideal into lived practice in a kind of hybrid materially spiritual space. In January 2013, I interviewed one of the current members of the governing board or "inner circle" of the resort, Osho's former physician, Swami Amrito, who strongly emphasized that this is neither an ashram nor a luxury hotel but rather a "Meditation Resort." It is, as he put it, an ideal wedding of *both* a sacred space for the pursuit of spiritual enlightenment *and* an attractive physical space for the enjoyment of sensual pleasure.[35] Today, the Osho resort is advertised as a spiritual-sensual paradise that boasts luxury accommodations, a swimming pool, a Jacuzzi, "Zennis" courts, "India's most modern and technically advanced kitchen facility,"[36] and, of course, the Zorba the Buddha restaurant, which offers an international array of "star quality Western, Asian, and Indian vegetarian food."[37] According to the Osho.com website, "This lush contemporary 28-acre campus is a tropical oasis where nature and the 21st Century blend seamlessly, both within and without. With its white marble pathways, elegant black buildings, abundant foliage and Olympic-sized swimming pool, it is the perfect setting to take time out for yourself."[38] A video advertisement for the resort likewise emphasizes this harmonious blend of spirit and body, daytime spiritual work and nighttime pleasures:

> The creative expression of many has been and remains to provide an environment supportive of the Osho proposal for a new man, a whole man, sometimes called Zorba the Buddha. Zorba for the person of celebration, Buddha for the person of meditation. Not one but both together. From . . . heated swimming pool, tennis courts, Jacuzzi, sauna and gymnasium in the daylight, to bistros, wine bars and late night celebration, dancing and partying with friends old and new in the night light.[39]

In the words of one visitor, whose reflections are featured in another video advertisement for the resort, "It was like a fantasy land. From the moment you walk into the welcome center, it was like state of the art design, shining marble floors, waterfalls, beautiful benches."[40] The promotional videos also go to great lengths to highlight the international and global nature of the resort, featuring mostly young, good-looking people from the United Kingdom, America, India, Europe, and Japan who represent Osho's harmonious multicultural vision: "In the resort . . . there's people from all over the world. Although there's a culture clash, but somehow in this place it becomes a unity of all people—like a global link, it connects all people together."[41]

Meanwhile, the Indian and American media have been equally enthusiastic in their reviews of the resort. *India Today* reported in 2002, "The 60 room guesthouse would put most five-star hotels to shame."[42] *Elle* magazine described the resort in equally glowing terms, as a unique mix of sacred space and five-star accommodations, of spiritual wisdom and physical comfort.

Yet the Osho resort is by no means simply a tourist holiday retreat; it is also a global spiritual center with diverse offerings. To give just one example of a day at the resort, on December 31, 2011, the following were available to guests: Vinyasa Flow, Tai Chi, Zen Archery, Silent Sitting Meditation, Whirling Celebration, OSHO Chakra Breathing Meditation, OSHO Vipassana Meditation, Dance Celebration, Laughing Drums Meditation, AcuEnergetics, OSHO Nadabrahma Meditation, OSHO Kundalini Meditation, Awareness Techniques for Every Day Life, and finally the New Year's Eve Party. The next two days included an even broader array of offerings, including Chi Kung, Zennis, Emotional Freedom, OSHO Nataraj Meditation, OSHO No Dimension Meditation, OSHO Mahamudra Meditation, Men and Women on the Path of Love, No-Mind, Art Therapist Intensive, Jazz Café, and Variety Show.[43]

The Osho resort and its manifold spiritual and psychological offerings are not, however, inexpensive. Simply visiting the resort for a day involves a number of fees, including a registration free (which includes a mandatory HIV test), an entry fee, and the purchase of red and white robes to be worn inside the resort—all totaling roughly $100 for a single-day visit, not including additional fees for using the swimming pool, Jacuzzi, sauna, and gym. Those who choose to stay at the Osho Guesthouse pay roughly the same rates as those staying at five-star hotels in India, well over $100 per night during the regular season. Courses at the Multiversity are also not inexpensive, ranging from a few hundred to over a thousand dollars depending on the type and length of a particular course. For example, a six-day "Tantra Intensive" course offered in January 2013 cost 50,750 rupees, at that time a little over $1,000.[44]

The eclectic spiritual offerings and high cost of the resort are largely reflected in its current clientele. By my count during several trips between 2011 and 2013, roughly 75 percent of the visitors at the resort were non-Indian; and of these, more than half were Europeans, followed by smaller numbers of American, British, Brazilian, Israeli, and Japanese guests. The Indian guests were almost entirely wealthy middle and upper class. (It is worth noting that the lower-end working staff at the

globalization

resort—including cleaning, janitorial, food service, and laundry staff—was 100 percent South Asian, and by no means upper class.)

While the early Pune ashram of the 1970s had attracted large numbers of hippies, young people, and spiritual seekers backpacking around India, the current Osho resort tends to draw a far more affluent clientele, largely screening out those who cannot afford the high entrance fees and costs of the various courses. More than one local businessman told me that they believe this to be one reason why the resort now draws fewer (though wealthier) visitors than it did in previous decades—a charge that critics of the current leadership have echoed.[45] At the same time, the very nature of the Pune community has also been transformed from an ashram in which *sannyasins* came to live for long periods of time into a more transient sort of tourist resort, in which guests come to visit for short periods, and even the teachers come and go more freely. Dillon recalls:

> Gradually towards the end of the 90s there was kind of a new quality coming in to the whole resort as resort and many of the older people were gradually drifting away. Many of the group leaders that were there started moving toward the West and actually circulating around the West rather than working in Pune. It's nothing like it was, the way it used to be. There were actually people living there, making their lives there, or at the very least they were coming for six months and then going back to the West for six months and earning more money and coming back. So there was a very solid community of people that were living together over many years. . . . But that fullness of participation started to diminish gradually over the 90s.[46]

As we saw in chapter 2, the early Pune ashram was always something of an "anti-commune" and as much a business as a spiritual retreat; however, the new Osho resort has clearly evolved from its hippie ashram roots much more explicitly in the direction of an international business.

THE OSHO RESORT AS A UNIQUELY EMBODIED SACRED SPACE

The unique form of sacred space that we find at the Osho resort is very much an embodied, sensual, and material sort of space. All those who enter the resort—whether for a luxury tourist visit or for a spiritual retreat—are marked physically in several ways. First, before even entering the resort, all visitors must take an HIV test, which is performed on the spot through a blood sample. Up to the mid-1980s, as we saw in chapter 4, the Rajneesh movement was infamous for its promiscuous sexuality and Neo-Tantric excesses, but following the AIDs epidemic, it became increasingly concerned with sexual hygiene.[47] While members are no longer given special "AIDs kits" with the warming that "AIDs will destroy two thirds of the world's population," the legacy of these sexual anxieties persists at the resort to this day. Second, while inside the grounds, all visitors and residents are marked by special robes, maroon for daytime and white for evening use. Finally, physical hygiene is also a central concern of the resort, and all visitors are given special instructions on how to wash their hands, how to place food on their trays, how to conduct themselves physically in the meditation hall, and so on. Meanwhile, handling currency is forbidden inside the grounds, and the stated rationale is that paper money is unhygienic.

First-time visitors are also shown an introductory video that not only explains the lifestyle and spiritual practices at the resort but also highlights the need for physical hygiene. The video is also quite notably racialized in several telling ways. For example, the main character in the film who illustrates precisely what not to do in the meditation hall is a young Indian male, who coughs, speaks loudly on his cell phone to his mother, and has very smelly feet (depicted by an animated stink cloud). Finally, at the end of the clip, he lets loose a long, audible fart (again followed by an animated green stink cloud). Meanwhile, the large majority of the other characters in the film are white non–South Asians, who respectfully follow the rules of comportment and hygiene.[48]

Two of the main focal points of spiritual practice at the resort are also very much embodied spaces. The first is the meditation hall, a huge pyramid-shaped structure that emerges from a small lake, inside of which lies a vast white space with white marble floors and dazzling lighting. As a promotional video for the resort describes it, the meditation hall is an ideal combination of sacred space and twenty-first-century technology, harmoniously blending a pristine spiritual and aesthetic atmosphere with the latest state-of-the-art environmental controls and audiovisual systems:

> Rising out of a body of water, the twenty-eight-meter pyramid structure was completed in the autumn of 2002. The soundproof auditorium enjoys the latest in international technology. The air-quality systems both condition and purify. It has computerized, multidimensional lighting and sound systems and a seating capacity for 5000.[49]

This is the primary space for the practice of Osho's unique meditations, such as Dynamic, Kundalini, and other "chaotic" methods. As we saw in chapter 2, Osho's meditations are explicitly "embodied" and intensely physical techniques aimed at shaking the individual free of our normal social and mental conditioning and projecting us into a state of ecstatic, godlike liberation. As Osho himself described his "chaotic" methods, these are new bodily techniques adapted to the new bodily situation of modern human beings, who now live in a highly technological society and a largely artificial environment that demands radical catharsis:

> Modern man is a very new phenomenon. No traditional method can be used exactly as it exists because modern man never existed before. . . .
>
> The body has changed so much. It is not as natural as it was in the days when Patanjali developed his system of yoga. It is absolutely different. It is so drugged that no traditional method can be helpful. . . .
>
> I use chaotic methods rather than systematic ones because a chaotic method is very helpful in pushing the center down from the brain. . . . Through chaotic methods the brain is nullified. . . . If you do my method of Dynamic Meditation vigorously, unsystematically, chaotically, your center moves to the heart. Then there is a catharsis.[50]

A second key space at the resort is a large dance pavilion, where guests perform various dance arts from around the world, ranging from the Sufi "whirling dervishes" to the sacred dance techniques of George Gurdjieff to popular Bollywood styles. Thus a video advertisement for the resort concludes with a celebration of dance and features a montage of clips depicting every form of sacred and secular dance taking place at the resort, including fire dancing, disco, break dancing, and finally free-form silent movement.[51] Indeed, dance in every possible form is a central part of Osho's uniquely embodied spirituality and is a key intersection between the physical fun and religious transcendence that is at the heart of the "Zorba the Buddha" ideal. As Osho-Rajneesh himself put it, dance is the supreme means to bring the individual out of the mind and back into the body, thus reintegrating the intellectual and physical aspects of the person into a single, dynamic flow of experience:

> Mentation alone won't do: the body has to be brought in. That is why, in *my* meditation techniques, I do not take you as divided: you are one. . . . If your mind is feeling happy, allow your body to dance. Don't create a division. Let yourself come deep down into the body, and allow the body to flow to your innermost core. Become a flow![52]

Ultimately, when dance is performed fully as an embodied, flowing meditation, the very idea of the "dancer" disappears. The dancing ego itself dissolves in the pure flow experience until solely the dance remains:

Let the dance flow in its own way; don't force it. Rather, follow it, allow it to happen. It is not a doing but a happening. Remain in the mood of festivity. You are not doing something very serious; you are just playing, playing with your life energy, playing with your bioenergy . . . you are flowing and blowing. Feel it. . . .

Forget the dancer, the center of the ego; become the dance. That is the meditation. Dance so deeply that you forget completely that "you" are dancing and begin to feel that you are the dance. . . . The dancer must go, until only the dance remains.[53]

Here we see another example of the way in which Osho-Rajneesh skillfully merges traditional religious ideas such as the Buddhist concept of "no-self" with the postmodern "death of the subject." In the Osho resort's dance pavilion, the ascetic Buddhist ideal of *anatman* and the consumer ideal of embodied sensuality meld as one in a kind of joyous, playful ecstasy.

A GLOBAL, LATE CAPITALIST, AND NEOLIBERAL SACRED SPACE

Thus the Osho resort offers some critical insights not just into the nature of sacred space at this particular site in South Asia but also into the complex dynamics of sacred space and bodily practice in the context of globalization and late capitalism. If sacred space acts as a kind of "focusing lens" in Smith's sense, highlighting what is most significant to a given community, then the unique sacred space of the Osho resort also helps focus on the larger dynamics of global tourism, sensual pleasure, and transnational capitalism, which are particularly significant to this community.

Among other things, the Osho resort highlights some of the key shifts in the role of sacred space and the body itself in the "deterritorialized" context of late twentieth- and early twenty-first-century spiritual life. As David Harvey suggests, late or postmodern capitalism has brought about a profound alteration in our experience of space and time—a remarkable kind of "space-time compression." With the ever-increasing speed of global travel, transportation, and commerce, spatial barriers have largely collapsed in a new world of rapid transit and instant communication that has fundamentally altered our sense of space itself:

The satellite communications systems deployed since the early 1970s have rendered the unit cost and time of communication invariant with respect to distance. . . . It is now possible for a large multinational corporation . . . to operate plants with simultaneous decision making with respect to financial, market, input costs, quality control and labour processes in more than fifty different locations across the globe. Mass television ownership coupled with satellite communication makes it possible to experience a rush of images from different spaces almost simultaneously, collapsing the world's spaces into a series of images on a television screen. The whole world can watch the Olympic Games, the World Cup, the fall of a dictator, a political summit, a deadly tragedy . . . while mass tourism, films made in spectacular locations, make a wide range of simulated or vicarious experiences of what the world contains available to many people. . . .

We have, in short, witnessed another fierce round in that process of annihilation of space through time that has always lain at the center of capitalism's dynamic.[54]

The Osho-Rajneesh movement not only emerged *simultaneously* with this shift from organized to late capitalism (during the 1960s and 1970s), but with its broad transnational audience and its wildly eclectic practices, it also very much reflects a new kind of late capitalist spirituality. And with its fusion of East and West, its waves of tourists from around the globe, its complex multinational financial structure, and its hybrid mix of sacred and secular space, the new Osho resort itself is in many ways an epitome—indeed, a global epicenter or node—of the sort of late capitalist space-time compression that Harvey is describing. Much of Osho's message was aimed precisely at creating this sort of collapse of space and time—that is, at dissolving traditional national and spatial boundaries such as East and West, India and Europe, and opening a place for his new vision of humanity: "The days of division are over, the days of the politicians are over. We are moving in a tremendously new world, a new phase of humanity—and that phase is that there can only be one world now. . . . Then there will be a tremendous release of energies. The East has its treasures, the religious technologies, and the West has its treasures, the scientific technologies. And if they can meet, this very world can be a paradise."[55]

At the same time, as authors such as Bryan S. Turner and Mike Featherstone suggest, the shift from modern to postmodern or late forms of capitalism has also been accompanied by a shift in attitudes toward sensual pleasure and the physical body. If early modern forms of capitalism were characterized—in Max Weber's terms—by an ideal of innerworldly asceticism and restraint in consumption, the postmodern consumer ethic is characterized more by "living for the moment, hedonism, self-expression, the body beautiful, paganism, freedom from social obligations [and] the exotica of faraway places."[56] The body ceases to be a vessel of sin or an unruly source of desires that must be disciplined; rather, the body is proclaimed the ultimate source of gratification and aesthetic pleasure. In late capitalist consumer culture, Turner suggests, we see a progressive shift "from an emphasis on the control of the body for ascetic reasons to the manipulation of the body for aesthetic purposes."[57]

All of these trends—the emphasis on the body beautiful, sensual pleasure, freedom from social obligations, and above all the "exotica of faraway places"—are clearly celebrated at the new Osho resort. Along with its wildly eclectic and quite postmodern collage of spiritual styles drawn from every corner of the planet, the resort also focuses on the body and its pleasures in every possible sense, from dance and chaotic meditations, to partying and wine bars. All of this, meanwhile, is also "consumptive" in both the sensual and the commercial sense sof the word, inhabiting a new kind of sacred space that celebrates both consumption by the senses and spiritual consumerism as a business model. Osho's central ideal of "this very body the Buddha"[58] melds seamlessly with his view that "wealth is a perfect means which can enhance people in every way, can make their lives rich in all," and with his declaration "I am a spiritual materialist."[59]

In this sense, the Osho resort reflects yet a third trend in the dynamics of late or deterritorialized capitalism—namely, the progressive expansion of the logic of capital to more and more aspects of human life.[60] As we saw in chapter 4, the Rajneeshpuram experiment in Oregon was a remarkable embodiment of the "commodification of everything," or the transformation of everything—including spiritual pursuits—into a good to be bought and sold. As Featherstone notes, "The tendency in modern societies is for religion to become a private leisure pursuit purchased in the market like any other consumer culture lifestyle."[61] Yet the new Osho Meditation Resort appears to take this logic a step further by absorbing "sacred space" itself into the ostensibly "secular" space of the marketplace. Established on the ideal of Zorba the Buddha, the Osho resort not only embodies this merger of sacred and commercial space but celebrates it as the highest ideal of fully realized spiritual-yet-sensual human being.

Finally, the Osho resort could also be described as a kind of "neoliberal sacred space." As Carrette and King observe, spirituality today is not only increasingly reduced to yet another commodity in the capitalist marketplace; more importantly, spirituality is also increasingly marketed as a tool to help individuals become more "efficient, productive" employees of the capitalist workforce.[62] This neoliberal trend is made quite explicit in many of the Osho resort's promotional materials. Not only does the resort explicitly accommodate—and even celebrate—the late capitalist marketplace, but it also claims to help make individuals more efficient producers in that marketplace. "Osho active meditations [are] meditations designed for people living in today's fast-paced and stressful world," one promotional video for the resort states, explaining that the Osho residential program of "work as meditation" can help individuals to cultivate the spiritual energy to go back and be successful in their regular working lives in the business world: "Work as meditation: to support the experience of a creative and relaxed awareness on returning to the marketplace."[63] The same video then goes on to quote a young female visitor who recounts the ways in which the resort has given her much needed time out for herself so that she can relax and rejuvenate in order to return to "the West" and enter the workforce as a productive member:

> It's just for me . . . it's just about me: the more I put in, the more I can flower from the experience and that's . . . something that I can then take in to a regular job in the West perhaps. I really hope that I can put this into practice in the outside world.[64]

Here we see perhaps the most remarkable transformation of the Pune center as it has evolved from the 1970s to the present. No longer a wild commune full of hippie dropouts seeking a radical political and spiritual alternative to mainstream society, the resort is now marketed as a temporary, spa-like respite from the hectic working world that will ultimately allow one to return to the marketplace as a more contented and efficient employee/citizen.

markets

CONCLUSIONS: THE SPIRITUALITY OF "SECOND WAVE NEOLIBERALISM"

As I have argued in the preceding chapters, the Osho-Rajneesh movement is not only a reflection but also an embodiment of some of the most important social and economic trends of the last five decades, serving as a kind of microcosm of the shifting dynamics of global capitalism between India and the United States since the 1960s. If the Rajneesh community of the 1980s embodied many aspects of Reagan-era neoliberalism, the new Osho resort likewise embodies many aspects of global capitalism during the 1990s and what some have called the "second wave of neoliberalism," which spread to India and other parts of Asia during the Clinton and Blair eras. "By the end of the Roaring Nineties," as Steger and Roy observe, "neoliberalism in its various permutations and modifications had successfully spread to most parts of the world. Its powerful advocates in the West had employed the compelling narrative of inevitable market globalization to convince people that the liberalization of trade and minimally regulated markets will result in high economic growth and dramatic improvements in living conditions worldwide."[65]

In the course of this "inevitable market globalization," few domains of culture were left unaffected. As Harvey suggests, one of the key features of neoliberalism is precisely the commodification not just of every *material* thing, but also of *nonmaterial* things, which were once assumed to exist outside of the marketplace: "The commodification of sexuality, culture, history, heritage . . . these all amount to putting a price on things that were never actually produced as commodities."[66] Here we could add to Harvey's list the commodities of "meditation," "sacred dance," and "Tantric ecstasy," all of which are on offer at the Osho resort, side by side with books, videos, clothing, and more conventional wares.

It would, however, be a serious mistake to dismiss the Osho resort as simply a kind of religious "sellout" or just another example of the co-opting of spirituality by commercialism and consumerism. Rather, I would argue, the resort represents a far more interesting and complex reshaping of "sacred space" itself in the context of late capitalism and global neoliberalism. With its hybridized form of "space-time compression," its radical fusion of traditional Indian techniques and modern Western psychology, its central emphasis on the body and physical pleasure, and its explicit blending of spiritual and commercial enterprises, the resort is very much a kind of "focusing lens" in Smith's sense. That is, it highlights in a particularly acute way the ideals that are most significant to this community. As such, the unique form of sacred space embodied in the Osho resort is an ideal place to study the complex dynamics of global spirituality in the twenty-first century.

CHAPTER 6

OSHO®?

The Struggle over Osho's Legacy in the
Twenty-First Century

In 1989 Osho changed his name to OSHO and requested that
everything previously branded with RAJNEESH . . . be
rebranded OSHO. Osho International Foundation registered
the mark OSHO and to this day continues to follow his
guidelines to protect his name and his work.
—Osho International Foundation, "Trademark Information"

Things can be copyrighted, thoughts cannot be copyrighted,
and certainly meditations cannot be copyrighted. They are
not things of the marketplace.
—Osho-Rajneesh, *Om Shantih Shantih Shantih*

[handwritten annotation: how sell then?]

While Osho's ideas and practices continue to spread across the planet in
a new transnational context, they have also become the focus of intense
legal and financial disputes in the twenty-first century. By the dawn of the
new millennium, the Osho movement had grown into a vast, complex,
and extremely valuable global entity—really as much a multinational
corporation as a spiritual movement. In 2000 *India Today* estimated that
the "Osho Inc." empire included some "750 meditation centres across 80
countries . . . 1500 books published in 40 languages . . . 400 tapes of
music and sermons . . . 800 signature paintings; 10,000 exclusive photographs; diamond robes and accessories, Rolls Royce fleet and properties."[1] Not surprisingly, as is often the case with multinational entities,
the expansion of this corporate empire has also generated its share of
complex legal issues.

Tensions surrounding the guru's legacy began to build shortly after his death, when the Rajneesh Foundation in Pune changed its name to the Osho International Foundation (OIF), which is now housed in Zurich. Ironically, even though Osho himself declared on at least one occasion that his "meditations cannot be copyrighted," they quickly were, which inevitably led to a variety of disputes over the rights to their use and profits. Beginning in 1992, the OIF began to file trademark applications in the United States for all books, tapes, meditations, and other materials related to the name Osho; and today, the OIF claims to be the sole and registered owner of all of the copyrights of Osho's works and all of the trademarks, designs, and logos of his various practices.[2] Since 2000, this move has led to a series of legal disputes with rival Osho groups, most importantly with the New Delhi–based group Osho Dhyan Mandir, and their website Oshoworld.com, over the right to use the name Osho itself. Many new legal disputes have arisen more recently. Among others, there have been disputes over the Osho resort property, which many critics claim is being sold off and/or transferred for the financial advantage of the small group of (primarily non-Indian) *sannyasins* who run the Pune center.[3] There have also been battles over Facebook pages used by groups that advertise Osho's name and techniques but are not under the OIF umbrella.[4] And finally, most recently, serious questions have been raised about the authenticity of Osho's will, which some Indian critics claim was forged, again in order to benefit a small group of individuals at the top of the Pune organization.[5]

In many ways, this legal debate about intellectual property (IP) reflects a larger tension within the global Osho community today, between the nationalist and transnational elements in Osho's contemporary following. The primary leaders of the "inner circle" in Pune today are non-Indians. Foremost among them are Osho's British physician, George Meredith (aka Swami Devaraj and now known as Swami Amrito), and two Canadians, Michael O'Byrne (Swami Jayesh) and Darcy O'Byrne (Swami Yogendra). These three in particular have been dubbed the "three dictators" by critics of the Pune leadership.[6] Meanwhile, the primary opposition has been led by Indian followers such as Yogesh Thakkar (Swami Premgeet) and Ma Yoga Neelam, who allege that these foreign administrators have grossly commercialized Osho's message and abused it for their own personal profit.[7] Clearly, larger issues of nationalism and probably identity politics are a part of these contemporary legal debates.

Disputes over legacy are not unique to the Osho movement, of course. In fact, these sorts of struggles over intellectual property have become increasingly common within religious movements, which more and more frequently have found themselves drawn into the complex legal tangles of transnational capitalism and commerce.[8] As Allison Fish has shown in the case of modern forms of yoga such as Bikram Yoga, these South Asian practices are increasingly becoming "globally franchised businesses" within the legal framework of global capitalism. Practices such as yoga have often developed into a "valuable, competitive market commodity where rival actors . . . secure financial interests through IP claims of copyright, patent and trademark."[9] But at the same time, some local organizations have resisted the commercialization of traditional spiritual practices, arguing that these are "public goods" that cannot be privatized and commodified. And finally, the Indian state has also become involved, claiming that yoga is part of India's national and cultural heritage and therefore needs to be defended against global commercial piracy.[10]

Beyond India, meanwhile, similar wars over copyright and trademark have been waged by a variety of other new religious movements. The Church of Scientology, for example, has fought several massive legal battles over its confidential materials, which were leaked to the media in the 1990s and now circulate widely on the Internet. Over the last two decades, Scientology has engaged in a series of intense and extremely costly battles over the dissemination of its higher-level materials, which the church has claimed are both copyrighted and trade secrets, in addition to being esoteric religious teachings.[11]

In short, the debate over intellectual property within the Osho movement is a reflection of a much larger trend in contemporary global spirituality, as religious ideas and practices are increasingly commodified and drawn into the same legal struggles as other sorts of widely exchanged commodities. And yet, because these are also regarded as "spiritual" practices that derive from a particular region (India, in this case), there are also many followers who argue that they belong to the domain of "religion" not commerce, and that religious phenomena cannot be restricted by trademark or copyright. In many ways, the question of the relationship between spirituality and intellectual property is rapidly becoming one of the most complex, contested, and interesting issues of the twenty-first century. And it is also, we will see, reframing and redefining the person of Osho himself, crafting yet another new legal and corporate identity for a new global economic context.

However, it would be a serious mistake to reduce the Osho movement in the twenty-first century to a mere series of legal squabbles over intellectual property and finance. Despite the fierce legal disputes over Osho's legacy, thousands of individuals across the globe continue to find his teachings and practices profoundly meaningful. For many Osho followers today, his eclectic, iconoclastic ideal of Zorba the Buddha is ironically the best possible guide to navigating the strange new world of global telecommunications and late capitalist economics, where the boundaries between spirituality and economics, religion and corporate law, have become not only blurred but are often completely invisible. In the words of William Foster, a *sannyasin* from the Oregon period and today an expert on global telecommunications, "The internet makes in many ways having a central organization irrelevant. The issue now is where are the real leaders in consciousness? Where are the centers of energy?"[12] This may well be key questions for Osho's followers in the coming decades.

IN THE ABSENCE OF THE LIVING MASTER

Osho himself seems to have anticipated that problems would arise after his departure from the physical body. On several occasions, he noted the profound difference between a thriving movement in which the living master is present and a movement after his passing, when it tends to become increasingly bureaucratic, institutionalized, and dogmatic—in short, increasingly "religious." The former is a living, vital Buddhafield, while the latter is an empty, hollow corpse:

> While I am here, it is a myth—an alive myth with a heart, beating . . . When I am gone it will be a lie. And this is the misery: that by the time people come to know the flower it is gone. When the flower is gone, they will worship for centuries and centuries. They will worship the past, the dead, the grave.[13]

And yet many *sannyasins* have suggested that even after Osho's death, the age of the Internet and other media might actually open the way to a far more universal proliferation of Osho's message to a whole new global audience. As Sarito Carol Neiman put it in the foreword to *The Autobiography of a Spiritually Incorrect Mystic,* "Since Osho's death, both CNN and the Internet have been born. The utopian vision that Osho spoke of so often—of a world without the divisions of national boundaries, of race or religion, gender or creed—is now at least imaginable."[14] Another *sannyasin,* named Shantam Prem, expressed an equally optimistic hope that Osho would in fact see another kind of apotheosis in the digital age, transmitting his message in wholly new media through new technologies for an even broader global audience: "It will be a spring of global spirituality in the age of iPods and Facebook."[15]

And yet, as in other global empires—spiritual or secular—that have entered the digital age, Osho's legacy has become enmeshed in the complex legal, cultural, and political disputes surrounding intellectual property. Osho himself addressed the questions of copyright and trademark explicitly in a talk delivered in 1988. Here he directly attacked the idea that meditation techniques could be copyrighted, and offered a critique of attempts to apply the corporate and legal logic of "the West" to India's spiritual traditions. In the process, he also slipped in a satirical critique of Transcendental Meditation, noting that "TM" is also a registered trademark (™):

> Just today a letter has arrived from Germany. Our sannyasins are doing a meditation called The Four Directions. The letter says, "In your commune people are doing a meditation called The Four Directions, and we have the copyright over it." I have told Neelam, my secretary, to write to them, "Things can be copyrighted, thoughts cannot be copyrighted, and certainly meditations cannot be copyrighted. They are not things of the marketplace." Nobody can monopolize anything. But perhaps the West cannot understand the difference between an objective commodity and an inner experience.
>
> Maharishi Mahesh Yogi has copyrighted transcendental meditation and just underneath in a small circle you will find written TM—that means trademark! For ten thousand years the East has been meditating and nobody has put trademarks upon meditations. And above all, that transcendental meditation is neither transcendental nor meditation . . . just a trademark.
>
> I have told Neelam to reply to these people, "You don't understand what meditation is. It is nobody's belonging, possession. You cannot have any copyright. Perhaps if your country gives you trademarks and copyrights on things like meditation, then it will be good to have a copyright on stupidity. That will help the whole world to be relieved. . . . Only you will be stupid and nobody else can be stupid; it will be illegal."[16]

Despite explicit statements like these, copyright and trademark would quickly become serious issues in the wake of Osho's death. Indeed, the current OIF maintains several pages on the Osho.com website devoted to copyright and trademark information relating to Osho's name, books, and meditations. OIF lawyers point out that trademarks were registered for Osho's (then Rajneesh's) work as early as the 1970s, specifically for his logos and name. They are also not shy about using corporate language to describe the trademarks, and state quite explicitly that this is very much a matter of branding: "Osho and the foundation he selected have always used these symbols and marks to identify—or in today's language, to 'brand'—every aspect of his work: books, meditations, buildings, foundations, centers."[17] In this regard, moreover, the OIF was following the lead of many other contemporary gurus and spiritual movements, who have similarly used the language of branding, trademark, and copyright.[18]

Already by 2000, however, disillusioned *sannyasins* were complaining that the leadership of the Pune community was descending into pure profit-driven commercialism. According to Osho's former secretary, Ma Yoga Neelam, the community had deteriorated from an organism as Osho had envisioned it into "an organisation where commerce was the keyword,"[19] as the Pune center was transformed from a real commune into a mere luxury resort where wealthy tourists simply came to relax for a few days. "The commune is being turned into a corporation," she complained,[20] and meanwhile,

> short-term visitors, particularly the fly-by-night western *sannyasins* who came for having pure fun in the form of indulging more in MedClub activities rather than looking into their inner selves were given more importance. . . . And the long-term *sannyasins* who used to come here for a few months to create an energyfield were discouraged. Of course, it was Osho's vision to *add* modern facilities in order to cater to the modern man, but the three inner circle members picked only this fragment, to project it as Osho's vision.[21]

Neelam and others were particularly upset that the rights to Osho's name, books, and techniques had been transferred outside of India, to Zurich and New York. Interestingly enough, she complains not *that* they have been copyrighted, but rather, about *where* the copyrights are located. Although she goes out of her way to say this is not a question of nationality and that Osho's work is meant for a global audience, she is clearly bothered that these assets have been transferred to entities outside of his homeland in India:

> I'm not saying that the copyrights should come to India because I'm an Indian. I am Osho's *sannyasin* who does not differentiate between any nationalities. Osho always insisted that the international headquarters of his commune must form the nucleus of all activities, be it meditation techniques, publishing works or whatever. Since Pune is rightfully the commune's headquarters, there is no question of having copyrights anywhere in the world. New York is merely the extension of Pune's headquarters and cannot pose as Osho's international headquarters.[22]
>
> When Osho left Pune for Oregon, all the rights were transferred there and then when he left the USA and finally came to Pune, second time round, all

these copyrights, his books, watches, robes—whatever there was—Osho wanted them to come back to Pune. He always wanted it that way. However, as we found out recently, the copyrights never came back to Pune, much to our shock.[23]

This dispute over the "Indian" versus the "global" nature of Osho's legacy has been a recurring theme throughout these legal debates. As *India Today* reported in 2000, much of the tension lay along national lines, as growing numbers of Indian *sannyasins* began to voice their anger that the movement was not only becoming commercialized but also "Westernized" by this inner circle of non-Indians running the Pune center: "Many of the rebel Oshoites are outraged that India, Osho's homeland, has been completely sidelined by the 'western' leadership that has injected a commercial agenda into the soul of the cult. . . . Swami Keerti, a former spokesperson who left the commune last February, says, 'We are very agitated about the secret shifting of the headquarters from Pune to the U.S.'"[24]

Finally, it is also worth noting that some of the most prominent Indian *sannyasins* have also recently made contact with India's most powerful political leaders, including those on the far right of the ideological spectrum. Thus in June 2012, Swami Satya Vedanta—aka Vasant Joshi, who was Rajneesh's first biographer—made a public appearance in order to present Osho's books to none other than Narendra Modi (fig. 17). A member of the right-wing Bharatiya Janata Party, Modi served as chief minister of the state of Gujarat and was overwhelmingly elected as prime minister during the 2014 general elections. As *Sannyas News* reported, this public photo op with Modi was a clear strategy on the part of *sannyasins* who are critical of the Pune group to align themselves with India's political elite:

> Indian ex-inner circle members who were kicked out from the main organisation/Ashram/Resort in Pune are doing their best to reach everywhere through networking with the Indian political leadership.
>
> For example a few weeks ago they were presenting books to the Rajasthan Assembly, and as one can see from the accompanying photo, Satya Vedant, under the banner of Osho Nisarga is presenting Osho books to one of the most powerful right wing leaders of India, Mr. Narendra Modi.
>
> Narendra Modi was just recently on the cover of *Time* Magazine as India's most vaunted political figure.[25]

It does seem more than a little ironic that the works of Osho-Rajneesh—once dubbed India's most dangerous guru and a spiritual iconoclast who opposed all forms of governmental, religious, and bureaucratic

FIGURE 17. Swami Satya Vedant presenting Osho books to
Narendra Modi. *Sannyas News,* June 8, 2012.

regulation—should now sit on the shelf of one of India's most conservative political leaders.

OSHO IN THE COURTS

The first major legal battle over Osho's trademarks and copyrights
began in 2000, when the OIF took action against the New Delhi–based
group Osho Dhyan Mandir. The OIF's claims to both trademarks and
copyrights are extensive and assert its sole control over all names,
designs, works, and techniques associated with Osho. The current
Osho.com website contains detailed pages on intellectual property
issues. On its trademark page, it states quite forcefully that the OIF is
the sole owner not simply of all the meditations, techniques, designs,
and logos associated with Osho, but also of the very name Osho:

> All trade names, trademarks, service marks, logos and trade styles on this
> site are owned by Osho International Foundation. Proper use is limited to
> use in connection with the products and services of the mark owner and no
> other use is permitted without the owner's prior written permission. The fol-
> lowing marks are owned by OIF: OSHO and the OSHO SIGNATURE

DESIGN, OSHO ACTIVE MEDITATIONS, OSHO KUNDALINI MEDI-
TATION, OSHO GOURISHANKAR MEDITATION, OSHO NADAB-
RAHMA MEDITATION, OSHO NATARAJ MEDITATION, OSHO
DYNAMIC MEDITATION, SPIRITUALLY INCORRECT, OSHO REBAL-
ANCING, OSHO DIVINE HEALING, OSHO CRANIO-SACRAL BAL-
ANCING, OSHO TIBETAN PULSING, OSHO MYSTIC ROSE, OSHO
TIMES, OSHO ZEN TAROT, OSHO TRANSFORMATION TAROT,
OSHO MEDITATION RESORT, OSHO MULTIVERSITY, NO-THOUGHT
FOR THE DAY AND THE SWAN LOGO.[26]

Likewise, on its copyright page, the website makes it clear that the OIF
should be regarded as the sole owner of all works, videos, recordings,
music, and photographs relating to Osho:

> OSHO International Foundation is the sole and registered owner of all of the
> copyrights to all the published and unpublished words and works of Osho,
> as author in all mediums, including audio, video, electronic, multimedia, and
> written forms, which were the sole original works created by the Author, as
> well as photographs of the Author, and is the owner of the copyright to
> various derivative works and other writings, music, art, and other products
> created or otherwise associated with the Author.
>
> The word "copyright" means the entire copyright and design right, visual
> rights, sound recording rights, and any and all analogous rights subsisting
> under international treaties and the laws of each and every jurisdiction
> throughout the world.
>
> You may not copy, reproduce, sell, distribute, publish, display, perform,
> modify, create derivative works, transmit, or in any way exploit any mate-
> rial, works or intellectual property owned by the OSHO International Foun-
> dation without explicit permission.[27]

While the OIF is the most visible and most vocal claimant of Osho's
materials, Osho Dhyan Mandir, based in New Delhi, is arguably the
most powerful and popular rival to the Pune community. Publishing its
own magazine, *Osho World,* and its own extensive catalog of Osho's
books online, Osho Dhyan Mandir also operates its own spiritual
retreat center near New Delhi called Oshodham, which makes many of
the same claims to spiritual and material well-being as does the resort in
Pune. Its current website declares:

> Oshodham has blossomed on the outskirts of Delhi offering a clean, green,
> aesthetic and peaceful environment for those on the inner journey. In tune
> with nature, a beautiful space has been created for group and individual
> meditations both indoors and outdoors. The cherubic sound of gurgling
> water bodies and fountains with the chirping of birds help the meditators to
> go deep on the path of awareness through meditation. Today, meditators
> from all over India and abroad converge here to meditate and celebrate.

Over 150 people can be accommodated to take part in three-day or three weeks meditation camps and groups. Oshodham is open all round the year for meditations.[28]

In the 2000 case, the OIF was objecting to Osho Dhyan Mandir's use of the name Osho in the domain name for the website Osho World (www.oshoworld.com). This raised much larger and more profound questions as to whether a word such as Osho is a personal name or whether it is a more generic title (in the sense of the Japanese term for a Buddhist teacher), and also whether religious titles themselves can become intellectual property. Osho Dhyan Mandir pointed to quotations from Osho, such as the one cited above, that explicitly reject the idea of copyrighting or trademarking religious ideas. The OIF, however, pointed out that Osho frequently contradicted himself and that trademarks and copyrights are designed to prevent the abuse of Osho's teachings. According to Osho's former legal secretary, Ma Anando, "the godman was full of contradictions. The views he expressed on copyright to a particular person cannot be taken as the final word. . . . The aim is to protect these priceless works from being used in a distorted manner."[29]

The case went before the National Arbitration Forum (NAF), which is headquartered in the United States but maintains a panel of over 1,600 arbitrators from thirty-five different countries. In the Osho dispute, the NAF decided in favor of Osho Dhyan Mandir and rejected the OIF's claims to the trademark of the name Osho. Here the NAF noted that Osho himself had little interest in intellectual property issues and did not exploit this particular title for commercial gain (though the NAF did raise the question of whether he did so with the title Bhagwan). More importantly, the decision also noted that allowing a group to trademark a name such as Osho would open the door to the trademarking of other titles, such as Christ or Buddha:

> There is no evidence that Bhagwan Shree Rajneesh (Osho) ever commercially exploited the name or mark OSHO during his natural life . . . or that he or his estate, if one was ever established, ever authorized either Party or any one else to utilize his name or mark. . . . The record also reflects that Osho himself had little regard for or concern with intellectual property rights, including any related to the use of his chosen name. . . .
>
> To grant Complainant's request for relief would be to permit virtual monopolization on the Internet by Complainant of any domain name which includes the name of a great spiritual teacher and leader. While making no judgment on the relative merits or validity of the world's religions or spiritual movements or any leader thereof, this Arbitrator finds that permitting this would be as improper as doing the same with Christianity, Judaism,

Islam, Zoroastrianism, Hinduism, Buddhism, Taoism, Confucianism, Shintoism or any of the several hundred other of the world's religions and/or spiritual movements.[30]

Later that same year, in the wake of the NAF ruling, a new group called Osho Friends International (OFI) was formed. The group was led by prominent dissidents within the Osho community, such as Ma Yoga Neelam, Swami Chaitanya Keerti, and others who had challenged the "aggressive and dominating" style of the Pune community and had effectively been cast out. Rejecting what they saw as blatant commercialization, they argued that Osho's works and techniques should be freely available all over the world.[31] Thus OFI filed a petition with the U.S. Patent and Trademark Office (USPTO) to cancel several trademarks claimed by the OIF. These included the trademark on the name Osho, along with those on techniques such as Osho Kundalini Meditation and Osho Rebalancing. Arguing that the Master's message is for the benefit of all humanity and therefore can never be fettered by claims to intellectual property, OFI bears as its slogan "OSHO: Everybody's birthright—nobody's copyright."[32]

Once again, in 2009, the USPTO decided against OIF, ruling that the name Osho is a generic adjective and should be freely available to competitors.[33] The decision actually quoted Osho's own satirical critique of Transcendental Meditation (TM™) mentioned above and found that Osho had also authorized members to found centers worldwide and use the name Osho in order to be more widely recognized. Finally, the USPTO also examined scholarly works, such as Paul Heelas's work *The New Age Movement*, noting that the academic community also refers to "Osho" in a generic sense as a "religious and meditative movement and not as a trademark."[34]

And yet, despite the verdicts from two major entities—both located in the United States—the OIF continues to assert its rights over the *global* circulation of Osho's name, techniques, and associated paraphernalia. At the time of the writing of this book, the Osho.com website maintains the same copyright and trademark information and argues that these rulings affect only the United States and not the forty or more other countries where Osho's name continues to be protected.[35] As such, this dispute is in many ways a kind of microcosm of the larger problems in global intellectual property disputes, as various groups struggle to negotiate between national and international laws, as well as between the opinions of entities such as the NAF or the USPTO and local courts in countries such as India, Germany, Switzerland, or elsewhere.

Yet these disputes are also a microcosm of a much larger and more complex debate as to whether religious ideas, figures, and practices can be regarded as intellectual property at all. At least in these two Osho cases, the official answer has been no. But in many other cases involving techniques such as Bikram Yoga or the Church of Scientology's confidential levels of advanced training, the court record has been far more mixed and contentious. In the case of Bikram Yoga, the founder, Bikram Choudhury, has been extremely aggressive in enforcing copyrights in relation to the teaching of his yoga system, particularly his method of "hot yoga." However, in 2012, a U.S. district court ruled that he does not in fact have copyright protection for the series of breathing exercises and yogic postures that constitute Bikram Yoga, finding that non-Bikram studies may also offer these techniques.[36]

The case of Scientology is even more complicated. The confidential upper levels of Scientology were first introduced as court evidence in 1985 in a civil case brought by ex-Scientologist Larry Wollersheim and were shortly thereafter leaked to the media and eventually onto the Internet in the 1990s. Wollersheim cofounded the website "Fight Against Coercive Tactics Network" (FACTNet), which was designed to expose Scientology's negative activities and disseminate information—including confidential material—about the church. Initially, Scientology's lawyers deployed multiple arguments that combined religious and commercial logic when expedient. At certain points, they used a First Amendment argument, by claiming that Scientology's confidential materials were religious documents and that disclosure of them would be a violation of the group's religious freedom.[37] Yet at other moments, they presented more straightforwardly corporate arguments, claiming that the documents were both copyrighted materials and "trade secrets" (that is, information that has economic value from not being generally known); the disclosure of these secrets, the church's lawyers claimed, could cause "irreparable spiritual injury if a rival church . . . were allowed to disseminate them."[38] In 1995, however, the federal district court ruled against Scientology, finding that there were no copyright or trade secret violations and that FACTNet's use of the Scientology materials was simply fair use.[39] Even after Judge Kane's decision, however, Scientology's war with FACTNet dragged on for several more years, until a settlement was finally reached in 1999. According to the terms of the settlement, if FACTNet is ever found guilty of violating church copyrights, it is permanently enjoined to pay the church $1 million.[40]

In sum, the intellectual property disputes surrounding Osho's name and work are symptomatic of a much broader trend in twenty-first-century spiritual life. As religious movements are drawn ever more into the logic of the commercial marketplace, they are increasingly forced to adopt the same legal strategies as do other multinational corporations. At the same time, as we will see, they also create tension with many of their followers, who are often disillusioned by the ever more blatant commercialization and bureaucratization of their spiritual practices.

OSHO'S LAST WILL AND TESTAMENT: FORGERY IN THE AGE OF DIGITAL TECHNOLOGY?

Perhaps the most remarkable dispute in the complex story of Osho's legacy is the fight over his alleged will, which many critics now believe is a fraudulent document.[41] The will was first submitted during a separate dispute between the OIF and the Osho Lotus Commune, which is the parent organization of the Osho UTA Institut, the largest Osho meditation center in Europe. In 2010, the Osho Lotus Commune filed a petition with the Office for Harmonization in the International Market (located in Spain), asking that it follow the lead of the American office and declare the OIF's claims to trademark invalid.[42] The German group is quite explicit in their opinion that the OIF's claims have little to do with any serious effort to protect Osho's legacy but are really primarily about power—the control of his massive and lucrative legacy. In their opinion, the OIF's case is in direct contradiction of Osho's central ideal of freedom and his fundamental rejection of institutional and bureaucratic control:

> This case is just about one thing: Whether OIF is able to use a trademark registration to monopolize the name "Osho" in order to gain power to decide who is to be permitted to use the name "Osho" for meditation centers, meditation programs, therapy, training courses, festivals and so on. . . .
> Ultimately, this is an attempt to use a trademark to establish a worldwide franchising system with which OIF would be able to use licensing agreements to control all Osho centers. . . . OIF is seriously attempting to sell us this attempt as "Osho's vision"!
> Osho's vision was freedom. The vision of Michael Byrne (also known as Jayesh) is power and control.[43]

In support of its claim to sole possession of trademark, the OIF submitted a document described as the "last will and testament" of Osho, signed on October 15, 1989, along with a sworn affidavit by lawyer

Swami Niren (Philip Tölkes). The will in question is a very short document—less than a page—but it does contain the following key sentence:

> I, Osho . . . hereby devise and bequest any and all right, title in any form owned by me, now or in the future, including but not limited to all ownership, publishing or related rights, to all my work, published to date or in the future, in any form, to "Neo Sannyas International Foundation."[44]

The Neo Sannyas International Foundation, we should note, was the entity that became the Osho International Foundation or OIF in 1990. As such, this document—if authentic—would turn over all rights to all Osho-related materials worldwide to the sole control of the OIF.

Not long after this document was submitted, however, serious questions began to be raised about it. Most importantly, critics quickly noticed that the signature at the end of the will appears to be not just similar but 100 percent identical in every minute detail to a signature penned by Rajneesh on a document from 1976. The two signatures have been scrutinized on a microscopic, dot-by-dot level by multiple independent experts—one from Bologna Italy, one from Aurangabad, and one from New Delhi—who have concluded that the signature on the "will" can only be the same as the signature on the 1976 letter. The signature in question, they conclude, must have been copied, which would mean that the will is a forgery. As N. R. Parik, the expert graphoanalyst from Aurangabad, put it, "I am of the opinion that the questioned signature . . . has been prepared by scanning and printing process and the admitted signature . . . has been used as a model signature for presenting a similar and fraudulent signature."[45]

The implications of this alleged forgery are, of course, enormous. Not only would it invalidate the OIF's claims to complete control of Osho's name, works, and meditations, but it would also implicate the very top leadership at the Pune center in serious criminal activities. Thus, on December 8, 2013, Yogesh Takkar (Swami Prem Geet), on behalf of Osho Friends International, lodged a complaint, arguing that the signature on the will had been faked in order to gain control of Osho's intellectual property,[46] and "to claim the rights and income from Osho's intellectual property worth millions."[47] Shortly afterward, the Pune police issued a notice to the administrators of the ashram asking them to produce the original will.[48] Significantly, however, in January 2014, the OIF chose to withdraw the will from the European court proceedings. While they did not admit it is a forgery, they argued that they "did not wish to present any document which would distract the attention of the OHIM from the key evidence and issues of the case at hand."[49] Critics of the OIF, on the other hand, see this maneuver as simply a desperate attempt at "damage control," and evidence that the document must have been forged.[50]

OSHO'S "PERSONHOOD" IN THE AGE OF FACEBOOK

Despite the strong rulings of the NAF and the USPTO, the war over Osho's status in cyberspace is far from over. On the contrary, not long after the USPTO decision in 2009, the dispute over Osho's name in the digital realm shifted to social media platforms such as Facebook, which has become one of the primary means by which Osho groups (like many other alternative spiritual groups) advertise their services, attract new members, and communicate with followers today. After losing the 2009 ruling, the OIF launched a new series of attacks on the many small Osho-related individuals and communities who have a Facebook presence, such as "Osho Pulsation," "UTA Institut," "Osho Times," and "Osho Diamond Breath." A long complaint about the OIF's aggressive policy was posted on the blog of Osho Viha, an independent Osho center located in the San Francisco Bay area. In their view, this attack on Osho-related Facebook pages is not only a contradiction of Osho's own views of intellectual freedom but also in violation of international laws of trademark and intellectual property:

> OIF continues to claim that no one can use the *name* Osho to indicate an association with Osho *the person* in work that is related to Osho's spiritual teachings unless OIF gives them permission. At some point after losing the US case, OIF went out and registered trademarks in new jurisdictions like China and Venezuela, where there are not enough sannyasins to oppose the registrations. Based on these filings they claim to own an "international" trademark for Osho.
>
> OIF now argues that no one can use Osho's name descriptively in a business name on the Internet, because the Internet goes to the whole world, and OIF has Osho registered as a trademark in some jurisdictions.[51]

[handwritten margin note: own in some countries]

Facebook, Osho Viha points out, has an unusual "hands off" policy with regard to intellectual property disputes, refusing to settle disagreements between parties and requiring only a simple online form to register a trademark complaint.[52] However, this seems to be at odds with U.S. law, which would allow those accused of copyright violations to have a fair chance to respond to such charges rather than simply being banned from the site:

Facebook's terms, which appear on its website, state that Facebook will *not* adjudicate between parties in an intellectual property dispute. US law requires Facebook to allow people accused of copyright violations to object to the copyright claim, and if the accused responds and the claimant does not file an enforcement lawsuit within a specified time, the page must be put back up.

In contrast, if a claimant to trademark ownership fills out a scanty online form that could not possibly give enough information to actually determine the sufficiency of a trademark claim, Facebook will take down the page, will not allow the accused to respond, and will not put the page back up unless the claimant agrees to it.[53]

Finally, Osho Viha also argues that "Osho" in this case is being treated unfairly in comparison to the names and titles of other religious groups. For example, it seems unlikely that Facebook would accept anyone's claim that "Jesus" or "Buddha" could be titles claimed by one specific group and ban all others who use that the name on their pages. And yet, that is ironically what has happened with the name Osho and pages using it to advertise their services:

> Both "Jesus" and "Buddha" are trademarks in the US for specific products, but Facebook would not take down all pages with these names in the title. For example, Facebook would not take down a page for the First Church of Jesus Christ, because they would acknowledge that "Jesus" in the church name is a reference to the historical person, not a trademark use. They would not take down a page titled Buddha Sanctuary, as they would recognize this as a reference to the historical Buddha.
>
> Yet Facebook treats Osho differently. For Facebook Osho is not a person with a name, and people associated with Osho are not allowed to refer to Him in their page names. For Facebook, Osho is only a trademark.[54]

The debate over Osho on Facebook raises another series of profound questions and ironies. Among others, it highlights the ironic fact that customers who use Facebook grant the company "a non-exclusive, transferable, sub-licensable, royalty-free, worldwide license to use any IP content that you post on or in connection with Facebook (IP License)."[55] While users still own the intellectual property—such as photos and videos—Facebook has the right to use and disseminate that material freely.[56] The case of the Osho groups on Facebook, conversely, highlights the fact that individual Facebook users do not in fact have the right to disseminate materials as widely as they would like. In other words, while Facebook is largely unfettered by IP law because it has the right to use all of the content its customers provide, its customers are often even more strictly bound by trademark and copyright because of

Facebook's tendency to simply side with the party that bothers to file a trademark claim.

RECENT WARS IN THE PUNE ASHRAM

The fight over Osho trademarks in cyberspace, however, is only the tip of an iceberg of accusations and legal challenges in the twenty-first century. More recently, Indian critics of the Pune community have also alleged that members of the inner circle have secretly transferred ashram funds to their own accounts. According to Yogesh Thakkar (aka Swami Premgeet), the members of the inner circle have set up a private company called Osho Multimedia and Resorts Pvt Ltd, to which they have been transferring the benefits of the Osho charitable trust: "As a result, the trust is being deprived of income and benefits. For example, any income accrued from visitors staying at the Osho Guest House (held by the trust) gets directly siphoned off to Osho Multimedia and Resorts Pvt Ltd."[57] In Thakkar's view, this is not just unethical but illegal: "According to the Bombay Public Trust Act, the trustees can't directly transfer any benefits for personal favour . . . the trustees can't be the beneficiaries. . . . The public charitable trust established by Osho is gradually getting turned into a private limited company."[58]

Meanwhile, another series of accusations has centered on the alleged transfer of key portions of the Pune ashram land, which is located in an extremely valuable and increasingly upscale part of the Koregaon Park neighborhood. Critics claim that the Pune inner circle has transferred parts of the valuable Pune property through "gifts" to a somewhat suspicious entity in New Delhi: "The transfer had allegedly been made to a little known, obscure 'Darshan Trust', registered in Delhi and controlled by Mukesh Sarda, a trustee of the Osho International Foundation."[59] Critics of the Pune leadership now wonder if this is not an attempt to exploit, sell off, and profit from the pricey ashram property "by selling it piece-meal."[60] At the same time, the critics argue, entry fees and course costs have risen dramatically, even as the number of visitors has declined steeply. While the ashram once attracted 1,200–1,500 visitors a day, it now brings in a mere 150. The number of courses offered by the Multiversity is also far fewer than a decade before, and critics claim that offerings have declined by as much as 90 percent.[61] Ironically, many of the critics now charge that the Pune leadership has transformed the ashram into a "religion"—that is, a religion in the negative sense of the term often used by Osho-Rajneesh

FIGURE 18. Cartoon satirizing the current leadership of the Osho commune in Pune, by Sudi Narayanan, *Osho News*, 2014. Used by permission of the artist.

to critique the institutional, dogmatic, fear-based forms of mainstream traditions:

> The Ashram, in its current state is a religion. Just by removing Osho's pictures does not make it a non-religion. It has everything that it takes to make a religion, i.e. fear, rules, suppression, serious and controlled responses. On the contrary, it would be impossible to make a religion out of a place, where love, freedom, dancing, and singing can co-exist with all the differences of the sannyasins around the world.[62]

The various charges against the "dictators" in the Pune inner circle are summarized in a satirical cartoon published in *Osho News* in 2012 (fig. 18). Conceived by Dhanyam (the head of the Osho Viha center in California) and drawn by Swami Anand Teertha (aka Sudi Narayanan, an Indian *sannyasin* living in Atlanta), the cartoon depicts the members of inner circle smiling, sipping wine, and protecting their treasure chests inside the Osho Resort—now renamed the "Pune Fort"—while surrounded by thousands of angry critics carrying signs such as "Osho's Will Was Forged," "False Copyright," and "We Demand CBI Inquiry."[63] In an interview in May 2014 the artist explained:

> This particular cartoon was my spontaneous reflection of what is happening in Osho's original ashram back in India. Following Osho's passing in 1990, the management of Osho's meditation resort restructured themselves and fired several of his older followers. This was seen as an effort to focus the activities of ashram into more of a book publishing house and procure copy-

rights on everything related to Osho. . . . Having been to the Ashram myself recently a few times, I have experienced the same level of concerns that the older intimate Osho disciples experience.[64]

It is significant, however, that these wars over copyright and trademark in cyberspace are also being waged primarily in cyberspace, through digital publications such as *OshoNews*, *OshoWorld*, *OshoWork*, *OshoFriendsInternational*, and blogs such as *OshoViha*. The greatest tool in the attempt to control Osho's legacy, in other words, is also the greatest tool in the effort to challenge and contest that control.

SPIRITUAL LIFE IN THE AGE OF MULTINATIONAL CORPORATIONS

All of these accusations and lawsuits, of course, have had an impact on the spiritual life and morale of *sannyasins,* both in India and around the world. As *India Today* reported in 2000, the atmosphere of joy and celebration that once suffused the Pune ashram and much of the surrounding city had been replaced by an aura of tension and hostility. Pune streets that once thronged with red-clad, dancing young people were instead filled with rumors about power struggles and underhanded deals:

> The merriment and laughter that used to ring around the commune have now been replaced with a pregnant silence, full of suspicion and hatred. The reason: battle lines have been drawn and the Bhagwan's very legacy is being torn apart by a bitter power struggle to retain control over his teachings and meditation practices. Says Swami Ganja Vedant, an old hand at the ashram: "Greed is spreading like a terminal cancer all over the commune."[65]

Both long-term *sannyasins* and members of the local Pune community whom I interviewed confirmed this feeling that the atmosphere of the ashram had changed dramatically in the last two decades. One Israeli *sannyasin* recalled the thousands of red-clad young people who once freely roamed the streets of the city in the 1970s, 1980s, and 1990s, and lamented the mere dozen or so who now remain, mostly huddled in the protective environs of the five-start resort. Waiters, shopkeepers, and local businessmen whom I interviewed echoed this basic assessment: the ecstatic and playful chaos of the early Pune ashram had been progressively replaced by a new sort of suspicious bureaucracy that seemed closer to an international corporate hotel than to a vibrant, thriving spiritual commune.[66]

Nonetheless, despite the spiritual malaise that may have descended upon some portions of the global Osho community in the twenty-first century, most *sannyasins* continue to find meaning in the movement in spite of these convoluted legal squabbles. While some *sannyasins* regard these legal disputes as an intense object of contention that is critical to Osho's entire legacy, most seem to see them as a boring, annoying, and quite embarrassing distraction from Osho's message, which has little or nothing to do with legal wrangling. "All that stuff—people suing each other—I have no interest in any of that," responded William Foster when I asked him about the recent disputes over Osho's legacy. Instead, his concern is more about where the new "centers of energy" might be found, where the new nodes of spiritual power and excitement might be located in the new global order; in this sense, having a single physical ashram such as Pune might be irrelevant, and it might be far more useful to have a decentralized global network of spiritual centers.[67]

Longtime Osho practitioner Aneesha Dillon expressed a similar sentiment when I asked her feelings about the present Pune center. In her view, the golden days of the vibrant Pune commune are over, which is a sad thing in many ways. But it is ultimately a good thing, she thinks, since it has opened new possibilities for a wider array of individual and small group practices all over the world:

> There was a difficult parting, I would say. There was a lot of heartbreak around the recognition that those days are over. So in a way, there has been a lot of regret about the loss of the commune. But I just have to see it as a change, and actually it's spread out in a much more global way with a constant circuiting and networking of traveling group leaders that are constantly going to these different centers all over the place and bringing along his work. Of course, we always include the Dynamic Meditation in it and the Kundalini, and that richness as far as I can see is now floating around and available out there. So it actually all feels like a good thing.[68]

Other *sannyasins,* such as Swami Satya Vedant, were even more optimistic about the future of Osho's work in a new global context. In the absence of the living master, he said, it is now up to a new generation of *sannyasins* to create a self-generating network that might continue to spread his work without the trappings of a centralized religious institution, bureaucracy, or control:

> Osho always insists that he has no followers, only fellow travelers, because following is so easy and cozy. Then the individual is not responsible; one can put the responsibility on someone else, God, guru, Jesus, Buddha, whatever. But slowly Osho begins withdrawing his support to our projections, like a bird luring its young from the nest. And that became the acid test. Creating something that depended on Osho's presence was one thing, but, to create

something that be self-regenerating, self-growing, without any outer help, relying only on each individual's inner sources—who could have anticipated it? Who would have thought it possible—that today his Work would go on expanding "beyond our minds" as he forecast?[69]

Quite apart from the bitter legal battles, Osho's work continues to be circulated, discussed, practiced, and reinterpreted by a vast assortment of groups worldwide. Perhaps the most important transformation that has taken place in the wake of Osho's demise is the shift from the "ashram" or "commune" model, in which individuals lived full-time in a self-sustaining alternative society, toward a new, decentralized model, in which individuals gather semiregularly at centers or even personal homes across the globe. There are still, to be sure, a few small intentional communities and ashrams today that have been inspired by Osho's message. These include the Osho Cocom in Goa, India, the Osho Tapoban in Nepal, the Gondwana Sanctuary and the Samaya Ashram in Australia, and the Desert Ashram in Israel, among others.[70] However, far more prevalent today are the fluid and decentralized centers scattered worldwide, where individuals come for shorter periods to engage in meditation, take courses, and experience a brief spiritual retreat before returning to the workaday world. This vast and loose network of centers includes the Osho UTA in Germany, Osho Humaniversity in the Netherlands, Osho Amritdham in Jabalpur, India, Osho Afroz in Greece, Instituto Osho in Brazil, Osho Madhuban in Canada, Osho Leela in the United Kingdom, Osho Work in Russia, Osho Varazze in Italy, Osho Academy in Sedona, Arizona, and Osho Viha in the Bay Area, to name but a few.[71] Some of these, such as Osho Leela, offer short-term "community experience" programs, in which guests may live, practice, and work in the center for a week or more for a basic fee;[72] but many are simply local sites where individuals can gather to practice Osho meditations on an informal basis.

For example, the Osho Humaniversity is one of the largest centers for alternative spirituality and therapy in Europe, located on the beautiful North Sea coast of Holland. Like the Multiversity in Pune, this center offers a wide selection of day and weekend sessions, such as "Zen Acting—the Power to Win," "Shaking Day," and "Humaniversity Encounter," as well as a variety of individual sessions ranging from "Bioenergetics," "Rebirthing," and "Trauma Release" to "Acu-Energetics," "Ayurvedic Consultation," and "Colon-Hydrotherapy."[73] One of the first programs advertised on the center's website is a fourteen-day "Tourist Retreat," which promises to help "release your emotional burdens so that you can be free to live your life to the fullest." This retreat has a rigorous "round-the-clock schedule" from early morning wake-up until the evening class after dinner; yet in keeping with Osho's Zorba the Buddha ideal, it concludes with "time in the Boozeria, our famous nightclub, where you can . . . dance till early in the morning."[74]

Much of the contemporary practice of Osho's teachings worldwide, we should note, also continues to center heavily on Neo-Tantra and sexuality. For example, according to the events listed on OshoNews. com, a large number of short Osho workshops and classes were being offered across the globe in early 2015. Of these, more than half focused on Tantra and sexuality, such as "Sexuality Free from Guilt" in Tuscany, "Master Lover Weekend" in Oslo, "Tantra Cacao Ceremony" in London, "Soul Mate Training" in Greece, and "Tantric Pulsation Training" in Miasto, Italy.[75]

In the United States today, the Osho movement bears little resemblance to the Oregon ashram of the 1980s. Rather, it is now primarily a loose network of individuals and small local centers, where *sannyasins* come together in far more sporadic and informal ways. As Swami Anand Teertha described the new global movement, Osho's message has ironically been spread even more widely than ever, in spite of—or perhaps because of—this more decentralized network of nodes and hyphal knots:

> Osho movement has never happened (and will never happen) in masses. The movement's nature is more close to an individual love affair than a mass phenomenon usually found around religious institutions or ideologies. Human beings are becoming more independent and informed these days, Osho's messages are widely read and appreciated especially among the younger generations. The Osho gatherings that usually happen in smaller settings are widely happening throughout the world. His books are even more widely available and popular these days. This is same in India and abroad.[76]

Thus, we now find Osho "meet-ups" in Marin County, Atlanta, Dallas, New York, Vancouver, and elsewhere, where *sannyasins* get together periodically for meditations and socializing, while maintaining their regular lives and careers. Yet the older model of the full-time commune, in which members dedicate their lives 24/7 to life in an ashram, has largely fallen by the wayside.

As we saw in the previous chapter, this seems to be in keeping with the broader neoliberal trend that we see in the Osho-Rajneesh movement and in twenty-first-century spirituality more broadly. Increasingly in developed neoliberal societies, spirituality is a largely privatized and individualized activity that might enhance one's personal well-being and even enhance one's ability to function in the workaday world.

CONCLUSIONS: FASHIONING A NEW "OSHO" IDENTITY IN THE AGE OF INTELLECTUAL PROPERTY

In sum, the legal disputes surrounding Osho's legacy highlight yet another key historical development in the expansion of global capitalism—namely, the progressive absorption of everything, including the most "intangible" of phenomena, such as meditations and spiritual practices, not simply into consumer culture but also into the legal apparatus of the marketplace. In the process, the Osho-Rajneesh movement itself has undergone profound transformations as it has been renegotiated through the matrices and networks of national and international IP law. Among other things, the community has been fractured and redefined along national (Indian) versus transnational ("Western") lines, along insider ("inner circle") versus outsider lines, and along the lines of conflicting interpretations of Osho's teachings and legacy.

As Rosemary Coombe suggests in her work on intellectual property and the legal construction of communities, there is a subtle but powerful sort of "constitutive character of intellectual property law" that has not just restrictive but also "productive capacities." Indeed, IP law like other forms of law also serves to constitute and produce identities, both of individual subjects and of communities. The law, in a very real sense, helps to fashion the "author" as the creator of expressive works; and it also helps fashion communities as collective subjects through their claims to possess certain cultural goods, such as traditional knowledge:

> Identities do not exist before the law but are forged in relation to law and the subject position it affords. . . . Both the subject position of the author and specific forms of authorial creativity are legitimated by copyright law. . . . Intellectual property laws are one means by which attachments and entitlements to "intangibles" such as expressive works and heritage goods are forged.[77]

Increasingly in the twenty-first century, "intangibles" here include not only "secular" kinds of expressive and heritage goods, but also "spiritual" intangibles, such as meditation techniques, yoga positions, and even religious titles. As Fish has shown in the case of yoga, IP law is serving to produce and constitute new forms of global commercial yoga such as Bikram and other hugely successful methods. Finally, in the case of the Osho movement, IP law is being used to produce new forms of multinational corporate spirituality, with a wide range of conflicting interpretations.

Ultimately, I would argue, not only the Osho movement but also the very "person" of Osho-Rajneesh himself have undergone yet another profound change of identity. As we have seen in the preceding chapters, the protean and rather postmodern character of Osho-Rajneesh has undergone a variety of transformations over the decades, from Chandra Mohan Jain to Acharya Rajneesh to Bhagwan Shree Rajneesh to Maitreya to Osho. In the twenty-first century, he has undergone a new series of identity shifts through the matrix of IP law, first as Osho®, then as a contested signature on a last will and testament, and now as a trademark on Facebook. As Osho himself put it, the "new man" must be a "liquid human being," always adapting to the present moment.

Conclusion

The Spiritual Logic of Late Capitalism

I am widely misunderstood. I don't think that it is in any way disrespectful to me. This is a compliment. The more widely I am misunderstood the better. . . . Gautam Buddha was not so widely misunderstood—he was misunderstood only in Bihar.

I am misunderstood all over the world!

—Rajneesh, *The Sword and the Lotus*

We need to think ourselves beyond the nation. . . . We are entering a postnational world.

—Arjun Appadurai, *Modernity at Large*

There is . . . a crying need to articulate a secular *revolutionary* humanism that can ally with those religious-based humanisms . . . to counter alienation in its many forms.

—David Harvey, *Seventeen Contradictions and the End of Capitalism*

During her visit to India in October 2011, the American pop singer, producer, and activist Lady Gaga addressed the media and discussed her views on creativity and spirituality. Earlier that same year, Lady Gaga had drawn attention to her interest in Indian philosophy when she included a quote from Osho himself on her Twitter account: "Creativity is the greatest form of rebellion." When journalists asked her further about her interest in Osho, she spoke enthusiastically about her love of his works and particularly the implications of his radical ideas for other aspects of life, such as art, society, and politics:

Oh yes Osho! I read a lot of Osho's books and I have been reading a lot about (Osho's views on) rebellion, which is my favorite so far. And how creativity is the greatest form of rebellion in life. It's important to stand up for what you believe in and to fight for equality. Equality is one of the most important things in my life—social, political, economic equality—these are all things I fight for in my country as a citizen. So I read Osho because not only do I love his work and what he writes about, but I guess I am kind of an Indian hippie![1]

In January the following year, Lady Gaga sent out yet another tweet, expressing her love of Osho and his work: "Thinking about an OSHO tattoo," she informed her 18 million Twitter followers.[2]

This international media story inspired a longtime *sannysasin* named Anand Subhuti to write a book about his own experience with Osho, which was initially published with a title directed at the pop star herself: *Lady Gaga, This is Osho*. Quickly realizing that he could not use the name Lady Gaga without permission, however, he withdrew the book. Unfortunately, Amazon.com did not remove the image of the book from the website, where it soon drew the attention of the singer's managers and lawyers. As Subhuti recalled, "When Lady Gaga's managers in Los Angeles got to hear about it, they freaked. After all, when you're managing a $90 million-a-year pop star you don't want other people cashing in on her fame. Overnight, I got a 'cease and desist' ultimatum from a firm of New York City lawyers representing Gaga. . . . The letter was aggressive and intimidating, as one would expect NYC lawyers to be."[3]

In many ways, the example of Lady Gaga's fascination with Osho-Rajneesh is emblematic of the guru's ongoing legacy in the twenty-first century. Even two decades after his death, his ideas and methods continue to circulate globally, being reread, reworked, and often wildly transformed in the shifting context of transnational tourism, entertainment, social media, and intellectual property disputes. As we see in the case of Lady Gaga's tweet about the Osho tattoo, his name and "brand" also continue to be commodified in fascinating new ways, appearing not only on a myriad of books, DVDs, and websites with its registered trademark, but even on the arm, leg, or belly of an international pop star.

To conclude this narrative of Osho-Rajneesh's complex global journey from India to America and back again, I would like to discuss several key aspects of his legacy and his significance for the study of religion and globalization today. While most Americans probably no longer remember Osho-Rajneesh except as "that sex guru with all the Rolls-Royces from the 1980s," he remains one of the most influential figures of the twenty-first century, even if that influence is often implicit and obscured rather than explicit or immediately visible.

THE NEW AGE, NEOLIBERALISM, AND THE SELLING OF SPIRITUALITY

Perhaps Osho-Rajneesh's most pervasive influence has been on the loose and eclectic body of contemporary spirituality commonly referred to as "New Age." Of course, the various beliefs and practices we label "New Age" are by no means singular or monolithic but in fact wildly diverse and heterogenous. These include everything from astrology, tarot cards, and crystals to alternative forms of healing such as aromatherapy to elements of Eastern religions such as Reiki, yoga, and chakra meditation to various forms of spirit communication such as channeling. However, despite their remarkable diversity, most of the phenomena we call New Age do have some common historical origins and family resemblances. Some scholars trace the historical roots of the New Age all the way back to the Western esoteric tradition, that is, to the current of alternative spirituality that runs through the Christian, Jewish, and pagan traditions since the early centuries CE.[4] However, most agree that, as a modern phenomenon, New Age spirituality really first began to appear in the late nineteenth century and then reached its full flowering in the United States, the United Kingdom, and Europe during the 1960s and 1970s. The phrase itself is most commonly associated with the astrological shift from the Age of Pisces—said to be a period of violence, conflict, and suffering—to the Age of Aquarius—said to be a new era of harmony, peace, and spiritual development.[5] During the 1960s, New Age ideas were still fairly esoteric and largely limited to the counterculture; however, in the 1970s and 1980s, the New Age emerged forcefully into popular culture, particularly through the appearance of best-selling books such as *Out on a Limb,* the spiritual memoir of actress Shirley MacLaine, which was made into a hugely successful TV miniseries in 1987. Suddenly ideas such as reincarnation, channeling, astral projection, and visits from UFOs were part of mainstream conversation.[6] As Kathryn Lofton recently put it in *Oprah: The Gospel of an Icon,* "The so-called New Age religion, which took shape in the late Sixties and Seventies, introduced to the mass culture an eclectic mix of world religious traditions, pop psychology, quantum physics and occult practices. Practices that before had been seen either solely in other parts of the globe or on the far margins of U.S. religious creativity found cultural success in paperback editions."[7]

Various scholars have characterized the New Age in different ways. As Lofton suggests, some of the primary themes that unify New Age spirituality include "an optimistic view of the future, a rejection of any form of authoritarian doctrine or hierarchy, an ethic of self-empowerment, an eclecticism of beliefs and practices, and a press to use science for spiritual ends."[8] Other authors such as Roy Wallis identify another key feature of the New Age, which he calls a kind of "epistemological individualism" and "revelational indeterminacy"; by this he means that the individual is "the ultimate locus for the determination of truth" and that "the truth may be revealed in diverse ways and through diverse agents. No individual or collectivity possesses a monopoly on truth."[9] Paul Heelas makes a similar point when he describes the New Age as a kind of "celebration of self and sacralization of modernity"; that is, New Age spirituality tends to see the individual self as inherently divine and as the primary source of truth, and it tends to affirm and sanctify key features of modernity, such as the values of freedom, science, and technology.[10]

Finally, one other common feature of much of New Age spirituality, which goes hand in hand with this celebration of self and the sacralization of modernity, is a positive attitude toward consumer capitalism. Kimberly Lau suggests in *New Age Capitalism* that New Age spirituality tends to appropriate non-Western and ancient traditions such as yoga, tai chi, aromatherapy, and macrobiotic diets, transforming them into billion-dollar industries in the marketplace.[11] Jeremy Carrette and Richard King make a similar argument in *Selling Spirituality,* in which they maintain that much of the New Age not only affirms the logic of modern capitalism but also fits well with a neoliberal economy that aims to create more productive, efficient laborers in the workforce. Not only has the "wisdom of ancient civilizations become commodified in order to serve the interests of spiritual consumers in the New Age marketplace of religions"; but "spirituality as a cultural trope" itself has also been "appropriated by corporate bodies and management consultants to promote efficiency, extend markets and maintain a leading edge in a fast-moving information economy."[12]

With its central emphasis on individualism, free will, and eclecticism, much of New Age spirituality does fit very well with a kind of "consumer" approach to the sacred, in which the seeker is empowered to pick and choose from a vast global marketplace of religious goods, piecing together his or her own personal worldview. This sort of market-place approach to spirituality is embraced by some of the great New Age centers, such as Sedona, Arizona, where one can shop at self-described "metaphysical department stores" such as "Center for the New Age." Here, we can browse among a huge assortment of spiritual goods and services ranging from psychic readings and chakra alignment to crystals, books, videos, and even "canned vortex" (collected by vegan hippie nudists, according to the label). In my own hometown of Columbus, Ohio, we have a huge, twice-yearly New Age convention called the "Universal Life Expo," which hosts over 300 vendors selling everything from jewelry, clothing, wands, and mandala paintings to psychic readings, communication with angels, and ghost-busting services.

Virtually all of these trends in the New Age as it developed in the 1960s, 1970s, and 1980s were clearly articulated by Osho-Rajneesh from his earliest lectures onward. While Osho-Rajneesh did at certain moments make dire predictions about the future of humanity, he also clearly saw civilization entering a critical moment or turning point, with a choice between self-destruction or a transition to a new age and the birth of a "new man for the new millennium."[13] As we have seen throughout this book, moreover, he always placed central emphasis on the divinity and freedom of the individual, celebrating the inherent Buddha-hood of the self and employing all manner of techniques to liberate the self from any form of social conditioning. At the same time, from his early critiques of Gandhi onward, Osho-Rajneesh called for a "modern" (and also "postmodern") kind of spirituality, which would embrace modern economic ideas, technology, and science while rejecting the superstition and prejudice of the past. And few contemporary teachers were more eclectic or syncretic than Osho-Rajneesh, who not only read widely and voraciously but also created a spiritual movement that experimented with every imaginable meditative and psychological technique, weaving them together into new, hybrid forms such as Dynamic Meditation.

Not surprisingly, Osho's work has been cited by both scholars and popular authors as one of the primary influences on the New Age.[14] His writings have been praised by none other than Deepak Chopra, arguably the most prominent New Age guru and advocate of alternative medicine, well known through his appearances on *Oprah* and other popular television shows. According to a quote featured prominently on many Osho websites, "These brilliant insights will benefit all those who yearn for experiential knowledge of the field of pure potentiality inherent in every human being. This book belongs on the shelf of every library and in the home of all those who seek knowledge of the higher self."[15]

But beyond its intellectual influence on the New Age, the Osho-Rajneesh movement itself was a key node in the emerging global networks of New Age spirituality as they spread from America and Europe to Asia and beyond. The early Pune ashram was a mecca for spiritual tourists during the 1970s, influencing a whole generation of seekers who in turn brought this hybrid mix of Eastern meditation and Western psychology back to Europe and America. Likewise, the Oregon ashram was one of the primary centers of the New Age movement in the 1980s, drawing young people from all over the world to Rajneeshpuram to engage in this complex mélange of spiritual practice and secular business. And finally, the new Pune center remains a key node in a global spirituality today, with its wildly eclectic Multiversity as a kind of model of the New Age in a twenty-first-century context.

But above all, Osho-Rajneesh's central ideal of Zorba the Buddha and his affirmation of material wealth have been hugely influential in the development of "New Age capitalism" since the 1970s. From its earliest days in Bombay to the new resort in Pune, the Osho-Rajneesh movement has been quite unapologetic in its embrace of capitalism and even freely makes use of the language of branding, marketing, and the multinational corporation.

NEO-TANTRA AND GLOBAL SEX FOR THE NEW MILLENNIUM

Besides his huge influence on New Age spirituality in general, Osho-Rajneesh probably made his greatest impact in the transmission and reinterpretation of South Asian Tantra for new audiences in America and Europe. As we saw in chapter 3, Tantra in its traditional South Asian contexts is incredibly diverse and not primarily focused on sexuality.[16] When sexual practices do occur in Tantric rituals, they are usually not particularly "sexy"—that is, they are less a matter of achieving optimal sexual pleasure than of acquiring material and spiritual power.[17] It was British Orientalist scholars, Christian missionaries, and Hindu reformers in the nineteenth century who equated Tantra with sexual practices and identified it as the most disgusting and depraved aspect of Hinduism in modern times. Ironically, this negative view of Tantra was turned completely on its head during the 1960s and 1970s, particularly in the United States and Europe, where it was assimilated into the counterculture movement and sexual revolution. Rather than a depraved perversion, Tantra was reimagined as a much-needed celebration of sexuality and a sure antidote to the prudery and repression of the modern West.

Osho-Rajneesh was not only one of the first to redefine Tantra during this period; he was also one of the most infamous and influential. As an Indian teacher, he endowed the modern reinterpretation of Tantra with a certain authority and gravitas, while as a guru who attracted thousands of young people from America and Europe, he played a key role in the translation (or, arguably, mistranslation) of Tantra to a non-Indian audience. This is really the heart of his idea of Neo-Tantra—a modern reworking of certain aspects of this ancient tradition, explicitly adapted to the needs, desires, and appetites of contemporary Americans and Europeans. No longer an esoteric path based on difficult rituals and aimed at the acquisition of spiritual power, Tantra remerged in the late twentieth century as a hugely popular path based on spontaneous pleasure and sexual liberation.

Today, there are literally hundreds of popular forms of New Age Tantra, ranging from the "Church of Tantra" and "Tantric Temple" to the "New Tantrik Order in America." Quite significantly, most of these popular forms of Tantra either cite Osho-Rajneesh as a key influence or were themselves developed by current or former *sannyasins*. Thus, as Mark A. Michaels and Patricia Johnson note in their popular text, *Tantra for Erotic Empowerment*,

> The term Neo-Tantra was . . . used by Bhagwan Shree Rajneesh (Osho) to describe his system, which melded Tantric philosophy with a variety of other spiritual and psychological approaches. Osho has influenced almost all Western Tantra teachers, so much of what is available in the West can accurately be described as Neo-Tantra.[18]

Urban Tantra: Sacred Sex for the Twenty-First Century, is another popular Tantric manual, by self-described sex and life coach Barbara Carrellas. The author not only thanks Osho in her acknowledgments but also cites him as her key inspiration in tracing the link between sex and spiritual bliss, with a lengthy quotation from Osho's *Book of Secrets*: "Once you get a big enough bite of that great cosmic orgasm, you realize that sex is not the only way to have bliss. You can then find bliss in everyday, ordinary aspects of life. Osho, the visionary (and controversial) spiritual teacher, explains how sex brings us to bliss."[19]

Indeed, citing Osho as a primary inspiration seems to be not only common but almost expected in these popular works on Tantric sex.

Thus, Diana Richardson's *Tantric Orgasm for Women* credits Osho as the key figure who pointed out the profound connection between sexual pleasure and spiritual awakening:

> My source of Tantric inspiration and guidance is my spiritual master, Osho. Osho, or Bhagwan Shree Rajneesh . . . teaches meditation not as a practice but as a way of life. He is a mystic who brings the timeless wisdom of the East to bear upon the urgent questions facing men and women today. . . . Osho says "Tantra is the transformation of sex into love through awareness."[20]

Citing an exotic Indian mystic appears to be a key strategy for endowing these popular paperbacks with an aura of legitimacy and authority. In other words, it is a way of indicating that these are not just superficial knockoffs of the *Joy of Sex* but rather have the spiritual imprimatur of an Eastern sage.

Finally, many of these popular Tantric texts are the work of *sannyasins* themselves, several of whom spent years with Osho-Rajneesh before going off on their own to teach various forms of Neo-Tantra. A good example is Aneesha Dillon, who was first trained at the Esalen Institute before working with Rajneesh in Pune and Oregon and then developing her own therapeutic mix of Wilhelm Reich and Neo-Tantra. Her book *Tantric Pulsation* clearly identifies her spiritual lineage with Osho-Rajneesh and his Tantric vision, which is "wholly life affirmative" and "rooted in acceptance, let-go meditation and celebration of life. This is a vision which embraces all human experience, from sex to superconsciousness."[21]

Another key example is Tantric teacher and self-help guru Margo Anand, author of the hugely popular books *The Art of Sexual Magic* and *Sexual Ecstasy: The Art of Orgasm*. Born Margo Naslednikov, she graduated from the Sorbonne in Paris before following Rajneesh and taking the name Ma Anand Margo. In the late 1980s, she helped found the "Sky Dancing Institute" and began publishing widely on a kind of New Age reworking of Rajneesh's version of Neo-Tantra.[22] Thus, her best-selling *Art of Sexual Ecstasy* praises Osho's work as "the most comprehensive and far-reaching perspective on a modern approach to Tantra for Western lovers."[23]

Despite Tantra's esoteric and typically "un-erotic" origins in South Asian history, now largely because of Osho, it is almost universally associated with sexual pleasure and social-political liberation. Uniquely situated as the exotic Indian guru speaking to a modern European and American audience, Osho-Rajneesh was the key link in the transmission of Tantra to the West in the years immediately following the sexual revolution.

TRADEMARK, COPYRIGHT, AND "SPIRITUAL PROPERTY" IN THE TWENTY-FIRST CENTURY

A third aspect of the legacy of Osho-Rajneesh is the complex question of religion and intellectual property, which, as we saw in chapter 6, has become a volatile and central issue in twenty-first-century spiritual life. This issue is linked to what David Harvey calls the "commodification of everything," in which, under neoliberal economics and policies, every form of exotic cultural knowledge, every yogic posture, and every spiritual technique has become a commodity and is claimed as exclusive property by a multinational corporation (or conversely, defended by an indigenous population or nation-state). And this devleopment in turn has led to a backlash on the part of various groups who argue that cultural and spiritual knowledge cannot be commodified or turned into property that can be trademarked or copyrighted.[24]

Osho-Rajneesh is a particularly acute example of this complex problem, in large part because he was himself so ambivalent and contradictory on the subject. On the one hand, as we have seen throughout this book, he was clearly one of the first and most ambitious global gurus to begin using the language of business, commerce, and the marketplace to promote his spiritual ideas. Not only was Osho-Rajneesh explicit about his embrace of capitalism, but he flaunted it in an outrageous manner, as in his absurd display of Rolls-Royces. Not surprisingly, trademarks and copyrights were added to his works and ideas from quite early on in the movement. On the other hand, Osho-Rajneesh also made statements that attacked the very idea of spiritual ideas becoming trademarked or copyrighted (particularly in his critique of rival practices such as TM). All of this has left parties on both sides of the debate with ample evidence to support their particular positions.

[margin note: want his ideas to spread more than make money]

However this specific debate over Osho's trademarks and copyrights plays out, it clearly raises a profound set of questions concerning spirituality and intellectual property that will likely affect every religious community in the twenty-first century. Can—or should—religious ideas and practices be treated like commodities, subject to intellectual property law? Are they simply goods that can be bought, sold, traded, and legally protected like any others? Or are they in fact examples of human creations that never were and probably never should be treated as commodities? Is Harvey correct when he argues that "the commodification of sexuality, culture, history, heritage . . . the extraction of monopoly rents from originality, authenticity, and uniqueness (of works or art, for example)—these all amount to putting a price on things that were never actually produced as commodities"?[25]

If we accept the former position—that spiritual ideas and practices should be treated as intellectual property like anything else in the marketplace, and, as such, can be trademarked or copyrighted—then where does that really end? As the National Arbitration Forum itself asked, could one by extension also claim intellectual property rights to aspects of Christianity or Buddhism?[26]Could one claim "Buddha" or "Christ" as a registered trademark? Could one copyright a Buddhist meditation technique or the Latin Mass?

Conversely, if we accept the latter position—that spiritual ideas and practices cannot be treated as intellectual property—are we perhaps returning to the idea that religion is somehow special, irreducible, or sui generis (of its own origin), transcending the messy realm of history, economics, and politics? This is of course the position for which an entire generation of scholars of religion—led by Mircea Eliade, America's most important scholar of religion in the twentieth century—was widely criticized and is today often dismissed.[27]

Or is there yet another way of thinking about spiritual ideas that would avoid the pitfalls of both neoliberal commodification and a nostalgic appeal to a transcendent, irreducible sacred? This may well prove to be one of the most pressing and increasingly common questions of the twenty-first century, as more and more religious groups—old and new alike—are drawn into the logic of the global capitalist marketplace and increasingly resort to the same legal arguments as do multinational corporations.

"KARMA COLA" OR POSTNATIONAL SODALITY? RETHINKING RELIGION, GLOBALIZATION, AND CAPITALISM

Finally, perhaps the most complex and interesting legacy that Osho-Rajneesh has left us is precisely his importance for rethinking the relations between religion, globalization, and capitalism in the twenty-first century. As I have argued throughout this book, the Osho-Rajneesh movement poses a significant challenge to most of the usual narratives of globalization. What we see in this movement is not simply a kind of Asian response to Western globalization but rather the emergence of multiple new nodes or "hyphal knots" in the complex mycelial networks of modern capitalism and spirituality. Emerging first in Pune, then in England and Europe, then in the United States, and then again in South Asia, these hyphal knots were key points of convergence in the new networks of tourism, commerce, spirituality, and also legal disputes that began to proliferate from the 1960s onward.

Most importantly, the Osho-Rajneesh movement raises a central question about religion and spirituality in the context of the new global economic regime that has been variously called late capitalism, deterritorialized capitalism, and neoliberalism. Can a truly "postnational" movement emerge in twenty-first-century global society, or will any such movement that attempts to transcend the boundaries of the modern nation-state inevitably become co-opted once again into the late capitalist marketplace and the hegemony of neoliberalism?

To date, most journalists and scholars looking at the Osho-Rajneesh movement have answered this question strongly in the negative. Already in 1994, the Indian writer Gita Mehta offered a fierce critique of the New Age appropriation and transformation of Indian spirituality, targeting Osho-Rajneesh's brand of Westernized mysticism as a particularly egregious example of the "marketing of the mystic East." Here she quotes Osho-Rajneesh as he describes his ideal of the *neo-sannyasin:* "My followers have no time. So I give them instant salvation. I turn them into neo-sanyasis." And yet, Mehta argues, the ordinary Hindu is likely to be deeply offended by this appropriation and radical transformation of traditional Indian ideas for a Western audience—and rightly so:

> When he comes upon two light-skinned strangers in the bazaar, sharing a chillum of hashish while they fondle each other, [he] is apt to think that the strangers are wearing the sadhu's orange robes of renunciation as an act of aggressive mockery. . . .
> It would appear that when East meets West all you get is the neo-Sanyasi, the instant Nirvana. . . . You have the Karma, we'll take the Coca-Cola, a metaphysical soft drink for a physical one.[28]

Others, such as Carrette and King, are even more pointed in their critique of Osho-Rajneesh. In their view, he is not only the most blatant example of the marketing of the mystic Orient, but also a clear case of the co-option of spirituality by the logic of neoliberalism, transforming even the most radical elements of religious thought into convenient commodities to be purchased by middle-class Western consumers to suit their busy lifestyle:

> Osho provided the perfect 1980s repackaging of "Asian" spirituality themes from the counter-cultural alternative scene of the 1960s. This time, however, there is no requirement to drop out to overcome your desires. Consumption and pursuit of wealth become techniques for attaining enlightenment itself.

This message was exactly what a generation of ex-hippies who now worked in the boardrooms of corporate America in the acquisitive Eighties wanted to hear. . . . The potentially radical elements in Rajneesh's philosophy are undermined by his privatized blend of western psychological discourse and Asian wisdom. The result . . . is a domestication of Asian philosophies according to the ideologies of contemporary consumerism.[29]

While it is not difficult to see why many critics would arrive at this cynical interpretation of Osho-Rajneesh, I would argue that it is at best a partial reading of this complex movement and its transnational history.[30] Even with its flagrant embrace of consumerism, the Osho-Rajneesh community was also in many respects an incredibly innovative, progressive, and creative attempt to create a radically new sort of postnational sodality, a new form of community even within the expanding networks of giant multinational corporations. As Rajneesh himself put it in 1985, this was in a sense his entire life's work:

I am not an American, and I am proud that I am not an American. Nor am I an Indian—then who am I? I am proud that I am nobody. That is where my whole journey has brought me—to nobodiness, to homelessness, to nothingness. . . . I have no religion, no country, no home. The whole world is mine.
   I am the first citizen of the universe. I am crazy. I could start issuing passports for universal citizenship.[31]

Despite its excesses and controversies, the early ashram in Pune during the 1970s was a remarkable space where a guru and his youthful followers were experimenting with a huge variety of spiritual, psychological, and sexual techniques, all designed to achieve a kind of radical freedom from the mainstream social, religious, and political regimes. The experiment in Oregon was an even more ambitious attempt to put this ideal into practice, through the creation of an entire utopian city, complete with organic farming, reclamation of land and water resources, and a whole new ideal of the integrated "Zorba the Buddha" spiritual yet physical lifestyle. As one *sannyasin,* Swami Anand Narayan, aptly notes, most Americans today only remember the outrageous wealth and the spectacular collapse of Rajneeshpuram, forgetting that this was also an incredibly progressive and briefly successful communal experiment: "Even today, people may not remember 'the Ranch' with its incredible vitality. . . . They may not remember the innovative agricultural project that reclaimed thousands of acres of semi-arid over grazed land in the middle of Oregon. But they can't forget those Rolls-Royces."[32] Finally, from the 1980s onward, the Osho-Rajneesh movement would spawn a whole new set of alternative sodalities around the world, including not only the new community in Pune but also rival communities in New Delhi, the Bay Area, and Germany, as well as a decentralized network of Osho teachers and practitioners now scattered worldwide. As Swami Satya Vedant put it in an interview in December 2013,

> Osho's vision and work show that we must now have a trans-political vision. . . . Osho brings that wisdom which is critical for our survival as a human species. He rebelled against the past so that the new can be created. His vision is that of a New Man/New Woman—one who learns to live with Awareness and reverence for Life. . . . Meditation and Love are the two wings which can raise his/her Consciousness higher into creating a world of integrity, creativity and collective wellbeing.[33]

While these utopian ventures were ultimately failures by most measures, they did at least articulate and partially embody many remarkable new ways of imagining human communities. At least in some respects, the Pune and Oregon experiments had much in common with the sort of "revolutionary humanism" recently advocated by Harvey in his critique of modern capitalism and his call for a radically new way of imagining social and economic relations. Harvey argues:

> There is . . . a crying need to articulate a secular *revolutionary* humanism that can ally with those religious-based humanisms (most clearly articulated in both Protestant and Catholic versions of the theology of liberation as well as in cognate movements within Hindu, Islamic, Jewish and indigenous religious culture) to counter alienation in its many forms and to radically challenge the world from its capitalist ways.[34]

The Rajneesh community did seem to achieve at least *some* of the ideals imagined by Harvey. Particularly during the early Oregon phase (before things got completely out of hand) we can see clear examples of several of Harvey's ideals for a revolutionary humanism, which would encourage "the greatest possible diversification . . . in ways of living and being, of social relations and relations to nature . . . within territorial associations, communes and collectives."[35] With its remarkably innovative use of land and water resources, its experiments in organic farming, and its massive program of recycling, the early Oregon community also embodied Harvey's ideal that "the appropriation and production of natural forces for human needs should proceed . . . with the maximum regard for the protection of ecosystems, maximum attention paid to the recycling of nutrients, energy and physical matter."[36]

Yet as we have seen repeatedly throughout this book, these more utopian and communal aspects of the Osho-Rajneesh movement always existed in tension with its simultaneous embrace of capitalism and consumerism. And in many ways, it was the latter that undid the former. That is, in the cases of the first Pune ashram, the Oregon experiment, and the new Pune resort, it has consistently been the movement's aggressive embrace of capitalism that has led to its most serious problems with local communities, government agencies, law enforcement, and its own members.

Thus, if it would be a mistake to dismiss the Osho-Rajneesh movement as a mere neoliberal commodification of spirituality, it would be no less a mistake to celebrate it naïvely as a postnational utopia. As Daniel Franklin Pilario aptly observes, Appadurai's ideal of the postnational movement perhaps does not fully take account of the often "asymmetric power present in these global disruptions."[37] There are, after all, massive differentials of wealth and poverty in the global economy, and there are real monetary and political constraints that determine who can and cannot participate in such postnational movements: "Personal and communal identities do not just move as freely in the social space, just as most people could not be jetsetters. Their movement is largely dictated by their social and economic locations. . . . When the cultural discourse on difference displaces itself into the economic, what is concealed behind this diversity is the asymmetry brought about by the march of global capital."[38] As it grew from an eclectic hippie ashram in 1970s India to a massive multinational network of corporate entities in the 1980s to the new international luxury resort of the contemporary Osho center, the Osho-Rajneesh movement has increasingly embodied this growing asymmetry in the march of global capital. Never exactly a religion for the poor, the current Osho-Rajneesh movement has become even more a spirituality designed for well-educated, middle- and upper-class consumers—in other words, for people with ready access to capital and the ability to travel freely across national boundaries. Meanwhile, even as affluent foreign visitors spend hundreds or thousands of dollars to participate in spiritual exercises at the new Osho resort, just outside the gate ordinary Indians on the streets of Pune continue to struggle with massive poverty and economic disparities in the new global economy.

In this sense, the Osho-Rajneesh movement embodies and perhaps epitomizes *both* the promise *and* the tensions of the emerging "postnational" world—that is, *both* the promise of new kinds of community that transcend the confines of national boundaries *and* the recurring tendency of these new forms to become co-opted once again into the logic of the marketplace and the multinational corporation. Indeed, it is a particularly acute example of the "split character of globalization": "On the one hand, it is in and through the imagination that modern citizens are disciplined and controlled—by states, markets and other powerful interests. But it is also the faculty through which collective patterns of dissent and new designs for collective life emerge."[39] The Osho-Rajneesh movement was an ambitious attempt to create radically new and imaginative forms of collective life; and yet, these collective experiments were consistently accompanied by new forms of discipline and control in a late capitalist context.

In sum, if the Osho-Rajneesh movement embodies the "spiritual logic of late capitalism" (to adapt a phrase from Fredric Jameson), it also embodies the deep "spiritual contradictions of capitalism" (to adapt a phrase from David Harvey).[40] Openly proclaiming itself the first movement to have "synthesized religion and capitalism," this was a remarkable sort of *hyphal knot* in the complex flows of spirituality and economics during the late twentieth and early twenty-first centuries. As such, it really challenges not only most current models of globalization but also most conventional models of charismatic religious movements. Early sociologists such as Max Weber had assumed that charismatic religions and capitalist bureaucratic organizations were fundamentally incompatible and irreconcilable. "In its economic substructure," Weber suggested, " . . . charismatic domination is the very opposite of bureaucratic domination . . . bureaucratic domination depends upon regular income . . . and a money economy. . . . Frequently charisma deliberately shuns the possession of money and of pecuniary income. . . . Charisma rejects all rational economic conduct."[41] And yet, as we have seen, the Osho-Rajneesh movement combined a form of charismatic and even ecstatic spirituality with the most elaborate apparatus of the late capitalist corporation. In this sense, it not only embodies a kind of "charismatic variant of a multinational corporation,"[42] but also what we might call a sort of re-enchanted capitalism. In the deterritorialized context of late capitalism, the fluid, flexible, ecstatic quality of charisma is by no means incompatible with the marketplace; on the contrary, it may even be the very epitome of an ever more volatile, fluid, and flexible global economy.[43]

This sort of "re-enchanted capitalism" is by no means unique to the Osho-Rajneesh movement. If anything, it would appear to be a growing trend throughout twenty-first-century religious life, from the "prosperity Gospel" espoused by globally popular televangelists such as Joel

Osteen,[44] to tremendously profitable New Age channelers such as JZ Knight, to huge multinational spiritual corporations such as the Church of Scientology.[45] Yet the Osho-Rajneesh movement is particularly interesting insofar as it was the first group to not only articulate this merger of spirituality and business but also to embrace and even celebrate it as a central "Zorba the Buddha" ideal.

At the same time, however, the Osho-Rajneesh movement also clearly epitomizes some of the deepest contradictions in global capitalism as it has evolved over the last several decades. As we have seen repeatedly in the history of the movement from Pune of the 1970s to America of the 1980s to India of the 1990s and 2000s, the Osho-Rajneesh community has retraced the "boom and bust" trajectory of global capitalism itself. From the collapse of the first Pune experiment and the flight to Oregon, the catastrophic implosion of Rajneeshpuram and the return to India, to the latest controversies surrounding the new Pune resort, the narrative of this community is the same narrative of "creative destruction" and "capital flight" that characterizes global capitalism more broadly: "The history of capital is rife with stories of localized booms and crashes in which the contradiction between fixed and circulating capital, between fixity and motion, is strongly implicated. This is the world where capital as a force of creative destruction becomes more visible."[46]

As we saw most clearly in chapters 3 and 4, moreover, the Osho-Rajneesh movement also embodies a deep tension between the idealistic rhetoric of freedom and the harsh realities of authoritarianism that are embedded in contemporary capitalism. As Harvey suggests, the ideal of individual freedom and radical liberty espoused by neoliberalism is often in profound tension with the growing authoritarianism of huge multinational corporations, which rarely offer much actual freedom to ordinary employees or citizens.[47] Perhaps nowhere was this deep tension more apparent than in the Rajneeshpuram experiment in Oregon. By 1985, Rajneesh's ideal of radical individualism, nonconformity, and spiritual freedom was quite obviously in tension with the brutal reality of a huge multinational corporation and a kind of paranoid, authoritarian police state under Sheela's regime. By 2014, the new Osho resort had also become enmeshed in an incredibly complex web of legal battles surrounding trademark, copyright, property, and virtually everything else in a new age of intellectual property disputes.

Thus, the Osho-Rajneesh movement is best understood not as a curious by-product of globalization and neoliberal economic policies;

rather, it is quite literally an embodiment and a sensuous incarnation of these expanding networks, with all their complexities, ambiguities, and contradictions. As a hyphal knot in which spirituality and commerce intersect, this is a movement that expresses—often in exaggerated form—the ambivalent nature of global capitalism itself: its most utopian ambitions, its most outrageous excesses, its most surprising successes, and its most catastrophic failures.

Notes

PREFACE

Epigraph: Osho, *Autobiography of a Spiritually Incorrect Mystic* (New York: St. Martin's Press, 2000), 171.

INTRODUCTION

Epigraphs: Bhagwan Shree Rajneesh, *Zorba the Buddha: Intimate Dialogues with Disciples* (Antelope, OR: Rajneesh Foundation International, 1982), 15; Mike Featherstone, *Consumer Culture and Postmodernism* (London: Sage, 2007), 110–11.

    1. "Guru and Ex-Secretary Trade Charges," *Associated Press*, November 4, 1985, www.apnewsarchive.com/1985/Guru-and-Ex-Secretary-Trade-Charges /id-7f95e884efe4e20fd12c2fc3e362ffa5.

    2. James S. Gordon, *The Golden Guru: The Strange Journey of Bhagwan Shree Rajneesh* (New York: Viking Penguin, 1987), 117. For the best scholarly treatment of this period in Oregon, see Lewis F. Carter, *Charisma and Control in Rajneeshpuram: The Role of Shared Values in the Creation of a Community* (Cambridge: Cambridge University Press, 1990). For a more popular documentary, see Oregon Public Broadcasting, "Rajneeshpuram," *Oregon Experience*, November 19, 2012, www.opb.org/television/programs/oregonexperience /segment/rajneeshpuram/.

    3. Les Zaitz, "25 Years after Rajneeshee Commune Collapses Truth Spills Out," *The Oregonian*, April 15, 2011, www.oregonlive.com/rajneesh/index .ssf/2011/04/part_one_it_was_worse_than_we.html. See also Win McCormack, ed., *The Rajneesh Chronicles: The True Story of the Cult That Unleashed the First Act of Bioterrorism on U.S. Soil* (Portland, OR: Tin House Books, 2010).

4. Scott Keys, "A Strange but True Tale of Voter Fraud and Bioterrorism," *The Atlantic,* June 10, 2014, www.theatlantic.com/politics/archive/2014/06 /a-strange-but-true-tale-of-voter-fraud-and-bioterrorism/372445/.

5. "Learn: Osho Multiversity," Osho.com, 2014, www.osho.com/learn.

6. See Rajneesh's interview with Jeff McMullen, "The Orange People," *60 Minutes* (Australia), July 26, 1985, video.au.msn.com/watch/video/the-orange-people/x101q8c: "My people are rich. In fact, only the very rich, educated, intelligent, cultured can understand what I'm saying. Beggars cannot come to me. Poor people cannot come to me. . . . I am the rich man's guru. . . . My conception of a beautiful flowering being is not that of austerity. It is of luxury."

7. See Osho, *Autobiography of a Spiritually Incorrect Mystic* (New York: St. Martin's Press, 2000), 207–19.

8. The few academic works on Osho-Rajneesh include Carter, *Charisma and Control;* Susan Palmer, *Moon Sisters, Krishna Mothers, Rajneesh Lovers: Women's Roles in New Religions* (Syracuse, NY: Syracuse University Press, 1996); Corinne Dempsey, *Bringing the Sacred Down to Earth: Adventures in Comparative Religion* (New York: Oxford University Press, 2011), 77–108; Judith M. Fox, *Osho-Rajneesh—Studies in Contemporary Religion* (Salt Lake City: Signature Books, 2002); Hugh B. Urban, "Zorba the Buddha: Capitalism, Charisma, and the Cult of Bhagwan Shree Rajneesh," *Religion* 26 (1998): 161–82; Urban, "Osho, From Sex Guru to Guru of the Rich: The Spiritual Logic of Late Capitalism," in *Gurus in America,* ed. Thomas A. Forsthoefel and Cynthia Ann Humes (Albany: SUNY Press, 2005), 169–92; Urban, "Zorba the Buddha: The Body, Sacred Space, and Late Capitalism in the Osho International Meditation Resort," *Southeast Review of Asian Studies* 35 (2013): 32–49.

9. See, among others Hugh Milne, *Bhagwan: The God That Failed* (New York: St. Martin's Press, 1986); Kate Strelley, *The Ultimate Game: The Rise and Fall of Bhagwan Shree Rajneesh* (San Francisco: Harper & Row, 1987); Tim Guest, *My Life in Orange: : Growing up with the Guru* (New York: Harcourt, 2004).

10. I use the phrase "history of religions" primarily in the more critical sense outlined by Bruce Lincoln, "Theses on Method," *Method and Theory in the Study of Religion* 8 (1996): 225–27. As Lincoln suggests, the task of the historian of religions is to analyze the temporal, material, social, and political aspects of those phenomena that are claimed to be transcendent and eternal: "To practice history of religions . . . is to insist on discussing the temporal, contextual, situated, interested, human, and material dimensions of those discourses, practices, and institutions that characteristically represent themselves as eternal, transcendent, spiritual, and divine." In this sense, my approach here is similar to historians of religions such as Steven Wasserstrom, *Religion after Religion: Gershom Scholem, Mircea Eliade, and Henry Corbin at Eranos* (Princeton, NJ: Princeton University Press, 1999); Tomoko Masuzawa, *The Invention of World Religions: Or How European Universalism Was Preserved in the Language of Difference* (Chicago: University of Chicago Press, 2005); Russell McCutcheon, *Manufacturing Religion: The Discourse on Sui Generis Religion and the Politics of Nostalgia* (New York: Oxford University Press, 1997); Ivan Strenski, *Why Politics Can't Be Freed from Religion* (Malden, MA: Wiley-Blackwell, 2010).

11. See Urban, "Osho"; Urban, "Zorba the Buddha"; and Urban, *Tantra: Sex, Secrecy, Politics, and Power in the Study of Religion* (Berkeley, CA: University of California Press, 2003).

12. Paul Heelas, *Religion, Modernity, and Postmodernity* (Malden, MA: Wiley-Blackwell, 1998).

13. Fredric Jameson, *Postmodernism: Or, the Cultural Logic of Late Capitalism* (Durham, NC: Duke University Press, 1991). See Urban, "Osho"; and Urban, *Tantra*, chap. 6. This point was also picked up by none other than Slavoj Žižek, *Living in the End Times* (London: Verso, 2011), 7: "[Tantra unites] spirituality and earthly pleasures, transcendence and material benefits, divine experience and unlimited shopping. It propagates the transgression of all rules, the violation of all taboos, instant gratification as the path to enlightenment."

14. See, for example, Mark Juergensmeyer, *Terror in the Mind of God: The Global Rise of Religious Violence* (Berkeley: University of California Press, 2003); Juergensmeyer, *Global Rebellion: Religious Challenges to the Secular State, from Christian Militias to al Qaeda* (Berkeley: University of California Press, 2008); Bruce Lincoln, *Holy Terrors: Thinking about Religion after September 11* (Chicago: University of Chicago Press, 2006); Scott M. Thomas, *The Global Resurgence of Religion and the Transformation of International Relations: The Struggle for the Soul of the Twenty-first Century* (New York: Palgrave Macmillan, 2005); Benjamin Barber, *Jihad vs. McWorld: Terrorism's Challenge to Democracy* (New York: Ballantine, 1996).

15. See, for example, Donald E. Miller, *Global Pentecostalism: The New Face of Christian Social Engagement* (Berkeley: University of California Press, 2007); Donald E. Miller, Kimon H. Sargeant, and Richard Flory, eds., *Spirit and Power: The Growth and Global Impact of Pentecostalism* (New York: Oxford University Press, 2004); Candy Gunther Brown, *Global Pentecostalism and Charismatic Healing* (New York: Oxford University Press, 2011); Ian Linden, *Global Catholicism: Diversity and Change since Vatican II* (New York: Columbia University Press, 2009); Philip Jenkins, *The Next Christendom: The Coming of Global Christianity* (New York: Oxford University Press, 2011).

16. Frank Lechner and John Boli, eds., *The Globalization Reader* (Malden, MA: Wiley-Blackwell, 2011), 386–425.

17. See Amanda Lucia, *Reflections of Amma: Devotees in a Global Embrace* (Berkeley: University of California Press, 2014); Tulasi Srinivas, *Winged Faith: Rethinking Globalization and Religious Pluralism through the Sathya Sai Movement* (New York: Columbia University Press, 2010); Smriti Srinivas, *In the Presence of Sai Baba: Body, City, and Memory in a Global Religious Movement* (Leiden: Brill, 2008); Lise McKean, *Divine Enterprise: Gurus and the Hindu Nationalist Movement* (Chicago: University of Chicago Press, 1996).

18. Srinivas, *Winged Faith*, 7.

19. Arjun Appadurai, *Modernity at Large: Cultural Dimensions of Globalization* (Minneapolis: University of Minnesota Press, 1996), 22.

20. Appadurai, *Modernity at Large*, 22–23, 158.

21. See Paul Stamets, *Mycelium Running* (Berkeley, CA: Ten Speed Press, 2005); "Thinking Like a Forest—Suzanne Simard," *To the Best of Our Knowledge,* May 5, 2011, www.ttbook.org/book/secret-language-plants. In mycological

terms, the formation of a *hyphal knot* is one key moment in the complex life-cycle of *mycelia,* which are the complex networks of fungi that pervade virtually all land masses on earth that support life. Each *mycelium* consists of millions of tiny, branching threads of cells called *hyphae,* many of which form vital symbiotic (or *mycorrhizal*) relationships with the roots of vascular plants, helping the latter to find and take up key nutrients from the soil. Under a single footstep there can be hundreds of miles of such *mycorrhizal* networks, forming an intricate, interconnected, living web throughout the ecosystem. More recently, we have learned that these fungal networks not only play a critical role in the *circulation of nutrients* between plants throughout an ecosystem, helping send resources (such as carbon, nitrogen, water, phosphorus) back and forth from one tree to another; but they also help *communicate* between plants, for example, by transmitting defense signals from tree to tree. When conditions are right, the *mycelium* will condense to form a *hyphal knot,* which in turn becomes a primordium or "pinhead" that will eventually grow into a mushroom, the fruiting body of the organism. When mature, the mushroom will release its spores, which then germinate under the soil and form new *hyphae,* to start the whole process all over again.

22. On this point, see Srinivas, *Winged Faith;* Srinivas, *In the Presence of Sai Baba;* Lucia, *Reflections of Amma;* McKean, *Divine Enterprise.*

23. Anthony Giddens, introduction to Max Weber, *The Protestant Ethic and the Spirit of Capitalism* (New York: Routledge, 2005), xix.

24. See Lucia, *Reflections of Amma,* 13, 231.

25. See Hermann Kulke and Günter-Dietz Sontheimer, eds., *Hinduism Reconsidered* (New Delhi: Manohar, 1991); Urban, *Tantra,* chap. 1.

26. Wilhelm Halbfass, *India and Europe: An Essay in Understanding* (Albany: SUNY Press, 1988), 228.

27. Swami Vivekananda, *The Complete Works of Swami Vivekananda* (Calcutta: Advaita Ashram, 1983), 3:189.

28. Vivekananda, *Complete Works,* 3:276–77. See also Sikata Banerjee, *Muscular Nationalism: Gender, Violence, and Empire in India and Ireland* (New York: NYU Press, 2012), 59; Halbfass, *India and Europe,*231.

29. Vivekananda, *Complete Works,* 5:67.

30. Halbfass, *India and Europe,* 232.

31. Vivekananda, letter to Swami Ramakrishnananda, March 19, 1894, in *Complete Works,* 6:326.

32. Robert S. Ellwood and Harry B. Partin, *Religious and Spiritual Groups in Modern America* (Englewood Cliffs, NJ: Prentice Hall, 1988), 194.

33. Philip Goldberg, *American Veda: How Indian Spirituality Changed the West* (New York: Harmony, 2010), 7.

34. On the idea of the "exotic Orient," see Urban, *Tantra;* Véronique Altglas, *From Yoga to Kabbalah: Religious Exoticism and the Logics of Bricolage* (New York: Oxford University Press, 2014).

35. See Robert S. Ellwood, *The Sixties Spiritual Awakening* (New Brunswick, NJ: Rutgers University Press, 1994), 143; E. Burke Rochford, *Hare Krishna Transformed* (New York: New York University Press, 2007), 12.

36. See Thomas Tweed and Stephen Prothero, eds., *Asian Religions in America: A Documentary History* (New York: Oxford University Press, 1999), 244–46.

37. Srinivas, *Winged Faith*, 7.

38. Srinivas, *Winged Faith*, 29; "Rather than assuming the West is central to the project of contemporary modernity and identity politics, the Sathya Sai movement encourages us to question the essentializing tropes of Euro-modernity and the truth claims vested within. In a sense, then, it allows for a new postulation of non-Euro-American pluralism and its ideological ally, cosmopolitanism, a cosmopolitanism from the margins of the global network" (326).

39. Lucia, *Reflections of Amma*, 8; on Bernard, see Robert Love, *The Great Oom: The Improbable Birth of Yoga in America* (New York: Viking, 2010).

40. Appadurai, *Modernity at Large*, 19, 8.

41. Rajneesh, *The Secret* (1978), quoted in Osho, *Autobiography*, 213.

42. See Ernest Mandel, *Late Capitalism* (London: Humanities Press, 1975); Jameson, *Postmodernism*; David Harvey, *The Condition of Postmodernity* (London: Blackwell, 1989).

43. Harvey, *Condition of Postmodernity*, 293.

44. Featherstone, *Consumer Culture and Postmodernism*, 110–11; see Jameson, "Postmodernism, or the Cultural Logic of Late Capitalism," *New Left Review* 146 (1984): 53–93.

45. Marshall Sahlins, *Waiting for Foucault, Still* (Chicago: Prickly Pear Press, 2002), 59.

46. As Sherry Ortner suggests, the terms "late capitalism" and "neoliberalism" both roughly describe the same phenomenon, a general shift in global capitalism that took place between the 1940s and 1970s. However, each narrates this shift in a slightly different way, the latter much more pessimistically: "If late capitalism and neoliberalism are two names for more or less the same set of changes in the capitalist system, the terminological shift from the first to the second signals . . . a change in the story or narrative in which the changes are embedded. The phrase 'late capitalism' was embedded in a narrative of 'globalization,' a concept that had positive as well as negative aspects, while 'neoliberalism' . . . is embedded in a much darker narrative, a story of a crusade powered by ideology and/or greed, to tilt the world political economy even more in favor of the dominant classes and nations." Ortner, "On Neoliberalism," *Anthropology of This Century* 1 (2011), http://aotcpress.com/articles/neoliberalism/.

47. David Harvey, *A Brief History of Neoliberalism* (Oxford: Oxford University Press, 2007), 26. See Manfred B. Steger and Ravi K. Roy, *Neoliberalism: A Very Short Introduction* (New York: Oxford University Press, 2010), 12: "A neoliberal governmentality is rooted in entrepreneurial values such as competitiveness, self-interest, and decentralization. It celebrates individual empowerment and the devolution of central state power to smaller localized units. Such a neoliberal mode of governance adopts the self-regulating free market as *the* model for proper government."

48. Harvey, *Brief History*, 165.

49. Jeremy Carrette and Richard King, *Selling Spirituality: The Silent Takeover of Religion* (New York: Routledge, 2004), 1. See also Andrea Jain, *Selling Yoga: From Counterculture to Pop Culture* (New York: Oxford University Press, 2014).

50. See R. Laurence Moore, *Selling God: American Religion in the Marketplace of Culture* (New York: Oxford University Press, 1994); John M. Giggie and Diane Winston, eds., *Faith in the Market: Religion and the Rise of Urban Commercial Culture* (New Brunswick, NJ: Rutgers University Press, 2002), 4.

51. See Steger and Roy, *Neoliberalism.*

52. Rajneesh, *The Secret of Secrets,* quoted in Osho, *Autobiography,* 242–43.

53. Ma Anand Sheela, interview with Australian television, 1985, www.youtube.com/watch?v = 9ib8MdHT61k. See "An Affair to Remember," *Open,* February 9, 2013, www.openthemagazine.com/article/international/an-affair-to-remember.

54. Harvey, *Condition of Postmodernity,* 44. See also Stephen Best and Douglas Kellner, *Postmodern Theory* (New York: Guilford Press, 1991).

55. Terry Eagleton, "Awakening from Modernity," *Times Literary Supplement,* February 20, 1987, 194.

56. Jameson, *Postmodernism;* Harvey, *Condition of Postmodernity,* 14.

57. Osho, *Autobiography,* 120. See Bhagwan Shree Rajneesh, *The Book of Wisdom: Discourses on Atisha's Seven Points of Mind Training* (Pune: Rajneesh Foundation, 1983), 151: "To choose me in my totality you will have to live a very inconsistent life—one moment this, another moment that. But that is my whole message. If one really wants to live life in all its richness, one has to be inconsistent, how to be *consistently* inconsistent, how to be able to move from one extreme to another . . . sometimes making love and sometimes meditating."

58. Bhagwan Shree Rajneesh, "The Greatest Joke There Is," *Bhagwan* 8 (1984): 24. See Osho, *Autobiography,* 152: "I have to tell jokes because . . . you are all religious people. You tend to be serious. I have to tickle you so that sometimes you forget your religiousness, you forget all your philosophies, theories, systems, and you fall down to earth . . . seriousness is a cancerous growth."

59. Osho, *Autobiography,* 151.

60. Weber, *Protestant Ethic and the Spirit of Capitalism,* 36, 67. See Stephen Kalberg, ed., *Max Weber: Readings and Commentary on Modernity* (Malden, MA: Wiley-Blackwell, 2005), 119.

61. Bhagwan Shree Rajneesh, *Beware of Socialism* (Rajneeshpuram, OR: Rajneesh Foundation International, 1984), 31.

62. See Carter, *Charisma and Control,* 72–78; Urban, "Osho."

63. Bryan S. Turner, *Regulating Bodies: Essays in Medical Sociology* (New York: Routledge, 1992), 47.

64. Osho, "I Am a Spiritual Playboy," Osho International, 2013. www.youtube.com/watch?v = TsyVpN-fOUA.

65. See Urban, *Tantra,* chap. 6; Urban, "Zorba the Buddha"; and chapter 3 below.

66. Osho, *Tantra: The Supreme Understanding* (London: Watkins, 2009), 98–99.

67. Rajneesh, interview with McMullen, "Orange People."

68. H. H. Gerth and C. Wright Mills, eds., *From Max Weber: Essays in Sociology* (New York: Oxford University Press, 1958), 246–47. See Urban, "Zorba the Buddha."

69. See Carter, *Charisma and Control*, 78; Urban, "Zorba the Buddha"; and chapter 4 and the conclusion below.

70. The few exceptions include Carter, *Charisma and Control*; Fox, *Osho-Rajneesh*; Urban, "Osho."

71. Among many others, see Vasant Joshi, *The Luminous Rebel: Story of a Maverick Mystic* (New Delhi: Wisdom Tree Publishing, 2010); Swami Gyan Bhed, *The Rebellious Enlightened Master: Osho* (Delhi: Diamond Pocket Books, 2006); Jack Allanach, *Osho, India, and Me: A Tale of Sexual and Spiritual Transformation* (New Delhi: Niyogi Books, 2013).

72. See Carrette and King, *Selling Spirituality*, 153–58; Bob Mullan, *Life as Laughter: Following Bhagwan Shree Rajneesh* (Boston: Routledge & Kegan Paul, 1983).

73. See "Harvest Bountiful at Rancho Rajneesh," *Sunday Oregonian*, April 22, 1984, D1; Scott Fagerstrom, "Guru's City Booms in the Desert," *The Columbian*, December 18, 1983, A1.

74. See Arjun Appadurai, ed., *Globalization* (Durham, NC: Duke University Press, 2001), 6.

75. See the bibliography for an extensive list of Osho-Rajneesh's writings, along with magazines, videos, and other material. Osho-Rajneesh's works are also all available electronically through the Osho International Foundation: "Osho Library," Osho.com, 2015, www.osho.com/iosho/library/the-books. The few good scholarly books include Carter, *Charisma and Control*; Fox, *Osho-Rajneesh*; Palmer, *Moon Sisters*; and Dempsey, *Bringing the Sacred Down to Earth*, chap. 3.

76. The University of Oregon Special Collections contain four large sets of materials: Rajneesh Artifacts and Ephemera Collection, 1981–2004, Coll. 275; Rajneesh Legal Services Corporation Records, Coll. 260; Rajneeshpuram, Accession #06–057; and Roshani Shay/Rajneesh Collection, Coll. 310. The Oregon Historical Society contains three collections: Max Gutierrez Collection, Org. Lot 506; Oregon Rajneesh History Collection, MSS 6030; and Papers Relating to Rajneeshpuram, 1982–1985, Religion MSS 1517.

77. Bryan R. Wilson, *Apostates and New Religious Movements* (Los Angeles: Freedom Publishing, 1994), 4.

78. Hugh B. Urban, introduction to *The Church of Scientology: A History of a New Religion* (Princeton, NJ: Princeton University Press, 2011).

79. Lewis F. Carter, "Carriers of Tales: On Assessing Credibility of Apostate and Other Outsider Accounts of Religious Practices," in *The Politics of Religious Apostasy: The Role of Apostates in the Transformation of Religious Movements*, ed. David Bromley (London: Praeger, 1998), 222–23.

80. See, for example, Timothy D. Lytton, *Holding Bishops Accountable: How Lawsuits Helped the Catholic Church Confront Clergy Sexual Abuse* (Cambridge, MA: Harvard University Press 2008).

81. See Rebecca Moore, *Understanding Jonestown and Peoples Temple* (London: Praeger, 2009).

82. Srinivas, *Winged Faith*, 47.

83. Appadurai, *Globalization*, 6.

CHAPTER I. RAJNEESH AND INDIA AFTER INDEPENDENCE

Epigraphs: Rajneesh, quoted in Vasant Joshi, *The Awakened One: The Life and Work of Bhagwan Shree Rajneesh* (San Francisco: Harper & Row, 1982), 1; Tom Robbins, quoted in "Friends of Osho," Osho.com, 2014, www.osho.com/read/osho/friends-of-osho.

1. Vasant Joshi, *The Awakened One: The Life and Work of Bhagwan Shree Rajneesh* (San Francisco: Harper & Row, 1982), 1.

2. Fox, *Osho-Rajneesh*, 1. See Sue Appleton, *Bhagwan Shree Rajneesh: The Most Dangerous Man since Jesus Christ* (Zurich: Neo-Sannyas International, 1987).

3. Joshi, *Awakened One*, 1.

4. See Ramchandra Guha, *India after Gandhi: The History of the World's Largest Democracy* (New York: Harper Perennial, 2008), 8–24; Paul R. Brass, *The Politics of India since Independence* (Cambridge: Cambridge University Press, 1994), 6; Christophe Jaffrelot, *The Hindu Nationalist Movement in India* (New York: Columbia University Press, 1995), 11–12.

5. See Steger and Roy, *Neoliberalism*, 91: "Nehru chose a democratic-socialist middle way between the capitalist West and the communist soviet bloc by rejecting both Western liberal economic ideas such as free trade and entrepreneurial individualism and Marxist-Leninist forms of authoritarian collectivism." See also Andrew Kennedy, *The International Ambitions of Mao and Nehru: National Efficacy Beliefs and the Making of Foreign Policy* (Cambridge: Cambridge University Press, 2011), 2.

6. Rajneesh, in Joshi, *Awakened One*, 165. See Bhagwan Shree Rajneesh, *Dimensions beyond the Known* (Los Angeles: Wisdom Garden Books, 1975), 7: "I am not a philosopher or a logician, but I always use logic. I am using this only for the purpose of leading your thinking to the point where you can be pushed out of it. If reasoning is not exhausted, one cannot go beyond it. I am climbing on a ladder, but this ladder is not my goal; it has to be given up. I use reasoning only to know what is beyond it. I do not want to establish anything by reasoning. What I want instead is to prove its uselessness. My statements will, therefore, be inconsistent and illogical."

7. See Carter, *Charisma and Control*, 40: "The most interesting feature of Bhagwan's reconstructed 'biography' is the shifting persona reflected in the changes of name applied to Mohan Chandra Rajneesh. Some stages of identity are undoubtedly based in fact, though other features may be seen as 'reconstructed Mythos.'"

8. See Urban, *Church of Scientology*, chap. 1.

9. Harvey, *Condition of Postmodernity*, 43–44.

10. Michel Foucault, *The Order of Things: An Archaeology of the Human Sciences* (New York: Vintage, 1994), 387. See Foucault, "What Is an Author?," in *The Foucault Reader*, ed. Paul Rabinow (New York: Pantheon, 1984), 118: "It is a matter of depriving the subject . . . of its role as originator and of analyzing the subject as a variable and complex function of discourse."

11. Best and Kellner, *Postmodern Theory*, 42. See also Eugene W. Holland, *Deleuze and Guattari's Anti-Oedipus: Introduction to Schizoanalysis* (New York: Routledge, 1999), 35: "Even to speak of 'the' subject in the singular is in

a sense to have already succumbed to the reversal and the illusions of sovereign subjectivity, for even the last of the syntheses . . . produces a subject that is always different from itself."

12. Fredric Jameson, "Cognitive Mapping," in *Marxism and the Interpretation of Culture,* ed. C. Nelson and L. Grossberg (Urbana: University of Illinois Press, 1988), 351.

13. Harvey, *Condition of Postmodernity,* 43–44. See also Jean-François Lyotard, *The Postmodern Condition: A Report on Knowledge* (Minneapolis: University of Minnesota Press, 1984).

14. See Bhagwan Shree Rajneesh, "A Liquid Human Being," *Bhagwan* 11 (1984): 10.

15. James S. Gordon, *The Golden Guru: The Strange Journey of Bhagwan Shree Rajneesh* (Lexington, MA: Stephen Greene Press, 1987), 13.

16. Osho, *Autobiography,* 129–67.

17. M. V. Kamath, reviews of *The Sound of Running Water* and *The Wisdom of the Sands,* by Bhagwan Shree Rajneesh, *Illustrated Weekly of India,* June 1, 1981, 70.

18. Osho, *Autobiography,* xvii.

19. See, for example, Appleton, *Bhagwan Shree Rajneesh.*

20. Ma Prem Shunyo, *My Diamond Days with Osho: The New Diamond Sutra* (Delhi: Motilal Banarsidass, 1993), 74.

21. Swami Gyan Bhed, *The Enlightened Rebellious Master: Osho* (New Delhi: Diamond Pocket Books, 2006).

22. Milne, *Bhagwan,* 94: "At first they could not believe that seemingly sophisticated, sensible people like myself could think that 'Mohan' was the true guru, and that we had given up everything to follow him. . . . It became clear that 'Mohan' was considered the *enfant terrible* of this particular clan. They did not seem to be very fond of him and frankly could not believe that he had now set himself up as a guru, an enlightened being."

23. Joshi, *Awakened One,* 15–16.

24. Osho, *Autobiography,* 20.

25. Carter, *Charisma and Control,* 42; see Joshi, *Awakened One,* 35–39.

26. Jaffrelot, *Hindu Nationalist Movement,* 11: "Hindu nationalism was constructed as an ideology between the 1870s and the 1920s. . . . Beginning in 1920, this doctrine crystallized. . . . Its primary concern was to maintain the basic elements of the traditional social order . . . of the Hindus while adapting that tradition to take account of certain aspects of western society. . . . In the 1920s certain Hindu ideologies felt threatened by the mobilization of Muslims."

27. Osho, *Autobiography,* 55–56; Gyan Bhed, *Rebellious Enlightened Master,* 65–73.

28. Rajneesh, quoted in Milne, *Bhagwan,* 96. See Osho, *Autobiography,* 24–25, 52–54.

29. Rajneesh, quoted in Joshi, *Awakened One,* 31. See Osho, *Autobiography,* 54.

30. Carter, *Charisma and Control,* 42; Joshi, *Awakened One,* 33–34.

31. Rajneesh, quoted in Carter, *Charisma and Control,* 44.

32. Rajneesh, *Dimensions beyond the Known*, 160. See Osho, *Autobiography*, 62–63: "That last year, when I was twenty-one, it was a time of nervous breakdown and breakthrough. . . . I was surrounded with nothingness, emptiness. . . . My whole concern was to go deeper and deeper into myself. . . . To everybody else during that one year I was mad. But to me that madness became meditation, and the peak of that madness opened the door."

33. Joshi, *Awakened One*, 52.

34. Rajneesh, *The Discipline of Transcendence*, quoted in Joshi, *Awakened One*, 61. See Osho, *Autobiography*, 72–73: "I felt a throbbing life all around me, a great vibration—almost like a hurricane, a great storm of light, joy, ecstasy. I was drowning in it. It was so tremendously real that everything else became unreal. The walls of the room became unreal, the house became unreal, my own body became unreal. . . . There is an awakening—compared to the reality of that awakening, this whole reality becomes unreal. . . . Suddenly it was there, the other reality, the separate reality—the really real, or whatsoever you want to call it. Call it god, call it truth, call it *dhamma*, call it Tao."

35. Osho, *Autobiography*, 68–69.

36. See Best and Kellner, *Postmodern Theory*, 42ff.; Foucault, "What Is an Author?"; Holland, *Deleuze and Guattari's Anti-Oedipus*, 35–36.

37. Joshi, *Awakened One*, 66.

38. Osho, *Autobiography*, 71.

39. Guha, *India after Gandhi*, 8–9, 24. See Jaffrelot, *Hindu Nationalist Movement*, 11–12; Brass, *Politics of India*, 6.

40. Joshi, *Awakened One*, 79.

41. Rajneesh, *Ecstasy: The Forgotten Language* (Pune: Rajneesh Foundation, 1978), 37.

42. Gordon, *Golden Guru*, 234.

43. Gordon, *Golden Guru*, 26. See Bhagwan Shree Rajneesh, "What Counts Is Consciousness," *Rajneesh* 2 (1984): 15: "Religion was giving opium to the people—'tomorrow,' 'after death.' Millions of people remained in that state of druggedness, under that chloroform."

44. Bhagwan Shree Rajneesh, *The Mustard Seed* (New York: Harper and Row, 1974), chap. 2; online version at Osho.com, 2015, www.osho.com/iosho /library/read-book/online-library-consolation-peace-master-5b822052-a4f?p = 04536ec62122d27aeb90c166c0eec28c&sri = 6c6bb319d6825ac07dcf1102ce973 ece. See also Rajneesh, *Ecstasy*, 149.

45. Joshi, *Awakened One*, 88; Carter, *Charisma and Control*, 45.

46. See, for example, Rajneesh, "*Ek Omkar Satnam: The True Name* (Pune: Rajneesh Foundation, 1974), www.oshorajneesh.com/download/osho-books /Indian_Mystics/The_True_Name_Volume_1.pdf.

47. Rajneesh, "Greatest Joke," 24.

48. Ma Yoga Laxmi, *Bhagwan Shree Rajneesh, Diary 1981* (Pune: Rajneesh Foundation, 1980), n.p.

49. A *sannyasin*, quoted in Carter, *Charisma and Control*, 48. As Vasant Joshi explained to me it in a interview in 2013, Rajneesh was not a "teacher, a mentor or a philosopher" at all but rather a being who has "*seen* the Truth from

an exalted state of consciousness beyond the confines of the human mind"; thus all of his words, actions, jokes, and even radical techniques were not so much "teachings" as practical tools to help awaken each of us to the same state of realization: "His provocation and his playful humor worked more as a device to unsettle one's fixed mindset and lift the person to a mature and an evolved state" (interview, December 24, 2013).

50. Dhanyam, interview, December 16, 2013.

51. Rajneesh, quoted in Gordon, *Golden Guru*, 85.

52. Bhagwan Shree Rajneesh, *Meditation: The Art of Ecstasy* (New York: Harper & Row, 1976), 28

53. Osho, *Autobiography*, 153. See Laxmi, *Diary 1981*, n.p.: "For centuries religion has lacked many things. One of the most important of them all is laughter. Seriousness is a kind of disease. It is the cancer of the soul. Laughter is as precious as prayer, or even more precious than prayer."

54. Rajneesh, "Greatest Joke," 23.

55. See June McDaniel, *The Madness of the Saints: Ecstatic Mysticism in Bengal* (Chicago: University of Chicago Press, 1998); Georg Feuerstein, *Holy Madness: The Shock Tactics and Radical Teachings of Crazy-Wise Adepts, Holy Fools, and Rascal Gurus* (New York: Paragon House, 1991); Rob Linrothe, ed., *Holy Madness: Portraits of Tantric Siddhas* (New York: Rubin Museum of Art, 2006); Urban, *Tantra*, chap. 6.

56. See Urban, *Tantra*, chap. 6.

57. Fox, *Osho-Rajneesh*, 3. Rajneesh made literally hundreds of references to Gurdjieff, as a quick search on the Osho library website will show: www .osho.com/iosho/library/library-search.

58. Gurdjieff, quoted in John Shirley, *Gurdjieff: An Introduction to His Life and Ideas* (New York: Penguin, 2004), 20.

59. P. D. Ouspensky, *In Search of the Miraculous: Fragments of an Unknown Teaching* (New York: Harcourt, Brace & World, 1949), 142–43.

60. Gordon, *Golden Guru*, 13.

61. Ouspensky, *In Search of the Miraculous*, 48–49.

62. Osho, "I Have No Biography," www.youtube.com/watch?v = gcoWjJW-wz8s.

63. Bhagwan Shree Rajneesh, "I Enjoy Disturbing People," *Sannyas News: Here and Now* 21 (1986): 3. See Swami Devageet, "Devageet on Shiva," *Sannyas News,* July 25, 1986, 4: "We are all dreaming, locked into a pseudo-reality which never breaks until something shocks us into another state of consciousness. Bhagwan, in order to enter our dreams, plays many games. He will use all kinds of ways; this is perhaps the only game where the end justifies the means. He may shock you into sudden awareness. . . . The whole object is for you, the seeker, to wake up."

64. Tom Robbins, quoted in "Who Is Osho?," Osho.com, 2013, www.osho .com/Topics/TopicsEng/who-is-osho.htm.

65. Carter, *Charisma and Control*, 44; Milne, *Bhagwan*, 19.

66. Gordon, *Golden Guru*, 27.

67. Carter, *Charisma and Control*, 44.

68. "Poona Period Caps Period of Growth for Rajneeshism," *The Oregonian*, July 2, 1985, www.oregonlive.com/rajneesh/index.ssf/1985/07/poona_era_caps_period_of_growt.html.

69. Susan J. Palmer and Arvind Sharma, eds., *The Rajneesh Papers: Studies in a New Religious Movement* (Delhi: Motilal Banarsidass, 1983), 30. See Affidavit of Eckart Flöther, United States Department of Justice, Immigration and Naturalization Service, January 7, 1982, in Rajneesh Legal Services Corporation Records, University of Oregon Special Collections and University Archives, Coll. 260, box 3, fol. 1094.

70. Gordon, *Golden Guru*, 234.

71. Ma Anand Sheela, "Glory," 18 (draft manuscript, October, 11, 1986), Roshani Shay/Rajneesh Collection, University of Oregon Special Collections and University Archives, box 11, fol. 27.

72. Carter, *Charisma and Control*, 29–30.

73. Osho, *Autobiography*, 140: "*Bhagwan* is a state of experience—nothing to do with an appointment, an election, a title or a degree. It is the experience of *bhagawatta*, of godliness, that whole existence is full of godliness, that there is nothing other than godliness."

74. Osho, *Autobiography*, 145.

75. Osho, *Autobiography*, 135. See Osho, *Tantra: The Way of Acceptance* (London: Pan Macmillan, 2011), 10: "Have you not watched the so-called religious people? They are always afraid—afraid of hell—and always trying to get into heaven. But they don't know what heaven is. . . . No one has ever gone to heaven, and nobody has ever gone to hell. . . . Heaven comes to you, hell comes to you—it depends on you."

76. Osho, *Autobiography*, 176. "I am proclaiming a new religion—the essential religion. In Islam it is known as Sufism, in Buddhism it is known as Zen, in Judaism it is known as Hasidism—the essential core. But I speak your language, I speak the way you can understand. I speak a very religionless language. I speak as if I am not religious at all. That's what is needed in this world. The twentieth century needs a religion completely free of superstitions, utterly nude and naked" (236).

77. Rajneesh, *Ecstasy*, 100.

78. See Jeffrey J. Kripal, *Esalen: America and the Religion of No-Religion* (Chicago: University of Chicago Press, 2008), 85–248 and 365. See chapter 3 below.

79. Vasant Joshi, aka Swami Satya Vedant, interview, December 24, 2013. "For seekers and his sannyasins, he functioned more as a Healer and not as a Teacher. His presence, words, gestures, pauses, silences all brought a sense of one being healed, transformed, rejuvenated. His provocation and his playful humor worked more as a device to unsettle one's fixed mindset and lift the person to a mature and an evolved state. It is a widely known fact that in his interactions with the host families and friends working with him his humor and playfulness came through delighting one and all" (ibid).

80. Ma Anand Sheela, "Glory," 10–11, 14. Another *sannyasin*, Kate Strelley, provides an almost identical account, describing an intense experience of loss of self and utter dissolution in the depthless eyes and hypnotic voice of the Master: "I was lost in those grave-laughing eyes now. I could feel myself nod-

ding as he went on. . . . I forgot planet earth, forgot *everything*. He spoke so beautifully, his words touched me so deeply that I felt he had always known me. The rhythm and tone of his words more than their content seemed to speak to me at some deep level. . . . I felt that he was communicating directly to my spirit, reawakening it" (*Ultimate Game*, 71).

81. Allanach, *Osho, India, and Me*, 11. For a similar account of a first meeting with Rajneesh, see Aneesha Dillon, *Tantric Pulsation: The Journey of Human Energy from Its Animal Roots to Its Spiritual Flower* (Cambridge: Perfect Publishers, 2005), 177: "Just before he stood up, he made eye contact with me and then held my gaze, looking at me all the way from a sitting to standing position. It couldn't have taken more than a few seconds, but it seemed like forever. . . . What was transmitted through this look, through the eye contact we had, I couldn't say, but it penetrated deep, deep inside me, and I felt I'd received such a vast amount of 'something' that I could barely contain it. My head fell down to the floor, and I started to cry. I was crying out of gratitude, out of the humbling experience of receiving such an incredible gift. . . . It was a transmission of divine energy."

82. Allanach, *Osho, India, and Me*, 11–12.

83. Milne, *Bhagwan*, 25.

84. Joshi, interview, December 24, 2103.

85. Milne, *Bhagwan*, 16. See also Ma Anand Sheela, *Don't Kill Him: The Story of My Life with Bhagwan Rajneesh* (New Delhi: Prakash Books, 2012): "I saw Bhagwan as extremely charismatic, brilliant, inspiring, powerful and loving, and I also saw Him being ridiculously manipulative, vengeful, self-serving and hateful. He disregarded all laws, moralities, ethics and legalities of every community, society and nation because He wanted to create a society of His own vision with its own laws and rules."

86. Gordon, *Golden Guru*, 234.

87. See Guha, *India after Gandhi*, 24; Kennedy, *International Ambitions*, 2.

88. Rajneesh, "Liquid Human Being," 10–11.

89. Holland, *Deleuze and Guattari's Anti-Oedipus*, 36. See Best and Kellner, *Postmodern Theory*, 284. Rajneesh's "liquid man" also foreshadowed Zygmunt Bauman's idea of "liquid modernity" by several decades. See Bauman, *Liquid Modernity* (Cambridge: Polity, 2000).

CHAPTER 2. THE "ANTI-GANDHI" AND THE EARLY RAJNEESH COMMUNITY IN THE 1970S

Epigraphs: Bhagwan Shree Rajneesh, *The Wisdom of the Sands*, vol. 1, *Discourses on Sufism* (Pune: Rajneesh Foundation, 1980), 21; Rajneesh, *Beware of Socialism* (Rajneeshpuram, OR: Rajneesh Foundation International 1984), 31.

1. See Rajneesh's critique of Gandhi in *The Secret of Secrets* (Pune: Rajneesh Foundation, 1983), 11–12; and Acharya Rajneesh, *The Mind of Acharya Rajneesh* (Mumbai: Jaico Publishing House, 1974), 190–91.

2. Steger and Roy, *Neoliberalism*, 91. See Lloyd I. Rudolph and Susanne Hoeber Rudolph, *In Pursuit of Lakshmi: The Political Economy of the Indian State* (Chicago: University of Chicago Press, 1987).

3. McKean, *Divine Enterprise*, 1.

4. Rudolph and Rudolph, *In Pursuit of Lakshmi*, 26. See also Steger and Roy, *Neoliberalism*, 91.

5. Rudolph and Rudolph, *In Pursuit of Lakshmi*, 27.

6. Achin Vanaik, *The Painful Transition: Bourgeois Democracy in India* (London: Verso, 1990), 56–57.

7. McKean, *Divine Enterprise*, 6. See Sushi Khanna, "The New Business Class, Ideology, and State: The Making of a New Consensus," *South Asia* 10 (1987): 59–60.

8. "The New Millionaires and How They Made It," *India Today*, October 31, 1987. See McKean, *Divine Enterprise*, 7.

9. "The Power and the Glory," *Sunday*, November, 8, 1987. See McKean, *Divine Enterprise*, 7.

10. Joshi, *Awakened One*, 83.

11. Rajneesh, *Secret of Secrets*, 11–12.

12. Joshi, *Awakened One*, 84–85.

13. Rajneesh, *Secret of Secrets*, 11–12.

14. Rajneesh, *Mind of Acharya Rajneesh*, 190–91.

15. Shiva has written a huge amount since the 1980s; see, for example, Vandana Shiva, *Staying Alive: Women, Ecology, and Development* (London: Zed Books, 1989). For a critique of her work, see Meera Nanda, "Is Modern Science a Western, Patriarchal Myth? A Critique of the Populist Orthodoxy," *South Asia Bulletin* 11, nos. 1 and 2 (1991): 32–61.

16. Rajneesh, *Mind of Acharya Rajneesh*, 190–91.

17. Rajneesh, *Secret of Secrets*, 11–12. See also Rajneesh, *Mind of Acharya Rajneesh*, 189: "The whole country is in a state of self-deception. Poverty is glorified. This is a great obstacle in our prosperity. We have to get rid of it. . . . The country's tragedy today is that it has adopted a 'philosophy of poverty' and thus almost closed the doors to riches and prosperity. But now we should tell ourselves 'Enough is enough' and should understand that possessions, material well-being, wealth—everything is needed to cultivate a desire of non-possession."

18. Gordon, *Golden Guru*, 26.

19. Bhagwan Shree Rajneesh, *The Wisdom of the Sands*, vol. 1, *Discourses on Sufism* (Pune: Rajneesh Foundation, 1980), chap. 2; online version at Osho. com, 2014, www.osho.com/online-library-masochism-surdas-violence-b12ef9b7-595.aspx.

20. Joshi, *Awakened One*, 44.

21. Rajneesh, *Beware of Socialism*, 20.

22. Rajneesh, *Beware of Socialism*, 18.

23. Rajneesh, *Mind of Acharya Rajneesh*, 163.

24. Rajneesh, *Mind of Acharya Rajneesh*, 156.

25. Rajneesh, *Mind of Acharya Rajneesh*, 172.

26. Rajneesh, *Mind of Acharya* Rajneesh, 173.

27. See Carter, *Charisma and Control*, 48; Urban, "Zorba the Buddha" (2013).

28. Rajneesh, *Beware of Socialism*, 26.

29. Rajneesh, *Beware of Socialism,* 29.

30. Rajneesh, *Beware of Socialism,* 171–72.

31. Rajneesh, *Beware of Socialism,* 182.

32. Rajneesh, *Mind of Acharya Rajneesh,* 156; see Rajneesh, *Beware of Socialism,* 11.

33. Rajneesh, *Mind of Acharya Rajneesh,* 181.

34. See Bhagwan Shree Rajneesh, *The Psychology of the Esoteric: The New Evolution of Man* (New York: Harper & Row, 1978), 43: "I use this chaotic method very considerately. Systematic methodology will not help now. . . . Consciousness must be pushed down to its source, to the roots. Only then is there the possibility of transformation. So I use chaotic methods to push the consciousness downward from the brain."

35. Rajneesh, *Psychology of the Esoteric,* 43.

36. Rajneesh, *Meditation,* 233.

37. Arthur Janov, *The Primal Scream: Primal Therapy; The Cure for Neurosis* (New York: Dell, 1970).

38. Rajneesh, *Meditation,* 33: "*Hoo* is hitting the same center of energy [the sex center] but from within. And when the sax center is hit from within, the energy starts to flow within. This inner flow of energy changes you completely. You become transformed: you give birth to yourself."

39. Osho, "Stop!," OshoDynamic.com, 2014, www.oshodynamic.com /stohtml.

40. Rajneesh, *Psychology of the Esoteric,* 43.

41. Rajneesh, *Meditation,* 28.

42. Joshi, *Awakened One,* 90.

43. Milne, *Bhagwan,* 56–57.

44. Allanach, *Osho, India, and Me,* 17. See also Gordon, *Golden Guru,* 7: "I found that during sessions I was expressing emotions that hadn't surfaced in several years of psychoanalysis and resolving conflicts that intellectual understanding had not affected. It was also an incredible physical workout. After I did Dynamic I felt purged and relaxed, alert and generally more intuitive and less judgmental. . . . It was democratic. I could—anyone could—do it. No priests or gurus were needed, no initiation or secret mantras. . . . Then after the activity, the calm and stillness, the quiet pleasures of a relaxed body and uncluttered mind might come of their own accord."

45. Appadurai, *Modernity at Large,* 85.

46. Osho, *Autobiography,* 228.

47. For traditional Hindu views on *sannyasa,* see Patrick Olivelle, *The Samnyasa Upanisads: Hindu Scriptures on Asceticism and Renunciation* (New York: Oxford University Press, 1992); for a popular work on *sadhus* in India today, see Dolf Hartsuiker, *Sadhus: India's Mystic Holy Men* (Rochester, VT: Inner Traditions, 1993).

48. Bhagwan Shree Rajneesh, *Tao: The Golden Gate* (Pune: Rajneesh Foundation, 1980), 12–13. See Carter, *Charisma and Control,* 48; Joshi, *Awakened One,* 4.

49. Rajneesh, interview by George Hunter, Immigration and Naturalization Service, Portland, OR, October 14, 1982, Rajneesh Legal Services Corporation

Records, University of Oregon Special Collections and University Archives, Coll. 260, box 2, folder 27, fol. 1070.

50. Osho, *Autobiography*, 228.

51. Rajneesh, *Ecstasy*, 36. See Rajneesh, *Meditation*, 110: "Sannyas means living moment to moment, with no commitment to the past."

52. Bhagwan Shree Rajneesh, "The New Man," *Rajneesh* 2 (1984): 37.

53. Guest, *My Life in Orange*, 38.

54. Aneesha Dillon, interview, December 30, 2013. See Rajneesh, *Meditation*, 109: "To me sannyas is not something very serious. . . . Live life as play and not as work. If you can take this whole life just as a play, you are a *sannyasin:* then you have renounced. Renunciation is not leaving the world but changing the attitude."

55. Guest, *My Life in Orange*, 40.

56. Joshi, interview, December 24, 2013.

57. Dillon, interview, December 30, 2013.

58. Dillon, *Tantric Pulsation*, 171.

59. Dillon, interview, December 30, 2013. Swami Prabodh Dhanyam had similar recollections of the Pune ashram: "I went to Pune in 1980 and expected a Zen-like Ashram, but found a loving, happy, harmonious, high-energy place with lots of laughter. . . . It was a place I wanted to live in. Osho, the energy, the people—this was paradise" (interview, December 16, 2013).

60. Dillon, *Tantric Pulsation*, 179. See also Strelley, *Ultimate Game*, 84–85: "Life in the Ashram had a timeless quality. . . . This was a big part of the Ashram's appeal for me: I had entered a never-never-land where time ceased to exist."

61. Dillon, interview, December 30, 2013.

62. Palmer, *Moon Sisters*, 46.

63. Dillon, *Tantric Pulsation*, 174.

64. "Poona Period Caps Period of Growth," *The Oregonian*, July 2, 1985, http://www.oregonlive.com/rajneesh/index.ssf/1985/07/poona_era_caps_period_of_growt.html.

65. See the conclusion to chapter 3 below; see also Kripal, *Esalen*, 364–65. Although initially fascinated by Rajneesh's work, Esalen cofounder Dick Price was horrified by the authoritarianism and violence that he witnessed upon his visit to the Pune community.

66. Guest, *My Life in Orange*, 42.

67. Ma Satya Bharti, *Death Comes Dancing* (London: Routledge and Kegan Paul, 1981) 72; see Fox, *Osho-Rajneesh*, 18.

68. Ma Prem Shunyo, *My Diamond Days with Osho*, 40. See Fox, *Osho-Rajneesh*, 21.

69. Interview, December 31, 2012. Most of the longtime *sannyasins* I interviewed described the early days in Pune in very similar terms.

70. Gordon, *Golden Guru*, 43.

71. Carter, *Charisma and Control*, 58.

72. Guest, *My Life in Orange*, 40–41.

73. Guest, *My Life in Orange*, 41.

74. Rajneesh, quoted in Joshi, *Awakened One*, 3.

75. Dillon, interview, December 30, 2013. Joshi described the early ashram as follows: "The international movement includes people from many profes-

sions and walks of life: lawyers, physicians, psychologists, educators, scientists, dentists, acupuncturists, journalists, writers, artists, architects, photographers, radical feminists, New Age seekers, 'flower children' housewives and catholic priests. . . . Most of Bhagwan's disciples are young—between the ages of twenty and forty" (*Awakened One,* 3).

76. Milne, *Bhagwan,* 127.

77. Guest, *My Life in Orange,* 185.

78. Gordon, *Golden Guru,* 235; "Poona Period Caps Period of Growth."

79. Carter, *Charisma and Control,* 57.

80. Rajneesh, *Secret of* Secrets, quoted in Osho, *Autobiography,* 242–43.

81. Fox, *Osho-Rajneesh,* 19.

82. Osho, *Autobiography,* 155.

83. Osho, *Autobiography,* 238.

84. Shobha Kilachand, "The Saffron Superstar," *Illustrated Weekly of India,* April 5, 1981, 20–24. See "Poona Period Caps Period of Growth"; Osho, *Autobiography,* 242.

85. *Sunday,* June 21, 1981, 24.

86. "Poona Period Caps Period of Growth."

87. Rajneesh, interview by George Hunter, Immigration and Naturalization Service, Portland, OR, October 14, 1982.

88. Rajneesh, *The Discipline of Transcendence,* quoted in Osho, *Autobiography,* 147.

89. Friedrich Engels, "Speech at the Graveside of Karl Marx," in *The Marx-Engels Reader,* ed. Robert C. Rucker (New York: W.W. Norton, 1978), 681–82.

90. Rajneesh, *The Last Testament: Interviews with the World Press* (Rajneeshpuram, OR: Rajneesh Foundation International, 1986), vol. 3, chap. 27; online version at www.osho.com/library/online-library-leonardo-da-vinci-dostoyevsky-poor-c896a8b6–507.aspx.

91. Appadurai, *Modernity at Large,* 8.

92. Bhagwan Shree Rajneesh, *The Dhammapada: The Way of the Buddha* (Pune: Osho International Foundation, 2014), vol. 6, chap. 6; online version at Osho.com, 2014, www.osho.com/iosho/library/read-book/online-library-pain-ecstasy-adventure-d30455a5-f85?p = 3d49c2b64d42e6796b86ef22aa8fc7c1.

93. Holland, *Deleuze and Guattari's Anti-Oedipus,* 115.

94. Scott Lash and John Urry, *The End of Organized Capitalism* (Madison: University of Wisconsin Press, 1987), 16. See also Claus Offe, *Disorganized Capitalism: Contemporary Transformations of Work and Politics* (Cambridge, MA: MIT Press, 1985).

95. Harvey, *Condition of Postmodernity,* 159.

CHAPTER 3. SEXUALITY, TANTRA, AND LIBERATION IN 1970S INDIA

Epigraphs: Osho, *The Book of Secrets: 112 Meditations to Discover the Mystery Within* (New York: St. Martin's Griffin, 1998), 20; Dennis Altman, *Global Sex* (Chicago: University of Chicago Press, 2001), 160.

1. Lonely Planet, *India* (Lonely Planet Publications, 2011), 786.

2. John Updike, *S.* (New York: Random House, 2013).

3. Osho, *Autobiography,* 132: "I have never taught 'free sex.' What I have been teaching is the sacredness of sex. . . . This is the idiotic Indian yellow journalism that has confined my whole philosophy to two words. I have published four hundred books—only one is concerned with sex."

4. See Bhagwan Shree Rajneesh, *The Book of Secrets III* (Pune: Rajneesh Foundation, 1976), 3–43; Osho, *Sex Matters* (New York: St. Martin's Griffin, 2003); Osho, *Tantra: The Science of Tantra,* DVD (Pune: Osho International Foundation, 2010); Osho, *The Tantra Experience: Evolution through Love* (Pune: Osho Media International, 2012).

5. Osho, *Tantra: The Way of Acceptance,* 102.

6. Rajneesh, *Psychology of the Esoteric,* 24. Rajneesh also regularly discussed the details of male and female anatomy, the vagina and clitoris, and the differences between male and female orgasm. See Ma Prem Shunyo, *My Diamond Days with Osho,* 236–38.

7. See David Gordon White, *Kiss of the Yogini: "Tantric Sex" in Its South Asian Contexts* (Chicago: University of Chicago Press, 2003); Urban, *Tantra,* chaps. 1 and 6.

8. See Urban, *Tantra,* chap. 6; Urban, "The Cult of Ecstasy: Tantrism, the New Age, and the Spiritual Logic of Late Capitalism," *History of Religions* 39, no. 3 (2000): 268–304.

9. Nik Douglas, *Spiritual Sex: Secrets of Tantra from the Ice Age to the New Millennium* (New York: Pocket Books, 1997), 15.

10. Lynn Collins, "The Secret to Tantric Sex," *Cosmopolitan,* May 2000, 240. See Urban, *Tantra,* 205.

11. See Richard King, *Orientalism and Religion: Post-Colonial Theory, India, and the "Mystic East"* (New York: Routledge, 1999); Urban, *Tantra,* chap. 1.

12. See Osho, *Tantra: The Way of Acceptance,* 131: "Tantra teaches you to reclaim respect for the body, love for the body. Tantra teaches you to look at the body as the greatest creation of existence. Tantra is the religion of the body. . . . Tantra is really juicy, very alive."

13. See Kripal, *Esalen,* 62–65; Urban, *Tantra,* chap. 6.

14. David Allyn, *Make Love, Not War: The Sexual Revolution, an Unfettered History* (New York: Routledge, 2001), 4.

15. Wilhelm Reich, *The Function of the Orgasm: Sex-Economic Problems of Biological Energy* (New York: Farrar, Straus and Giroux, 1973), 21.

16. Wilhelm Reich, *Reich Speaks of Freud: Wilhelm Reich Discusses His Work and Relationship with Sigmund Freud* (New York: Farrar, Straus and Giroux, 1967), 24.

17. See Wilhelm Reich, *Selected Writings: An Introduction to Orgonomy* (New York: Farrar, Straus and Giroux, 1973), 185.

18. See Allyn, *Make Love,* 4; Altman, *Global Sex,* 133.

19. Allyn, *Make Love,* 45. See Reich, *The Sexual Revolution: Toward a Self-Governing Character Structure* (New York: Farrar, Straus and Giroux, 1963).

20. Allyn, *Make Love,* 8: "In some respects the permissiveness of the era was just the logical extension of the commercial free market to include sexual goods and commodities."

21. Philip Jenkins, *Decade of Nightmares: The End of the Sixties and the Making of Eighties America* (New York: Oxford University Press, 2006), 24.

22. Altman, *Global Sex,* 104.

23. Altman, *Global Sex,* 6. "Changes in our understandings of and attitudes to sexuality are both affected by and reflect the larger changes of globalization. . . . As all . . . the world's peoples are brought within the scope of global capitalism, a consumer culture is developing which cuts across borders and cultures, and is universalized through advertising, mass media and the enormous flows of capital and people in the contemporary world. Increasingly sexuality becomes the terrain on which are fought out bitter disputes around the impact of global capital and ideas" (1).

24. Rajneesh, quoted in Joshi, *Awakened One,* 99. See Osho, *Autobiography,* 226.

25. Bhagwan Shree Rajneesh, *From Sex to Superconsciousness* (Delhi: Orient Paperbacks, n.d.), 34–35.

26. Rajneesh, *From Sex to Superconsciousness,* 34. See Rajneesh, *Mind of Acharya Rajneesh,* 94: "The simple truth is that sex is the beginning of love. The origin, the Gangotri of the Ganges of love is sex. . . . Every culture, every religion, every Guru, every seeker has attacked this Gangotri, this source, and the river has remained bottled up. . . . We never realize that ultimately sex energy travels and reaches the sea of love."

27. Rajneesh, *From Sex to Superconsciousness,* 157. See Osho, *Tantra: The Way of Acceptance,* 14: "Sex and superconsciousness are both the same energy. The serpent and the savior are not two. . . . There is no separation between divine love and human, four-lettered love."

28. Rajneesh, *Mind of Acharya Rajneesh,* 94. See Rajneesh, *Book of Secrets III,* 34: "In sex you are natural for the first time. The unreal is lost; the faces, the facades are lost, the society, the culture; the civilization is lost. . . . You are in a greater something—the Cosmos, the Tao."

29. Rajneesh, *From Sex to Superconsciousness*; online version at Osho.com, 2015, chap. 5, p. 11, www.osho.com/iosho/library/read-book/online-library-psychological-byron-level-cda44cf4-081?p = 686e09f4449fb1d5a3ac2adbe44 d3b69&sri = a784de53231aa66c713ebo4175efc29f.

30. Bhagwan Shree Rajneesh, *A Cup of Tea* (Rajneeshpuram: Rajneesh Foundation International, 1983), 88. See Rajneesh, *Book of Secrets III,* 33: "Tantra says do not try to go against sex, because if you go against sex and try to create a state of *brahmacharya*—celibacy, purity, it is impossible. . . . A person who suppresses sex starts seeing sex in everything. . . . This *brahmacharya* is perversion; it is unnatural."

31. Bhagwan Shree Rajneesh, *The Goose Is Out* (Antelope, OR: Rajneesh Foundation International, 1982), 106–7.

32. Rajneesh, *Meditation*; online version at Osho.com, 2015, chap. 4, pp. 10–11, www.osho.com/library/online-library-insanity-sex-energy-man-99614ea7-b4a.aspx. See Osho, *Sermons in Stones* (New York: Osho International, 1987), 139: "Reich started working on human energy. Naturally, if you work on human energy you are going to come to the source of all—that is sexual energy."

33. Aneesha Dillon, interview, December 30, 2013. See Dillon, *Tantric Pulsation*, 39–40: "When I arrived at Esalen, India was in fashion among a whole generation of young Americans, and travelers returning to the institute from the East were offering lectures on the chakra system, courses in yoga and many types of meditation. Altogether it was a heady cocktail of Western psychotherapy and Eastern spirituality."

34. Dillon, *Tantric Pulsation*, 41.

35. Gordon, *Golden Guru*, 51.

36. Gordon, *Golden Guru*, 51–52.

37. David Gordon White, "Tantrism," in *Encyclopedia of Religion*, vol. 13, ed. Lindsay Jones (New York: Macmillan, 2005), 8984.

38. See Urban, *Tantra*, 1–43.

39. André Padoux, "What do We Mean by Tantrism?" in *The Roots of Tantra*, ed. Katherine Ann Harper and Robert L. Brown (Albany: SUNY Press, 2002), 33.

40. André Padoux, "Tantrism: An Overview," in *Encyclopedia of Religion*, vol. 14, ed. Mircea Eliade (New York: Macmillan, 1986), 271–72. See Hugh B. Urban, "The Extreme Orient: The Construction of 'Tantrism' in the Orientalist Imagination," *Religion* 29 (1999): 123–46.

41. See Urban, "Extreme Orient;" Urban, *Tantra*, chap. 2.

42. Philip Rawson, *Tantra: The Indian Cult of Ecstasy* (London: Thames and Hudson, 1973); see Urban, "Cult of Ecstasy."

43. Garrison, *The Yoga of Sex* (New York: Julian Press), quoted in Douglas, *Spiritual Sex*, 222. For a similar celebration of Tantra, see Philip Rawson, *The Art of Tantra* (Greenwich, CT: New York Graphics Society, 1973), 9: "Tantra is a cult of ecstasy, focused on a vision of cosmic sexuality."

44. *Tantra*, directed by Nik Douglas; produced with Mick Jagger and Robert Fraser (1968); rereleased as *TANTRA: Indian Rites of Ecstasy* (New York: Mystic Fire, 1993).

45. See Urban, *Tantra*, 1–43, 203–63.

46. White, *Kiss of the Yogini*, 1–26. See Hugh B. Urban, *The Power of Tantra: Religion, Sexuality, and the Politics of South Asian Studies* (London: I.B. Tauris, 2010), introduction and chaps. 1–3.

47. See Urban, "Cult of Ecstasy;" Urban, *Tantra*, chap. 6.

48. Rajneesh, *Book of Secrets III*. For the original Sanskrit text and translation of this key text, see Jaideva Singh, *Vijnanabhairava Tantra or Divine Consciousness: A Treasury of 112 Types of Yoga* (Delhi: Motilal Banarsidass, 2010).

49. Dillon, *Tantric Pulsation*, 171.

50. Rajneesh, *Meditation*; online version at Osho.com, 2015, chap. 4, p. 11, www.osho.com/library/online-library-life-after-death-reich-ease-664fbfa7–9bf. aspx.

51. Osho, *Sermons in Stones*, 141–42.

52. Osho, *Sermons in Stones*, 140.

53. Osho, *Sermons in Stones*, 143.

54. Osho, *Sermons in Stones*, 141–42.

55. Bhagwan Shree Rajneesh, *Tantra Spirituality and Sex* (Rajneeshpuram, OR: Rajneesh Foundation International, 1983), 65. See Rajneesh, *Book of Secrets III*, 16.

56. Osho, *Tantra: The Science of Tantra*; *Osho Talks*, DVD (Pune: Osho International Foundation 2010). See Osho, *Tantra: The Way of Acceptance*, 112: "Tantrikas have been watching the phenomenon of lovemaking closely, because . . . the greatest experience of humanity is orgasm. So if there is some truth, we must be closer to realizing that truth in the moment of orgasm than anywhere else. . . . This is our greatest joy, so this joy must somehow be a door to the infinite."

57. Osho, quoted in Dillon, *Tantric Pulsation*, 175–76.

58. Rajneesh, *Book of Secrets III*, 31: "That is what tantra means: you can use sex as a jumping point. And once you have known the ecstasy of sex, you can understand what mystics have been talking about—a greater orgasm—a COSMIC ORGASM."

59. Osho, *Tantra: The Supreme Understanding*, chap. 1. See Osho, *Tantra: The Way of Acceptance*, 96: "Tantra says: Existence is an orgasm, an eternal orgasm going on and on and on. It is forever and ever an orgasm, an ecstasy."

60. Rajneesh, *Book of Secrets III*, 34.

61. Rajneesh, *Book of Secrets III*, 16.

62. See Holland, *Deleuze and Guattari's Anti-Oedipus*, 35.

63. Osho, *Tantra: The Way of Acceptance*, 128.

64. Osho, *Tantra: The Way of Acceptance*, 102. See Rajneesh, "Homosexuality," Roshani Shay/Rajneesh Collection, University of Oregon Special Collections and University Archives, Coll. 310, box 8, fol. 9: "Sex . . . creates an energy experience which no religion, no politician would like people to have. Because that will create the greatest revolution in the world. People will have a direct contact with existence—no holy scripture, no priest, no mediators."

65. Osho, *Tantra: The Way of Acceptance*, 112. "Sex energy has to be released. It has to flow all over your being. Then your body becomes orgasmic. . . . Only Tantra allows you total being and total flow. Tantra gives you unconditional freedom, whatsoever you are and whatsoever you can be. Tantra puts no boundaries on you" (135).

66. See Herbert Marcuse, "Political Preface, 1966," in *Eros and Civilization: A Philosophical Inquiry into Freud* (Boston: Beacon Press, 1966), xi-xii.

67. Osho, *Tantra: The Way of Acceptance*, 138.

68. Rajneesh, *Book of Secrets III*, 30.

69. Osho, *Tantra: The Supreme Understanding*, 99–100.

70. Osho, *Tantra: The Way of Acceptance*, 21. "Tantra is not ordinary indulgence, it is extraordinary indulgence. . . . It indulges in God himself. . . . Tantra says it can be known through drinking, it can be known through eating, it can be known through love" (121).

71. Ma Anand Sheela, "Glory," 15.

72. Gordon, *Golden Guru*, 79.

73. Guest, *My Life in Orange*, 47.

74. Gordon, *Golden Guru*, 79–80.

75. Gordon, *Golden Guru*, 79.

76. William Foster, interview, February 2, 2014.

77. Guest, *My Life in Orange*, 46.

78. Milne, *Bhagwan*, 26

79. Milne, *Bhagwan*, 134.

80. Rajneesh, interview by George Hunter, Immigration and Naturalization Service, Portland, OR, October 14, 1982.

81. Dillon, interview, December 30, 2013.

82. Palmer, *Moon Sisters*, 49. See also Rajneesh, *Light on the Path*, quoted in Ma Prem Shunyo, *My Diamond Days with Osho*, 238: "Man's wisdom is half unless the woman's wisdom is also absorbed, the wisdom cannot become whole."

83. Rajneesh, *The Book*, quoted in Palmer, *Moon Sisters*, 49–50; see Rajneesh, *A New Vision of Women's Liberation* (Pune: Rebel, 1987).

84. Palmer, *Moon Sisters*, 62.

85. Palmer, *Moon Sisters*, 51.

86. Allyn, *Make Love*, 8. See also Altman, *Global Sex*, 105: "This attempt to link sexuality with the political is far less fashionable today, where sexuality is more commonly linked with contemporary capitalism, and we increasingly think of ourselves as consumers rather than citizens."

87. Rajneesh, "Homosexuality," February 7, 1988. See also Rajneesh, *Yoga: The Alpha and the Omega* (Pune: Rajneesh Foundation, 1978), 9:262: "It is a perversion, a disease. . . . So when people come to me and confess that they are homosexuals, I say don't be worried . . . I will bring you out of it."

88. Russell L. Chandler and Tyler Marshall, "Guru Brings His Ashram to Oregon," *Los Angeles Times*, August 30, 1981, 12. See also Eric Floether, *Bhagwan Shree Rajneesh and His New Religious Movement in America* (Markham, Ont.: Intervarsity Press, 1983), 14: "Violent outbursts of uncontrollable rage, profanity and physical aggression took place in Rajneesh's encounter groups around the world. Hospitals in Poona were called upon to treat the broken bones of sannyasins who were attacked by fellow devotees working out their suppressed anger."

89. Affidavit of Eckart Flöther, United States Department of Justice, Immigration and Naturalization Service, January 7, 1982.

90. Kilachand, "Saffron Superstar," 20–24.

91. Strelley, *Ultimate Game*, 138.

92. Kripal, *Esalen*, 364.

93. Price, quoted in Kripal, *Esalen*, 365.

94. Bhagwan Shree Rajneesh, "This Is Not a Democracy," *Sannyas* 4, no. 78 (1978): 33–34.

95. Altman, *Global Sex*, 157. See Angus McLaren, *Twentieth-Century Sexuality: A History* (London: Blackwell, 1999), 1; Hugh B. Urban, *Magia Sexualis: Sex, Magic, and Liberation in Modern Western Esotericism* (Berkeley: University of California Press, 2005), 261–64.

96. Altman, *Global Sex*, 58, 106.

97. Herbert Marcuse, "Repressive Desublimation," in *Social Theory: The Multicultural and Classic Readings*, ed. Charles Lemert (Boulder, CO: Westview Press, 1993), 472. See also Marcuse, "Political Preface, 1966," xi–xii.

98. Altman, *Global Sex*, 162–63.

CHAPTER 4. RAJNEESHPURAM IN 1980S AMERICA

Epigraphs: Osho, *Autobiography of a Spiritually Incorrect Mystic* (New York: St. Martin's Press, 2000), 49; Arjun Appadurai, *Modernity at Large: Cultural Dimensions of Globalization* (Minneapolis: University of Minnesota Press, 1996), 170.

1. Gordon, *Golden Guru*, 100. See Chandler and Marshall, "Guru Brings His Ashram to Oregon.

2. Carter, *Charisma and Control*, 114.

3. Zaitz, "25 Years after Rajneeshee Commune Collapses"; Keys, "Voter Fraud and Bioterrorism."

4. Milne, *Bhagwan*, 17.

5. Ma Anand Sheela, interview with Australian television, 1985, www.youtube.com/watch?v = 9ib8MdHT61k. See "An Affair to Remember," *Open*, February 9, 2013, www.openthemagazine.com/article/international/an-affair-to-remember.

6. See Urban, "Osho"; Gordon, *Golden Guru*, 117–18; Carter, *Charisma and Control*, 78.

7. See Harvey, *Condition of Postmodernity*; Jameson, *Postmodernism*.

8. Lee Stokes, "Guru Mocks, Provokes from Greek Village," *The Bulletin*, February 26, 1986. See Swami Amrito, "Editorial: States of Terror," *Rajneesh Times International*, August 16, 1988, 2.

9. Carrette and King, *Selling Spirituality*; see also Jain, *Selling Yoga*.

10. Guest, *My Life in Orange*, 76, 188. See "Rajneeshpuram," Oregon Public Broadcasting, November 19, 2012.

11. Carter, *Charisma and Control*, 64. See Win McCormack, "Bhagwan's Bottom Line," *The State of Oregon*, November 1984, 28.

12. "Saint Goes Marching Out," *India Today*, June 16, 1981, 76.

13. "Sins of Bhagwan," *India Today*, June 15, 1982, 137.

14. Milne, *Bhagwan*, 190.

15. Guest, *My Life in Orange*, 188.

16. Rajneesh, *The Book of Books*, quoted in "Osho Is Interviewed by the INS," Oshoworld, 2015, www.oshoworld.com/biography/innercontent.asp?FileName = biography8/08–06-INS.txt.

17. Osho, *Autobiography*, 152.

18. Rajneesh, interview by George Hunter, Immigration and Naturalization Service, Portland, OR, October 14, 1982.

19. Aneesha Dillon, interview, December 30, 2013. See Swami Krishna Deva, "Interview," *Bhagwan* 2 (1984): 4: "Everyone on earth has dreamed of living a harmonious life in a self-sustaining and luxurious community. We actually have that chance here. So with Bhagwan's vision in mind, I came to Ranch Rajneesh in 1981 to put his teaching into practice."

20. Milt Ritter, interview, February 4, 2014. See "Greening of the Valley," *Rajneesh Times*, June 29, 1984, A3.

21. Sheela, *Don't Kill Him*.

22. Ritter, interview, February 4, 2014. See flyer for "Rajneeshpuram Chamber of Commerce," Oregon Rajneesh History Collection, Oregon Historical Society Research Library, MSS 6030.

23. Sharon Liddycoat, "Swami Tells of Life, Love at Rajneeshpuram," *Lane County Examiner*, March 20, 1986. See "Rancho Rajneesh Farming Activities," Papers Relating to Rajneeshpuram, 1982–1985, Oregon Historical Society Research Library, Religion MSS 1517.

24. Swami Deva Wadud, "Rajneeshpuram: 70 Percent Recycling," *Resource Recycling: Journal of Recycling, Reuse and Waste Reduction* 3, no. 2 (1984): 24–26; "Rajneesh Creeks Showing Signs of Recovery," *Northwest Horizons*, August 9, 1984, A8.

25. Ritter, interview, February 4, 2014. See also *City of Rajneeshpuram Preliminary Comprehensive Plan: Land Use* (Rajneeshpuram, OR, 1982); "Description of Farm Projects at Rajneeshpuram, Phases One and Two," Roshani Shay/Rajneesh Collection, University of Oregon Special Collections and University Archives, Coll. 310, box 6, fols. 5–15.

26. "Harvest Bountiful at Rancho Rajneesh"; Fagerstrom, "Guru's City Booms in the Desert." See also the transcript of Floyd McKay, KGW Channel 8, December 22, 1982, Papers Relating to Rajneeshpuram, 1982–1985, Oregon Historical Society Research Library, Religion MSS 1517.

27. Thomas N. Casey, Report of Investigation, Immigration and Naturalization Service, November 19, 1981, Rajneesh Legal Services Corporation Records, University of Oregon Special Collections and University Archives, Coll. 260, box 2, fol. 1050.

28. Preliminary Report on the Survey of the People of Rajneeshpuram, 9/14/83, Papers Relating to Rajneeshpuram, 1982–1985, Oregon Historical Society Research Library, Religion MSS 1517.

29. See Urban, *Church of Scientology*, chaps. 2 and 5.

30. Carter, *Charisma and Control*, 80.

31. Carter, *Charisma and Control*, 238 n. 38.

32. Carter, *Charisma and Control*, 78: "The Rajneesh movement uses corporations as a series of 'empty forms' into which they can move people or resources for transfer to other locations or application to other purposes. . . . The Rajneesh *charismatic* variant of the multinational corporation has many almost parallel organizations into which leaders and identities may be transferred. . . . A center which may be little more than a store front or paper entity can become a major point of control and coordination within weeks if the 'core' organizational members relocate there or transfer wealth . . . to it."

33. "Rajneeshpuram: The Second Annual World Celebration, 1983," Roshani Shay/Rajneesh Collection, University of Oregon Special Collections and University Archives, Coll. 310, box 7, fol. 2.

34. "Rajneesh Neo-Sannyas International Commune Organizational and Financial History" (1982), Roshani Shay/Rajneesh Collection, University of Oregon Special Collections and University Archives, Coll. 310, box 11, fol. 1.

35. Carter, *Charisma and Control*, 78. See, for example, the agreement between City of Rajneeshpuram and the Rajneesh Neo-Sannyas International Commune, July 1, 1983, Roshani Shay/Rajneesh Collection, University of Oregon Special Collections and University Archives, Coll. 310, box 7, fol. 4.

36. Gordon, *Golden Guru*, 116–17.

37. McCormack, "Bhagwan's Bottom Line," 28.

38. McCormack, "Bhagwan's Bottom Line," 28: "The profit-making arm of the Rajneesh corporate empire is Rajneesh Investment Corporation (RIC), a wholly owned subsidiary of RFI. The investment corporation holds title to Rancho Rajneesh and the entire city of Rajneeshpuram, as well as to Rajneesh properties in Rajneesh (Formerly Antelope) and Portland and in turn 'leases' these properties to the commune. These same properties are fully mortgaged to Rajneesh Services International Limited (RSI) in London."

39. McCormack, "Bhagwan's Bottom Line," 28.

40. "Rajneeshpuram," Oregon Public Broadcasting. See Gordon, *Golden Guru*, 117.

41. Rajneesh International Meditation University advertisements in *Bhagwan* 1 (1984): 13, and *Bhagwan* 3 (1984). See also the booklet for the Third Annual World Celebration, 1984, Roshani Shay/Rajneesh Collection, University of Oregon Special Collections and University Archives, Coll. 310, box 7, fol. 2.

42. Gordon, *Golden Guru*, 118.

43. Milne, *Bhagwan*, 245. See Carter, *Charisma and Control*, 117.

44. Carter, *Charisma and Control*, 77.

45. Harvey, *Condition of Postmodernity*, 14.

46. Rajneesh, interview by George Hunter, Immigration and Naturalization Service, Portland, OR, October 14, 1982, 28–29.

47. Guest, *My Life in Orange*, 200–201.

48. Guest, *My Life in Orange*, 127.

49. Gordon, *Golden Guru*, 114. See Osho, *Autobiography*, 146: "I always spend before I get. Just the idea that some money is coming, and I tell my people: Spend! Because who knows about tomorrow? Spend today. . . . I have lived thirty-five years without any money. It has always been coming. Somebody somewhere feels to send, and it comes. And now I have started believing that existence takes care, even of an expensive man like me."

50. Osho, *Autobiography*, 151. See Swami Anand Narayan, "Bhagwan Shree Rajneesh vs. The United States of America," *Viha Bay Area Connection*, April 1988, 2: "Few got the joke, however that Tom Robbins has called 'the greatest spoof on American consumerism ever staged.'"

51. "Rajneesh Followers Amass Fleet of 74 Rolls-Royces," *The Oregonian*, July 12, 1985, www.oregonlive.com/rajneesh/index.ssf/1985/07/rajneesh_followers_amass_fleet.html.

52. Milne, *Bhagwan*, 213–33.

53. Ritter, interview, February 4, 2014. See "Interim Citizen's Involvement Program," Interim Committee for Citizen Involvement, Madras OR, Papers Relating to Rajneeshpuram, 1982–1985, Oregon Historical Society Research Library, Religion MSS 1517.

54. See the map of Antelope and the letter of Ma Sat Probodhi, July 28, 1983, Papers Relating to Rajneeshpuram, 1982–1985, Oregon Historical Society Research Library, Religion MSS 1517.

55. Resolution of City of Antelope, no. 83, Roshani Shay/Rajneesh Collection, University of Oregon Special Collections and University Archives, Coll. 310, box 7, fol. 5.

56. Carter, *Charisma and Control*, 93.

57. See Catherine Wessinger, *How the Millennium Comes Violently: From Jonestown to Heaven's Gate* (New York: Seven Bridges Press, 2000); David Chidester, *Salvation and Suicide: An Interpretation of Jim Jones, the Peoples Temple, and Jonestown* (Bloomington: Indiana University Press, 2003).

58. Statement of Robert Harvey, March 29, 1982, Roshani Shay/Rajneesh Collection, University of Oregon Special Collections and University Archives, Coll. 310, box 1, fol. 1.

59. Open letter, December 21, 1984. Roshani Shay/Rajneesh Collection, University of Oregon Special Collections and University Archives, Coll. 310, box 1, fol. 2.

60. Roshani Shay/Rajneesh Collection, University of Oregon Special Collections and University Archives, Coll. 310, box 30, folder 2, fol. 1672.

61. Rajneesh Artifacts and Ephemera Collection, 1981–2004, University of Oregon Library Special Collections and University Archives, Coll. 275, series I, boxes 4, 5, 8, 13.

62. Oregon Big Game Hunters Association flyer, Roshani Shay/Rajneesh Collection, University of Oregon Special Collections and University Archives, Coll. 310, box 1, fol. 5.

63. "Flash: Attention Hunters!" flyer, Roshani Shay/Rajneesh Collection, University of Oregon Special Collections and University Archives, Coll. 310, box 1, fol. 5.

64. Guest, *My Life in Orange*, 193, 207–8.

65. Rajneesh visa application and letter from Rajneesh Foundation to Consulate General of USA, May 18, 1981, Rajneesh Legal Services Corporation Records, University of Oregon Special Collections and University Archives, Coll. 260, box 1, folder 1, fol. 1000. See also "Sins of Bhagwan," *India Today*, June 15, 1982, 135.

66. Thomas N. Casey, Report of Investigation, Immigration and Naturalization Services, November 19, 1981.

67. See the vast quantity of materials in Rajneesh Legal Services Corporation Records, University of Oregon Special Collections and University Archives, Coll. 260, box 3, f. 1130, and box 17, f. 1280. Among these is "Bhagwan Shree Rajneesh: Application for Immigration Fact Summary, March 2, 1983.

68. Letter of Swami Anand Santosh, Rajneesh Legal Services Corporation Records, University of Oregon Special Collections and University Archives Coll. 260, box 2, f.1030: "The only real question at the moment is how the American government is going to respond to this modern-day Christ. Will history show that America is indeed a land of religious freedom that can tolerate not only thousands of religious frauds but also the presence of an alive and lively enlightened master?" (4)

69. Swami Prem Niren, Memorandum, June 8, 1983, Rajneesh Legal Services Corporation Records, University of Oregon Special Collections and University Archives, Coll. 260, box 3, fol. 22, f. 1027.

70. Letter of Senator Mark O. Hatfield, May 6, 1982, Oregon Rajneesh History Collection, Oregon Historical Society Research Library, MSS 6030.

71. Frances Fitzgerald, "Rajneeshpuram," *New Yorker,* September 22, 1986, 91. See Rajneesh, "The New Man," *Rajneesh* 2 (1984): 37: "The days of the messiahs are over. Don't wait for Christ's coming again, and don't wait for Buddha's coming again. . . . That is what the old man used to believe—All nonsense! All holy cowdung!"

72. See Urban, *Church of Scientology,* chaps. 4–5.

73. Rajneesh Foundation International, *Rajneeshism: An Introduction to Bhagwan Shree Rajneesh and His Religion* (Rajneeshpuram, OR: Rajneesh Foundation International, 1983), 11: "Many Masters in the past did not create a canon of religious doctrine while they were alive. They worked directly with their disciples, trying to awaken in them the experience of enlightenment. After they had gone well-intentioned disciples created doctrines around their teachings, forming religious organizations to interpret clarify and spread the message. . . . Seeing the inevitability of this process, Bhagwan Shree Rajneesh is giving his spiritual direction to disciples who are creating a religion which will accurately reflect his teaching—while he is still alive."

74. Rajneesh Foundation International, *Rajneeshism,* 4.

75. Rajneesh Foundation International, *Rajneeshism,* 4, 12.

76. See *Rajneesh Times,* June 29, 1984, B1, and July 6, 1984, B1.

77. Rajneesh, *The Last Testament,* vol. 3, chap. 9; online version at Osho. com, 2015, www.osho.com/library/online-library-unconsciously-religion-belief-b1cc825b-77b.aspx.

78. Advertisement for the *Rajneesh Bible, Bhagwan* 11 (1984): 28.

79. Mahasattva Swami Krishna Prem, introduction to Bhagwan Shree Rajneesh, *The Rajneesh Bible* (Pune: Rajneesh Foundation International, 1985), 1:n.p.

80. Rajneesh, *Rajneesh Bible,* 1:9. See also Rajneesh, "Religion: The Spiritual Path," *Rajneesh Times,* April 6, 1984, B1–B6. Here Rajneesh outlines seven kinds of religion, culminating in the highest form, which is the religion of "ecstasy," based on joy, dance, and bliss.

81. There are two possible etymologies of our English term "religion." One is from Latin *re-ligare,* meaning "to reconnect or reunite," and the other is from *re-legere,* "to re-read or re-do carefully." See Jonathan Z. Smith, "Religion, Religions, Religious," in Smith, *Relating Religion* (Chicago: University of Chicago Press, 2004), 179–96.

82. Rajneesh, *Rajneesh Bible,* 594–95. See Rajneesh, introduction to *Rajneesh Bible,* 1:n.p.: "All these religions in the past are anti-life. Nobody is for life, nobody is for living, nobody is for laughter. No religion has accepted sense of humor as a quality of religiousness. Hence I say my religion is the first religion which takes man in its totality, in its naturalness, accepts man's whole as he is. And that's what holy means to me—not something sacred but something accepted in its wholeness."

83. Gordon, *Golden Guru,* 130.

84. Rajneesh, *Last Testament: Volume 3.* Online version at *Osho.com,* 2015, chapter 9. www.osho.com/library/online-library-unconsciously-religion-belief-b1cc825b-77b.aspx

85. Rajneesh, *The Last Testament,* vol. 3, chap. 14; online version at Osho. com, 2015, www.osho.com/library/online-library-adoration-collectivity-becoming-233f9f11–0b7.aspx. On Scientology and tax exemption, see Urban, *Church of Scientology,* chap. 5.

86. Gordon, *Golden Guru,* 127.

87. Dillon, interview, December 30, 2013.

88. "ABC's Nightline Halts Sheela during Wednesday Night Show," *The Dalles Chronicle,* September 20, 1984, 3.

89. Guest, *My Life in Orange,* 208.

90. Judy Mills and John Kaplan, "Peace Force Blends Mellow Thoughts, Tough Tactics," *Spokane Spokesman Review,* September 11, 1983.

91. Zaitz, "25 Years after Commune's Collapse." See "FBI Interview with Rajneesh Member Allen Thomas Gay on Wiretapping," Portland, OR, December 31, 1985, File # PD 250–3.

92. Ritter, interview, February 4, 2014. See Guest, *My Life in Orange,* 207.

93. Rajneesh Foundation International, *Rajneeshism,* 56–57. See Dempsey, *Bringing Heaven,* 89–90: "By late 1983, proclamations purportedly originating from Rajneesh and delivered to Sannyasins by Sheela became apocalyptic, anticipating nuclear annihilation and floods from which only Rajneeshee members would be spared. In early 1984 the AIDS scare provoked the formation of new rules restricting sexual practices and the prediction that the disease would cause mass destruction of which commune members would be the sole survivors."

94. *Rajneesh Times,* April 6, 1984, B6. A similar ad appears in *Rajneesh Times,* June 29, 1984, B2. See Swami Anand Madyapa, "Editorial," *Bhagwan* 11 (1984): 2: "We are living in a world of total cultural chaos . . . continuous warfare, famine, political assassinations, massive military arsenals and collapsing economies. . . . Bhagwan points the way out of this dilemma, while reminding us that the responsibility for resolving this crisis lies solely within each individual."

95. "Rajneeshpuram: The First Annual World Celebration, July 3–7, 1982," Papers Relating to Rajneeshpuram, 1982–1985, Oregon Historical Society Research Library, Religion MSS 1517. See "Bhagwan Shree Rajneesh: A Short Biography," 6–7, Rajneesh Legal Services Corporation Records, University of Oregon Special Collections and University Archives, Coll. 260, box 3, f. 1130.

96. Brochure printed by the Rajneesh Medical Corporation, P.O. Box 8, Rajneeshpuram, OR 97741, Rajneesh Artifacts and Ephemera Collection, University of Oregon Special Collections and University Archives, Coll. 275, Series I, box 11.

97. Gordon, *Golden Guru,* 131. See Guest, *My Life in Orange,* 174.

98. Altman, *Global Sex,* 77–78.

99. Guest, *My Life in Orange,* 207.

100. Ritter, interview, February 4, 2014. See "26 Accept Guru's Offer to Try Life in Utopia," *San Francisco Chronicle,* September 6, 1984; "The New Oregon Trail, *Sunday Oregonian,* September 16, 1984; "Guru Recruits Drifters," *Washington Post,* September 25, 1984.

101. Foster, interview, February 2, 2014.

102. Ritter, interview, February 4, 2014. See "Bhagwan's Medical Plan," *Oregon Magazine*, November 1985.

103. "Rajneeshpuram," Oregon Public Broadcasting.

104. Carter, *Charisma and Control*, 222.

105. "Bhagwan's Medical Plan," *Oregon Magazine*, November 1985.

106. Elroy King, "Feds Outline Background in Rajneesh Cases," *The Dalles Chronicle*, July 23, 1986.

107. Mark Wheelis and Masaaki Sugishima, "The Terrorist Use of Biological Weapons," in *Deadly Cultures: Biological Weapons since 1945*, ed. Mark Wheelis et al. (Cambridge, MA: Harvard University Press, 2006), 284–303.

108. Aubrey Meredith, "Assassination Plans Went as Far as Buying Arms," *The Oregonian*, November 1, 1985.

109. Zaitz, "25 Years after Commune's Collapse."

110. "Sheela Defects to Europe: Rajneeshism is Dead," *Hinduism* Today, November 1985, www.hinduismtoday.com/modules/smartsection/item.php?itemid = 348.

111. "Charged," *The Oregonian*, December 30, 1985. See Carter, *Charisma and Control*, 189.

112. "Guru's City Unconstitutional," *Register-Guard*, October 7, 1983, A1. Rajneesh himself would later deny that this was a religion and thus claim that there was no mixture of church and state: "Their whole case was that religion is being mixed with state. We don't *have* any religion, so how can we mix religion with state? . . . Here we don't have any religion, any church, any priest, no ritual, no congregation, nothing that you can point to as religious" (Rajneesh, *The Last Testament*, vol. 3, chap. 10, www.osho.com/library/online-library-wagner-frohnmeyer-religion-35d488fa-9a7.aspx).

113. Carl Abbott, "Utopia and Bureaucracy: The Fall of Rajneeshpuram, Oregon," *Pacific Historical Review* 59, no. 1 (1990): 77–103.

114. Gordon, *Golden Guru*, 182, 240.

115. Swami Amrito, interview, December 31, 2011, Pune.

116. Allanach, *Osho*, 435.

117. Milne, *Bhagwan*, 232; see Guest, *My Life in Orange*, 126.

118. Sheela, *Don't Kill Him.*

119. "Poona Period Caps Period of Growth for Rajneeshism," *The Oregonian*, July 2, 1985, www.oregonlive.com/rajneesh/index.ssf/1985/07/poona_era_caps_period_of_growt.html.

120. Les Zaitz, interview, December 13, 2013.

121. Gordon, *Golden Guru*, 240.

122. Gordon, *Golden Guru*, 210, 241.

123. Steger and Roy, *Neoliberalism*, 21.

124. Harvey, *Brief History*, 80, 165.

125. Michael Schaller, *Reckoning with America and Its President in the 1980s* (New York: Oxford, 1994), 181. See also Garry Wills, *Reagan's America: Innocents at Home* (Garden City, NY: Doubleday, 1987), 381.

126. Schaller, *Reckoning with America*, 181. See Haynes Johnson, *Sleepwalking through History: America in the Reagan Years* (New York: Anchor Books, 1991), 14: "An America yearning for reassurance about its place in the

world invested great faith in a Hollywood actor turned politician and suspended judgment on his leadership in hope that his promise would be realized. At a time when America desperately wanted to believe again, Reagan presented himself as the political wizard whose spell made everyone feel good."

127. Wills, *Reagan's America*, 381.

128. Rajneesh, *Book of Secrets III*, 30. See Osho, *Tantra: The Supreme Understanding*, 99–100.

129. Myles Meserve, "Meet Ivan Boesky, the Infamous Wall Streeter Who Inspired Gordon Gekko," *Business Insider*, July 26, 2012, www.businessinsider .com/meet-ivan-boesky-the-infamous-wall-streeter-who-inspired-gordon-gecko-2012–7?op = 1. See also John Paul Rollert, "Greed Is Good: A 300 Year History of a Dangerous Idea," *The Atlantic*, April 7, 2014, www.theatlantic.com /business/archive/2014/04/greed-is-good-a-300-year-history-of-a-dangerous-idea/360265/.

130. Steger and Roy, *Neoliberalism*, 31.

131. Steger and Roy, *Neoliberalism*, 32: "By October 1987 most stock values were seriously inflated. The disastrous correction came swiftly with the 'Black Monday' crash of the New York stock market, which lost a third of its value overnight. . . . Only a few years later, rising interest rates put a drastic end to another speculation-driven phenomenon: the real estate bubble that had been expanding during the 1980s finally burst in 1991, causing the collapse of hundreds of S&Ls."

CHAPTER 5. THE APOTHEOSIS OF A FALLEN GURU IN 1990S INDIA

Epigraphs: Osho, *Autobiography*, 145 (this quote is originally from *No-Mind: Flowers from Eternity*, talks given from December 1988 to January 1989); *Elle* magazine, quoted in "By the Media," Osho.com, 2014, www.osho.com/read /osho/by-press.

1. Aneesha Dillon, interview, December 30, 2013. See "Poona Resurgent," *Here and Now* 37 (April 1988): 37.

2. *Osho Multiversity Presents*, April 16, 1990.

3. Abhay Vaidya, "Will US Trademark Ruling Impact Osho's Work?," *DNA India*, January 18, 2009, www.dnaindia.com/india/report-will-us-trademark-ruling-impact-oshos-work-1222432.

4. Swami Amrito, interview, January 29, 2013.

5. Vanaik, *Painful Transition*, 55–56: "Thatcherism in the West is a response to the failure of the Fordist model of accumulation through mass production, mass consumption and mass employment. Thatcherism in India is the response to the failure of a larger and somewhat more generous Nehruvian vision of a populist welfarism and liberal democracy where both mass prosperity and popular power would systematically expand."

6. "The New Millionaires and How They Made It," *India Today*, October 31, 1987; "A Thriving Middle Class Is Changing the Face of India in a Land of Poverty: Its Buying Spree Promises Economic Growth," *Wall Street Journal*, May 19, 1988.

7. Steger and Roy, *Neoliberalism,* 91. "By the end of the Roaring Nineties, neoliberalism in its various permutations and modifications had successfully spread to most parts of the world. Its powerful advocates in the West had employed the compelling narrative of inevitable market globalization to convince people that the liberalization of trade and minimally regulated markets will result in high economic growth and dramatic improvements in living conditions worldwide" (119). See also Kanishka Chowdhury, *The New India: Citizenship, Subjectivity, and Economic Liberalization* (New York: Palgrave Macmillan, 2011).

8. McKean, *Divine Enterprise,* 7. See Brass, *Politics of India,* 287: "It was only after the appointment of P. V. Narasimha Rao as Prime Minster in July 1991 and his selection in turn of Manmohan Singh as finance minister that a more determined attempt to dismantle Nehru's system began. . . . Although most parties continued to pay lip service to Nehru's legacy, there was not much ideological commitment left in favor of it outside of the Communist Parties. . . . On the contrary there was a . . . consensus that the system of public sector enterprises had become an increasing burden on the economy."

9. "Osho International Meditation Resort," Osho.com, 2013, www.osho .com/medresort/Welcomemedresort.cfm.

10. Mircea Eliade, *The Sacred and the Profane: The Nature of Religion* (New York: Harcourt Brace Jovanovich, 1987), 20.

11. Jonathan Z. Smith, *Imagining Religion: From Babylon to Jonestown* (Chicago: University of Chicago Press, 1988), 54; see Joel O. Brereton, "Sacred Space," in *Encyclopedia of* Religion, vol. 12, ed. Lindsay Jones (New York: Macmillan, 2005), 7978–86.

12. News updates on Bhagwan, January 4, 1986, March 5, 1986, and April 12, 1986, Roshani Shay/Rajneesh Collection, University of Oregon Special Collections and University Archives, Coll. 310, box 8, fol. 8.

13. Swami Anand Narayan, "Bhagwan Shree Rajneesh vs. the United States of America, Part II," *Viha Bay Area Connection,* May–June, 1988, 2. See "Bhagwan Back at Poona Commune," *Rajneesh Newspaper,* February 4, 1987, 1.

14. See Bhagwan Shree Rajneesh, *Jesus Crucified Again: This Time in Ronald Reagan's America* (Mumbai: Rebel Publishing House, 1988).

15. Rajneesh Press Service, USA, press release, 1988, Roshani Shay/Rajneesh Collection, University of Oregon Special Collections and University Archives, Coll. 310, box 8, fol. 9. See Narayan, "Bhagwan Shree Rajneesh vs. The United States of America, Part II," 2.

16. "World Must Put U.S. 'Monster' in Its Place, Guru Says," *Chicago Tribune,* November 18, 1995, 5.

17. Bhagwan Shree Rajneesh, "Many More Communes Will Happen," *Sannyas News: Here and Now* 21 (1986): 1.

18. "News Update from Crete, March 4, 1986," Roshani Shay/Rajneesh Collection, University of Oregon Special Collections and University Archives, Coll. 310, box 8, fol. 8.

19. Stokes, "Guru Mocks, Provokes."

20. Osho, *Autobiography,* 145. See also "Biography," *Osho World,* 2015, www.oshoworld.com/biography/innercontent.asp?FileName = biography10/10–47-maitreya.txt.

21. "Buddha Merges into Bhagwan," *Rajneesh Newspaper*, November 19, 1986, 1.

22. Rajneesh, "I Am My Own Message," *Rajneesh Newspaper,* November 19, 1986, 5.

23. Osho, *Autobiography,* 77. See "Bhagwan Shree Rajneesh: The Buddha, Lord Maitreya," *Rajneesh Newspaper,* November 19, 1986, 1.

24. "Biography," *Osho World,* 2015. See also Osho, *Autobiography,* 278; Bodhena, "From California Back to Poona," *Osho News,* January, 8, 2013, www.oshonews.com/2013/01/from-california-back-to-poona/.

25. "In 1989 Osho changed his name to OSHO and requested that everything previously branded with RAJNEESH . . . be rebranded OSHO. Osho International Foundation registered the mark OSHO and to this day continues to follow his guidelines to protect his name and his work." Osho International Foundation, "Trademark Information," 2009, www.osho.info/trademark_information.asp.

26. "Rajneesh Ashram Update: Westerners Flooding Back to See Bhagwan" (February 1988), Roshani Shay/Rajneesh Collection, University of Oregon Special Collections and University Archives, Coll. 310, box 8, fol. 9. See "Poona Resurgent," *Here and Now* 37 (April 1988): 3.

27. Osho, *Autobiography,* 280.

28. *Osho Multiversity Presents,* October 16, 1990, 1

29. *Osho Multiversity Presents,* April 16, 1990, 2–12.

30. See Osho, *Autobiography,* 280. See Swami Gyan Bhed, *Rebellious Enlightened Master,* 580.

31. Ma Prem Shunyo, *My Diamond Days with Osho,* 218. She lists Amrito, Anando, Avirbhava, Chetana, David, Devageet, Hasya, Kavisha, Maneesha, Neelam, Nirvano, and Nitty, with a thirteenth member unnamed. According to Gyan Bhed, the list of twenty-one is Jayesh, Amrito, Anando, Amitabh, Anasha, Avirbhava, Chitten, Devageet, Garim, Hasya, Jayanti Bhai, Kaveesha, Mukta, Neelam, Plotinus, Prasad, Satya Vedanta, Tathagat, Turiya, Yogi, and Zareen (*Rebellious Enlightened Master,* 580).

32. Sheela Raval, "Osho's Legacy: Royalty Ruckus," *India Today,* July 3, 2000, archives.digitaltoday.in/indiatoday/20000703/religion.html.

33. Osho, *Autobiography,* 280.

34. Dillon, interview, December 30, 2013.

35. Swami Amrito, interview, January 29, 2013.

36. "OSHO: The Silent Explosion," Osho.com, 2015, www.osho.com /silent-explosion.

37. "Experiences from the Osho International Meditation Resort," Osho International, 2006, www.youtube.com/watch?v = d_aTWw3PJ4w.

38. "The Resort," Osho.com, 2014, www.osho.com/visit/accomodations /resort.

39. "OSHO: The Silent Explosion."

40. "Experiences from the Osho International Meditation Resort." Another visitor described the resort in similar terms: "I walked through the gate, and it was like an explosion. It was really amazing. I didn't realize how much in the previous years I had suppressed my joy and my expressiveness. And the moment that I walked in, it just went boom, and it was incredible" (ibid).

41. "Experiences from the Osho International Meditation Resort."

42. Sheela Raval, "New House for Old God," *India Today*, December 16, 2002, indiatoday.intoday.in/story/osho-ashram-bhagwan-rajneesh-ashram-in-pune-acquires-new-face-after-rs-50-crore-revamp/1/218327.html.

43. Osho International Meditation Resort, "Week Ahead, 31 Dec.–06 Jan." (Pune, 2011–2012).

44. Osho Multiversity, "Osho Multiversity Courses and Trainings, 30 Jan— 20 Feb" (Pune, 2013). See "Osho Living in Residential Programs & Osho Guesthouse" (Pune, 2013).

45. See Namrata Joshi, "The Salvation Slide," *Outlook India*, October 15, 2012, www.outlookindia.com/article.aspx?282474; Raval, "Osho's Legacy."

46. Dillon, interview, December 30, 2013.

47. Gordon, *Golden Guru*, 131. See Press Release from Rajneeshdham, Poona, February 5, 1988, Roshani Shay/Rajneesh Collection, University of Oregon Special Collections and University Archives, Coll. 310, box 8, fol. 9: "In March 1984 Bhagwan issued a public warning that AIDS would spread quickly from homosexuals to the heterosexual population. . . . Also in 1984 Bhagwan advised his disciples to guard against AIDS by wearing condoms and latex surgical gloves while making love. He cautioned them to avoid anal and oral sex and to stop kissing. These precautions were dismissed by many observers as fanatical and ridiculous. 'Now in many countries these procedures have been officially adopted—of course without mentioning my name,' said Bhagwan."

48. I viewed this introductory film during a visit on January 31, 2011.

49. "OSHO: The Silent Explosion."

50. Rajneesh, *Psychology of the Esoteric*, 41–42.

51. "OSHO: The Silent Explosion."

52. Bhagwan Shree Rajneesh, *The Supreme Understanding: Discourses on the Kenopanishad* (London: Routledge & Kegan Paul, 1980), 20.

53. Osho, *Meditation: The First and Last Freedom* (New York: Macmillan, 2004), 82–83.

54. Harvey, *Condition of Postmodernity*, 293. See Steger and Roy, *Neoliberalism*, 52: "A gigantic compression of time and space would have been impossible without the worldwide expansion of markets, the rise of transnational corporations, and the intensification of economic flows across the globe. Moreover, these economic developments were facilitated by the rapid transformation of information, communication, and transportation technology— 'digital revolution' epitomized by the proliferation of personal computers, the Internet, satellite TV . . . and global supply chains."

55. Osho, *Autobiography*, 213.

56. Featherstone, *Consumer Culture and Postmodernism*, 112.

57. Turner, *Regulating Bodies*, 164–65.

58. Bhagwan Shree Rajneesh, *This Very Body the Buddha: Discourses on Hakuin's Song of Meditation* (Pune: Rajneesh Foundation, 1978).

59. Rajneesh, interview by the Immigration and Naturalization Service, Portland, OR, August 26, 1983, Rajneesh Legal Services Corporation Records, University of Oregon Special Collections and University Archives, Coll. 260, box 2, folder 27, fol. 1070.

60. See Jameson, *Postmodernism*, 26; Mandel, *Late Capitalism*, 387.

61. Featherstone, *Consumer Culture and Postmodernism*, 110–11.

62. Carrette and King, *Selling Spirituality*, 29: "We are now seeing the corporatization of spirituality, that is the tailoring of those individualized spiritualities to fit the needs of corporate business culture in its demand for an efficient, productive and *pacified* workforce." A similar argument is made by Slavoj Žižek in his critique of Western Buddhism: "The Buddhist Ethic and the Spirit of Global Capitalism," The European Graduate School: Graduate and Postgraduate Studies, 2012, www.egs.edu/faculty/slavoj-zizek/videos/the-buddhist-ethic/.

63. "Experiences from the Osho International Meditation Resort."

64. "Experiences from the Osho International Meditation Resort."

65. Steger and Roy, *Neoliberalism*, 119.

66. Harvey, *Brief History*, 166.

CHAPTER 6. THE STRUGGLE OVER OSHO'S LEGACY

Epigraphs: Osho International Foundation, "Trademark Information," Osho.com, 2009, www.osho.info/trademark_information.asp; Osho-Rajneesh, *Om Shantih Shantih Shantih: The Soundless Sound, Peace, Peace, Peace* (Cologne: Rebel Pub. House, 1988), 264.

1. Raval, "Osho's Legacy."

2. Osho International Foundation, "Copyrights," Osho.com, 2013, www.osho.com/copyrights.

3. Namrata Joshi, "The Salvation Slide," *Outlook India*, October 15, 2012, www.outlookindia.com/article.aspx?282474.

4. "Facebook Discrimination: Osho Demoted from Personhood," *Osho Viha* (blog), August 2, 2013, oshoviha.blogspot.com.

5. Aditi Pai, "Trouble Brewing as Followers Allege Osho's Will Was Forged," *India Today*, December 16, 2013, indiatoday.intoday.in/story/trouble-brewing-as-followers-allege-oshos-will-was-forged-pune-police-investigating/1/331548.html.

6. Joshi, "Salvation Slide."

7. Abhay Vaidya, "Will US Trademark Ruling Impact Osho's Work?," *DNA India*, January 18, 2009, www.dnaindia.com/india/report-will-us-trademark-ruling-impact-oshos-work-1222432.

8. See Mario Biagioli, Peter Jaszi, and Martha Woodmansee, eds., *Making and Unmaking Intellectual Property: Creative Production in Legal and Cultural Perspective* (Chicago: University of Chicago Press, 2011), 1: "Once an arena of the law populated only by a technical subculture of attorneys and scholars, intellectual property (IP) has become a focus of vital concern and remarkably intense inquiry across an expanding range of disciplines and constituencies." On IP law and cultural goods, see also Ronald V. Bettig, *Copyrighting Culture: The Political Economy of Intellectual Property* (Boulder, CO: Westview Press, 1996); Rosemary Coombe, *The Cultural Life of Intellectual Properties: Authorship, Appropriation, and the Law* (Durham, NC: Duke University Press, 1999).

9. Allison E. Fish, "The Commodification and Exchange of Knowledge in the Case of Transnational Commercial Yoga," *International Journal of Intellectual Property* 13, no. 2 (2006): 190. See also Jain, *Selling Yoga,* chap. 4. Another good discussion is Andrew Ventimiglia, "Spirited Possessions: Intellectual Property Rights in the American Spiritual Marketplace" (PhD diss., University of California, Davis, 2015).

10. Fish, "Commodification and Exchange of Knowledge," 190. For similar debates regarding Islam and IP, see Ali Khan, "Islam as Intellectual Property: 'My Lord! Increase Me in Knowledge,'" *Cumberland Law Review* 31 (2000): 631–84.

11. See Urban, *Church of Scientology,* chap. 6.

12. William Foster, interview, February 2, 2014.

13. Rajneesh, *Ecstasy,* 102.

14. Sarito Carol Neiman, foreword to Osho, *Autobiography,* xiii.

15. "Amrito Replies to Critics," *Sannyas News,* October 4, 2009, sannyasnews.org/now/archives/429.

16. Osho-Rajneesh, *Om Shantih Shantih Shantih: The Soundless Sound, Peace, Peace, Peace* (Cologne: Rebel Pub. House, 1988), 264.

17. Osho International Foundation, "Trademark Information," Osho.com, 2009, www.osho.info/trademark_information.asp.

18. See Amanda Lucia, "Innovative Gurus: Tradition and Change in Contemporary Hinduism," *International Journal of Hindu Studies* 18, no. 2 (2014): 221–63; Mark Singleton and Ellen Goldberg, eds., *Gurus of Modern Yoga* (New York: Oxford University Press, 2013); Jacob Copeman and Aya Ikegame, eds., *The Guru in South Asia: New Interdisciplinary Perspectives* (New York: Routledge, 2014).

19. Vinita Deshmukh, "Osho's Secy Comes out of Cocoon, Seeks Transparency in Commune's Affairs," *Indian Express,* June 20, 2000, expressindia.indianexpress.com/ie/daily/20000620/ina20033.html.

20. Joshi, "Salvation Slide."

21. Deshmukh, "Osho's Secy Comes out of Cocoon."

22. Deshmukh, "Osho's Secy Comes out of Cocoon."

23. Deshmukh, "Osho's Secy Comes out of Cocoon."

24. Raval, "Osho's Legacy."

25. Parmartha, "Indian Sannyasins Make Moves on Political Leaders," *Sannyas News,* June 8, 2012, sannyasnews.org/now/archives/1956.

26. Osho International Foundation, "Trademarks," Osho.com, 2014, www.osho.com/trademarks.

27. Osho International Foundation, "Copyrights," Osho.com, 2014, www.osho.com/copyrights.

28. "Osho Dhyan Mandir," *Osho World,* 2014, www.oshoworld.com/oshodham/oshodham.asp.

29. Raval, "Osho's Legacy."

30. "Decision," *Osho International Foundation v. Osho Dhyan Mandir and Atul Anand,* Claim Number: FA0006000094990, July 28, 2000.

31. Vaidya, "Will US Trademark Ruling Impact Osho's Work?"

32. "Home," Osho Friends International, 2013, oshofriendsinternational.com/.

33. *Osho Friends International v. Osho International Foundation,* United States Patent and Trademark Office, January 13, 2009, 34.

34. *Osho Friends International v. Osho International Foundation,* 20. See Vaidya, "Will US Trademark Ruling Impact Osho's Work?"

35. "U.S. Trademark Case Osho Friends International," Osho.info, 2009. www.osho.info/testimonials.asp?intid = 16.

36. Ellen Rosen, "Yoga, AstraZeneca, Intel, UN: Intellectual Property," *Bloomberg,* December 17, 2012, www.bloomberg.com/news/2012–12–17 /yoga-astrazeneca-intel-un-intellectual-property.html. See *Bikram Yoga's College of India v. Evolation Yoga, LLC,* United States District Court, Central District of California, Case No. 2:11-cv-5506-ODW (SSx), 2012.

37. Joel Sappel and Robert Welkos, "Scientologists Block Access to Secret Documents," *Los Angeles Time,* November 5, 1985, pqasb.pqarchiver.com/latimes/access/64568420.html?dids = 64568420:64568420&FMT = ABS&FMTS = ABS:FT. See also Urban, *Church of Scientology,* chap. 6; Douglas E. Cowan, "Contested Spaces: Movement, Countermovement, and E-Space Propaganda," in *Religion Online: Finding Faith on the Internet,* ed. Lorne L. Dawson and Douglas E. Cowan (New York: Routledge, 2004), 233–49.

38. Ann Brill and Ashley Packard, "Silencing Scientology's Critics on the Internet: A Mission Impossible?" *Communications and the Law* 19, no. 4 (1997): 5. "The church not only sued for copyright infringement but for trade secret misappropriation. Copyright infringement occurs when someone violates the exclusive rights of a copyright owner to reproduce, distribute, perform, display, or make derivative works based on a copyrighted work. A trade secret is information that has economic value from not being generally known. A trade secret is misappropriated when it is disclosed or used by another without the consent of the trade secret rights holder" (3–4).

39. Mark Fearer, "Scientology's Secrets," in *Composing Cyberspace: Identity, Community, and Knowledge in the Electronic Age,* ed. Richard Holeton (Boston: McGraw-Hill, 1998), 352.

40. Courtney Macavinta, "Scientologists Settle Legal Battle," *CNET,* March 30, 1999, news.com.com/Scientologists+settle+legal+battle/2100–1023_3–223683 .html?tag = item. See Urban, *Church of Scientology,* chap. 6.

41. Pai, "Osho's Will." See Abhay Vaidya, "Osho's Will Surfaces Mysteriously," *First Post India,* September 19 2013, www.firstpost.com/india/oshoswill-surfaces-mysteriously-23-years-after-death-sparks-controversy-1119721. html.

42. Martin Viefhues, Formal Submission to the Office for Harmonization in the International Market, December 23, 2010.

43. "What Is the Story with the Trademark 'Osho' About?" Osho.de, 2014, www.osho.de/2012/03/trademark-about-en/.

44. "Last Will and Testament of Osho," October 15, 1989.

45. N.R. Parik, "Expert Opinion," November 6, 2013; see Nicole Ciccolo, "Technical Examination on the Will Dated 15th October 1989 Bearing the Signature 'Osho,'" 2013; both online at http://www.osho.de/alleged-last-willosho-en/.

46. Pai, "Osho's Will."

47. "Police Seek 'Original Will' of Osho from His Pune Ashram," *Deccan Herald*, December 16, 2013, www.deccanherald.com/content/374876/police-seeks-original-osho-his.html.

48. "Police Seek 'Original Will' of Osho."

49. Keltie, LLP, Letter to the Office for Harmonization in the International Market (Trade Marks and Designs), January 2, 2014.

50. "Withdrawal of Osho's Will," Osho.de, 2014, www.osho.de/withdrawal-of-the-will-en/.

51. "Facebook Discrimination."

52. "Reporting Trademark Infringements," Facebook, 2014, www.facebook.com/help/www/440684869305015/.

53. "Facebook Discrimination."

54. "Facebook Discrimination."

55. See "Statement of Rights and Responsibilities," Facebook, 2014, www.facebook.com/legal/terms. "For content that is covered by intellectual property rights, like photos and videos (IP content), you specifically give us the following permission, subject to your privacy and application settings: you grant us a non-exclusive, transferable, sub-licensable, royalty-free, worldwide license to use any IP content that you post on or in connection with Facebook (IP License)" (ibid).

56. "Facebook Privacy Notice," Snopes.com, October 17, 2103, www.snopes.com/computer/facebook/privacy.asp#wDCCS083DXeZgqiP.99.

57. Joshi, "Salvation Slide."

58. Joshi, "Salvation Slide."

59. Joshi, "Salvation Slide." According to the group Osho Work, the gift of property to the Darshan Trust "is a well-known legal maneuver designed to sidestep any local publicity about such a move in order to avoid public detection and possible objection." See "Osho: An Open Wave," OshoWork, 2015, oshowork.org/intro.html.

60. Joshi, "Salvation Slide."

61. Joshi, "Salvation Slide."

62. "Frequently Asked Questions," Osho Work, 2015, oshowork.org/faq.html.

63. "Current Affairs," *Osho News*, January 13, 2014, www.oshonews.com/2014/01/current-affairs/.

64. Swami Anand Teertha (Sudi Narayanan), interview, May 23, 2014.

65. Raval, "Osho's Legacy."

66. This sentiment was expressed to me repeatedly by local businessmen, shopkeepers, restaurant owners, and service people whom I interviewed in Pune between December 2011 and February 2013.

67. Foster, interview, February 2, 2014.

68. Aneesha Dillon, interview, December 30, 2013.

69. Swami Satya Vedant, interview, 2013.

70. See "Osho Cocom Eco Village Project," Ozenrajneesh.com, 2014, www.ozenrajneesh.com/ozenrajneesh/osho_cocom_goa_vision.html; "Osho Tapoban: An International Commune and Forest Retreat," tapoban.com, 2014, www.tapoban.com/; "Ashram in the Desert," Desertashram.com.il, 2014, www.desertashram.co.il/en/.

71. For a useful directory of Osho centers worldwide, see "Osho Links," Satrakshita.com, 2014, www.satrakshita.com/osho_links_eng.htm. For information on individual centers, see, for example, "Osho Humaniversity: School for Masters," Humaniversity.com, 2015, www.humaniversity.com/; "Osho UTA," Oshouta.de, 2014, www.oshouta.de/de/angebote/themen; "Osho Afroz," Oshoafroz.com, 2014, www.oshoafroz.com/site/; "Osho Amritdham," Oshoamritdham, 2014, www.oshoamritdham.com/.

72. See "Community Experience Programme," OshoLeela.co.uk, 2015, www .osholeela.co.uk/index.php?content = ev_cat_cep; "Community Experience Program," Humaniversity.com, 2015, www.humaniversity.com/community-experience-program.

73. "Individual Sessions," Humaniversity.com, 2014, https://www .humaniversity.com/individual-sessions.

74. "Tourist Program: A 14-Day Journey of Self-Discovery," Humaniversity.com, 2014, www.humaniversity.com/tourist-program.

75. "Events in Europe, Africa, Middle East," Osho News, 2015, www .oshonews.com/events-in-europe/.

76. Swami Anand Teertha, interview, May 23, 2014.

77. Rosemary Coombe, "Cultural Agencies: The Legal Construction of Community Subjects and Properties," in Biagioli, Jaszi, and Woodmansee, Making and Unmaking Intellectual Property, 81. See Coombe, Cultural Life of Intellectual Property; Johanna Gibson, Creating Selves: Intellectual Property and the Narration of Culture (London: Ashgate, 2006).

CONCLUSION

Epigraphs: Rajneesh, The Sword and the Lotus, republished as Osho, The Sword and the Lotus: Talks in the Himalayas (Cologne: Rebel Pub. House, 1997), 78; Arjun Appadurai, Modernity at Large: Cultural Dimensions of Globalization (Minneapolis: University of Minnesota Press, 1996), 158; David Harvey, Seventeen Contradictions and the End of Capitalism (New York: Oxford University Press, 2014), 287.

1. Nyay Bhushan, "Lady Gaga Reveals Love of Books by Indian Philosopher Osho," Hollywood Reporter, October 28, 2011, www.hollywoodreporter.com /news/lady-gaga-reveals-love-books-254661.

2. "Lady Gaga Thinking of Osho Tattoo," Osho Media, January 11, 2012, oshomedia.blog.osho.com/2012/01/lady-gaga-thinking-of-osho-tattoo/.

3. Anand Subhuti, "Lady Gaga, Swapping Rooms and Off to Goa," Osho News, April 30, 2014, www.oshonews.com/2014/04/lady-gaga-goa-subhuti/.

4. See Wouter J. Hanegraaff, New Age Religion and Western Culture: Esotericism in the Mirror of Secular Thought (Albany: SUNY Press, 1997).

5. See Marilyn Ferguson, The Aquarian Conspiracy: Personal and Social Transformation in Our Time (New York: Tarcher Cornerstone, 2009).

6. See Hanegraaff, New Age Religion, 40–41; Shirley MacLaine, Out on a Limb (New York: Bantam, 1986).

7. Kathryn Lofton, Oprah: The Gospel of an Icon (Berkeley: University of California Press, 2011), 52.

8. Lofton, *Oprah*, 79. See James R. Lewis and J. Gordon Melton, *Perspectives on the New Age* (Albany: SUNY Press, 1992), 7. As Lewis and Melton suggest, New Age spirituality tends to have the following features: an emphasis on healing, a desire to be modern and use scientific language; eclecticism and syncretism; a monistic and impersonal ontology; optimism, success orientation, and a tendency to evolutionary views; and an emphasis on psychic powers.

9. Roy Wallis, "Perspectives on *When Prophecy Fails*," *Zetetic Scholar* 4 (1979), 9–14; quoted in Lewis and Melton, *Perspectives*, 7.

10. Paul Heelas, *The New Age Movement: The Celebration of Self and the Sacralization of Modernity* (London: Blackwell, 1996).

11. Kimberly Lau, *New Age Capitalism: Making Money East of Eden* (Philadelphia: University of Pennsylvania Press, 2000).

12. Carrette and King, *Selling Spirituality*, 87, 1. See also Jain, *Selling Yoga*.

13. Osho, *New Man for the New Millennium* (New York: Penguin Books, 2000).

14. See Carrette and King, *Selling Spirituality*, 112–13, 144, 148, 152; see Heelas, *New Age Movement*, 22, 40, 68.

15. "Eminent Persons on Osho," *Osho World*, 2014, www.oshoworld.com /osho_now/eminent_osho.asp.

16. See also Urban, *Tantra*, introduction and chap. 1.

17. See White, *Kiss of the Yogini*, introduction; Urban, *Power of Tantra*, chap. 3.

18. Mark A. Michaels and Patricia Johnson, *Tantra for Erotic Empowerment: The Key to Enriching your Sexual Life* (Woodbury, MN: Llewellyn Publications, 2008), 1.

19. Barbara Carrellas, *Urban Tantra: Sacred Sex for the Twenty-First Century* (Berkeley, CA: Celestial Arts, 2007), 18.

20. Diana Richardson, *Tantric Orgasm for Women* (Rochester, VT: Destiny Books, 2004), 4–5.

21. Dillon, *Tantric Pulsation*, back cover advertisement. Another example is Osho *sannyasin* Ma Prem Shunyo, who now teaches a popular practice called "Meditantra." See "Meditantra: Prem Shunyo & Veet Marco," Meditantra, 2014, www.meditantra.com/.

22. Flyer for "Sky Dancing: A Day of Ecstasy and Celebration with Ma Anand Margo and Sw. Jivan Diwano" (April 23, 1988), Roshani Shay/Rajneesh Collection, University of Oregon Special Collections and University Archives, Coll. 310, box 4, fol. 2.

23. Margo Anand, *The Art of Sexual Ecstasy: The Path of Sacred Sexuality for Western Lovers* (Los Angeles: Jeremy P. Tarcher, 1990), 38.

24. See Fish, "Commodification and Exchange of Knowledge."

25. Harvey, *Neoliberalism*, 166.

26. "Decision," *Osho International Foundation v. Osho Dhyan Mandir and Atul Anand*, Claim Number: FA0006000094990, July 28, 2000.

27. On this debate, see Russell McCutcheon, *Manufacturing Religion: The Discourse on Sui Generis Religion and the Politics of Nostalgia* (New York: Oxford University Press, 2003); Robert Ellwood, *The Politics of Myth: A Study*

of C. G. Jung, Mircea Eliade, and Joseph Campbell (Albany: SUNY Press, 1999), 115.

28. Gita Mehta, *Karma Cola: Marketing the Mystic East* (New York: Vintage, 1994), 102–3.

29. King and Carrette, *Selling Spirituality,* 156.

30. See also Jain's useful critique of Carrette and King in *Selling Yoga.*

31. Bhagwan Shree Rajneesh, *Glimpses of a Golden Childhood* i(Rajneeshpuram, OR: Rajneesh Foundation International, 1985), 99–100.

32. Swami Anand Narayan, "Bhagwan Shree Rajneesh vs. the United States of America," *Viha: Bay Area Connection* (April 1988): 2.

33. Vasant Joshi (Swami Satya Vedant), interview, December 24, 2013.

34. David Harvey, *Seventeen Contradictions and the End of Capitalism* (New York: Oxford University Press, 2014), 287.

35. Harvey, *Seventeen Contradictions,* 296.

36. Harvey, *Seventeen Contradictions,* 296.

37. Daniel F. Pilario, "Back to the Rough Ground? Locating Resistance in Times of Globalization," in *Postcolonial Europe in the Crucible of Cultures: Reckoning with God in a World of Conflicts,* ed. Jacques Haers, SJ, and Norbert Hintersteiner (New York: Rodopi, 2007), 29.

38. Pilario, "Back to the Rough Ground?," 47.

39. Appadurai, *Globalization,* 6.

40. See Harvey, *Seventeen Contradictions.*

41. Gerth and Mills, *From Max Weber,* 246–47. See also Urban, "Zorba the Buddha" (1998).

42. Carter, *Charisma and Control,* 78. See also Urban, "Zorba the Buddha" (1998).

43. See Arjun Appadurai, *The Future as Cultural Fact: Essays on the Global Condition* (New York: Verso, 2013), 230: "The problem with charisma today is not its routinization but its ephemerality, its vulnerability to high-speed fame, short reputations, brief moments of credibility for elected leaders. Thus we may want to reflect on the volatility of charisma . . . as its major vulnerability."

44. See Kate Bowler, *Blessed: A History of the American Prosperity Gospel* (New York: Oxford University Press, 2013).

45. See Urban, *Church of Scientology,* chap. 4; Urban, "The Medium is the Message in the Spacious Present: Channeling, Television, and the New Age," in *Handbook of Spiritualism and Channeling,* ed. Cathy Gutierrez (Leiden: Brill, 2015), 319–39.

46. Harvey, *Seventeen Contradictions,* 78.

47. Harvey, *Seventeen Contradictions,* 79–80.

Selected Bibliography

LIBRARY AND SPECIAL COLLECTIONS

Jayakar Library. University of Pune, Pune, India.

Oregon Historical Society Research Library.

  Max Gutierrez Collection. Org. Lot 506.

  Oregon Rajneesh History Collection. MSS 6030.

  Papers Relating to Rajneeshpuram, 1982–1985. Religion MSS 1517.

Osho Library. Osho International Foundation, 2014. www.osho.com/iosho
/library/the-books.

University of Oregon Special Collections and University Archives.

  Rajneesh Artifacts and Ephemera Collection, 1981–2004. Coll. 275.

  Rajneesh Legal Services Corporation Records. Coll. 260.

  Rajneeshpuram. Accession #06–057.

  Roshani Shay/Rajneesh Collection. Coll. 310.

WORKS BY ACHARYA RAJNEESH/BHAGWAN SHREE RAJNEESH/
OSHO/OSHO-RAJNEESH

Osho. *Autobiography of a Spiritually Incorrect Mystic.* New York: St. Martin's
Press, 2000.

———. *The Book of Secrets: 112 Meditations to Discover the Mystery Within.*
New York: St. Martin's Griffin, 1998.

———. *Meditation: The First and Last Freedom.* New York: Macmillan, 2004.

———. *New Man for the New Millennium.* New York: Penguin Books, 2000.

———. *Sermons in Stones.* New York: Osho International, 1987.

———. *Sex Matters*. New York: St. Martin's Griffin, 2003.

———. *The Sword and the Lotus: Talks in the Himalayas*. Cologne: Rebel Pub. House, 1997.

———. *Tantra: The Science of Tantra*. DVD. Pune: Osho International Foundation, 2010.

———. *Tantra: The Supreme Understanding*. London: Watkins, 2009.

———. *Tantra: The Way of Acceptance*. London: Pan Macmillan, 2011.

———. *The Tantra Experience: Evolution through Love*. Pune: Osho Media International, 2012.

———. *Tantra, Spirituality, and Sex*. Nargol, India: Osho Chidvilas, 1994.

———. *Tantric Transformation: Discourses on the Royal Song of Saraha*. Rockport, MA: Element, 1994.

Osho-Rajneesh. *Om Shantih Shantih Shantih: The Soundless Sound, Peace, Peace, Peace*. Cologne: Rebel Pub. House, 1988.

Rajneesh, Acharya. *The Mind of Acharya Rajneesh*. Edited by Shireen Jamall. Bombay: Jaico Publishing House, 1974.

Rajneesh, Bhagwan Shree. *Beware of Socialism*. Rajneeshpuram, OR: Rajneesh Foundation International, 1984.

———. *The Book of Secrets III*. Pune: Rajneesh Foundation, 1976.

———. *The Book of Wisdom: Discourses on Atisha's Seven Points of Mind Training*. Pune: Rajneesh Foundation, 1983.

———. *A Cup of Tea*. Rajneeshpuram, OR: Rajneesh Foundation International, 1983.

———. *Dimensions beyond the Known*. Los Angeles: Wisdom Garden Books, 1975.

———. *Ecstasy: The Forgotten Language*. Pune: Rajneesh Foundation, 1978.

———. *Ek Omkar Satnam: The True Name*. Pune: Rajneesh Foundation, 1974. www.oshorajneesh.com/download/osho-books/Indian_Mystics/The_True_Name_Volume_1.pdf.

———. *From Sex to Superconsciousness*. Delhi: Orient Paperbacks, n.d.

———. *Glimpses of a Golden Childhood*. Rajneeshpuram, OR: Rajneesh Foundation International, 1985.

———. *The Goose Is Out*. Antelope, OR: Rajneesh Foundation International, 1982.

———. *The Greatest Challenge: The Golden Future*. Pune: Rebel Pub. House, 1988.

———. "The Greatest Joke There Is." *Bhagwan* 8 (1984): 23–24.

———. *I Am the Gate*. Bombay: Life Awakening Movement, 1972.

———. "I Am My Own Message." *Rajneesh Newspaper* 1, no. 8 (November 19, 1986): 5.

———. "I Enjoy Disturbing People." *Sannyas News: Here and Now* 21 (1986): 3.

———. *Jesus Crucified Again: This Time in Ronald Reagan's America*. Mumbai: Rebel Pub. House, 1988.

———. *The Last Testament: Interviews with the World Press*. Rajneeshpuram, OR: Rajneesh Foundation International, 1986.

———. "A Liquid Human Being." *Bhagwan* 11 (1984): 10–13.

———. "Many More Communes Will Happen." *Sannyas News: Here and Now* 21 (1986): 1.

———. *Meditation: The Art of Ecstasy.* New York: Harper & Row, 1976.

———. *The Mind of Acharya Rajneesh.* Mumbai: Jaico Publishing House, 1974.

———. "The New Man." *Bhagwan* 2 (1984): 37.

———. *A New Vision of Women's Liberation.* Pune: Rebel, 1987.

———. *The Psychology of the Esoteric: The New Evolution of Man.* New York: Harper & Row, 1978.

———. *The Rajneesh Bible.* Pune: Rajneesh Foundation International, 1985.

———. "Religion: The Spiritual Path." *Rajneesh Times,* April 6, 1984, B1–B6.

———. *Sambhog se samadhi ki aur.* Bombay: Jivan Jagruti Kendra, 1969.

———. *The Secret: Discourses on Sufism.* Pune: Rajneesh Foundation, 1980.

———. *The Secret of Secrets.* Pune: Rajneesh Foundation, 1983.

———. *Secrets of Discipleship.* Bombay: Life Awakening Movement, 1972.

———. *The Supreme Understanding: Discourses on the Kenopanishad.* London: Routledge & Kegan Paul, 1980.

———. *Tantra Spirituality and Sex.* Rajneeshpuram, OR: Rajneesh Foundation International, 1983.

———. *Tao: The Golden Gate.* Pune: Rajneesh Foundation, 1980.

———. "This Is Not a Democracy." *Sannyas* 4, no. 78 (1978): 33–34.

———. "Until the Vatican Is Destroyed Humanity Will Not Know What Freedom Is." *Here & Now* 32 (1987): 5.

———. *This Very Body the Buddha: Discourses on Hakuin's Song of Meditation.* Pune: Rajneesh Foundation, 1978.

———. "What Counts Is Consciousness." *Rajneesh* 2 (1984): 15.

———. *The Wisdom of the Sands.* Vol. 1, *Discourses on Sufism.* Pune: Rajneesh Foundation, 1980.

———. *Yoga: The Alpha and the Omega.* Vol. 9. Pune: Rajneesh Foundation, 1978.

———. *Zorba the Buddha: Intimate Dialogues with Disciples.* Antelope, OR: Rajneesh Foundation International, 1982.

WORKS BY OTHER *SANNYASINS* AND BY THE OSHO-RAJNEESH FOUNDATIONS

Allanach, Jack (Swami Krishna Prem). *Osho, India, and Me: A Tale of Sexual and Spiritual Transformation.* New Delhi: Niyogi Books, 2013.

Anand, Margo. *The Art of Sexual Ecstasy: The Path of Sacred Sexuality for Western Lovers.* Los Angeles: Jeremy P. Tarcher, 1990.

Appleton, Sue. *Bhagwan Shree Rajneesh: The Most Dangerous Man since Jesus Christ.* Zurich: Neo-Sannyas International, 1987.

City of Rajneeshpuram Preliminary Comprehensive Plan: Land Use. Rajneeshpuram, OR, 1982.

Dillon, Aneesha. *Tantric Pulsation: The Journey of Human Energy from Its Animal Roots to Its Spiritual Flower.* Cambridge: Perfect Publishers, 2005.

Joshi, Vasant. *The Awakened One: The Life and Work of Bhagwan Shree Rajneesh.* San Francisco: Harper & Row, 1982.

———. *The Luminous Rebel: Story of a Maverick Mystic.* New Delhi: Wisdom Tree Publishing, 2010.

Ma Anand Sheela. *Don't Kill Him: The Story of My Life with Bhagwan Rajneesh.* New Delhi: Prakash Books, 2012.

———. "Glory." Draft manuscript, October, 11, 1986. Roshani Shay/Rajneesh Collection, University of Oregon Special Collections and University Archives, box 11, fol. 27.

Ma Prem Shunyo. *My Diamond Days with Osho: The New Diamond Sutra.* Delhi: Motilal Banarsidass, 1993.

Ma Satya Bharti. *Death Comes Dancing.* London: Routledge and Kegan Paul, 1981.

Ma Yoga Laxmi. *Bhagwan Shree Rajneesh, Diary 1981.* Pune: Rajneesh Foundation, 1980.

Meredith, George. *Bhagwan: The Most Godless Yet Most Godly Man.* Pune: Rebel Publishing House, 1989.

Osho International Foundation. "Copyrights." Osho.com, 2014. www.osho.com/copyrights.

———. "Trademark Information." Osho.info, 2009. www.osho.info/trademark_information.asp.

———. "Trademarks." Osho.com, 2014. www.osho.com/trademarks.

Prasad, Ram Chandra. *Rajneesh: The Mystic of Feeling.* Delhi: Motilal Banarsidass, 1970.

Rajneesh Foundation International. *Rajneeshism: An Introduction to Bhagwan Shree Rajneesh and His Religion.* Rajneeshpuram, OR: Rajneesh Foundation International, 1983.

Sam. *Life of Osho.* London: Sannyas, 1997.

Shay, T. L. "Rajneeshpuram and the Abuse of Power" (1985). Roshani Shay/Rajneesh Collection, University of Oregon Special Collections and University Archives, Coll. 310.

Swami Amrito. "A Bankrupt Humanity." *Rajneesh Times International,* December 16, 1988, 9.

———. "Editorial: States of Terror." *Rajneesh Times International,* August 16, 1988, 2.

Swami Anand Narayan. "Bhagwan Shree Rajneesh vs. The United States of America." *Viha: Bay Area Connection,* April 1988, 1–2.

Swami Devageet. "Devageet on Shiva." *Sannyas News,* July 25, 1986, 4.

———. *Osho: The First Buddha in the Dental Chair.* Boulder, CO: Sammasati, 2013.

Swami Gyan Bhed. *The Rebellious Enlightened Master: Osho.* Delhi: Diamond Pocket Books, 2006.

Swami Krishna Deva. "Interview." *Bhagwan* 2 (1984): 4.

MAGAZINES, NEWSPAPERS, AND NEWSLETTERS

Bhagwan
Here & Now
NEWSensation

Osho Multiversity Presents
Osho News
Osho Times International
Osho World
Rajneesh
Rajneesh Newspaper
Rajneesh Times
Rajneesh Times International
Sannyas
Sannyas News
Viha: Bay Area Connection

OTHER WORKS

Abbott, Carl. "Utopia and Bureaucracy: The Fall of Rajneeshpuram, Oregon." *Pacific Historical Review* 59, no. 1 (1990): 77–103.

Allyn, David. *Make Love, Not War: The Sexual Revolution, an Unfettered History*. New York: Routledge, 2001.

Altglas, Véronique. *From Yoga to Kabbalah: Religious Exoticism and the Logics of Bricolage*. New York: Oxford University Press, 2014.

Altman, Dennis. *Global Sex*. Chicago: University of Chicago Press, 2001.

Appadurai, Arjun. *The Future as Cultural Fact: Essays on the Global Condition*. New York: Verso, 2013.

———, ed. *Globalization*. Durham, NC: Duke University Press, 2001.

———. *Modernity at Large: Cultural Dimensions of Globalization*. Minneapolis: University of Minnesota Press, 1996.

Aveling, Harry. *The Laughing Swamis: Australian Disciples of Swami Satyananda Sarasvati and Osho Rajneesh*. Delhi: Motilal Banarsidass, 1994.

Bell, Daniel. *The Cultural Contradictions of Capitalism*. New York: Basic Books, 1996.

Best, Steven, and Douglas Kellner. *Postmodern Theory*. New York: Guilford Press, 1991.

Brass, Paul R. *The Politics of India since Independence*. Cambridge: Cambridge University Press, 1994.

Carrette, Jeremy, and Richard King. *Selling Spirituality: The Silent Takeover of Religion*. New York: Routledge, 2004.

Carter, Lewis F. "Carriers of Tales: On Assessing Credibility of Apostate and Other Outsider Accounts of Religious Practices." In *The Politics of Religious Apostasy: The Role of Apostates in the Transformation of Religious Movements*, edited by David Bromley, 221–38. Westport, CT: Praeger, 1998.

———. *Charisma and Control in Rajneeshpuram: The Role of Shared Values in the Creation of a Community*. New York: Cambridge University Press, 1990.

Carus, W. Seth. *Bioterrorism and Biocrimes: The Illicit Use of Biological Agents since 1900*. Amsterdam: Fredonia Press, 2002.

Chandler, Russell L., and Tyler Marshall. "Guru Brings His Ashram to Oregon." *Los Angeles Times*, August 30, 1981.

Chowdhury, Kanishka. *The New India: Citizenship, Subjectivity, and Economic Liberalization.* New York: Palgrave MacMillan, 2011.

Copeman, Jacob, and Aya Ikegame, eds. *The Guru in South Asia: New Interdisciplinary Perspectives.* New York: Routledge, 2014.

Csordas, Thomas, ed. *Transnational Transcendence: Essays on Religion and Globalization.* Berkeley: University of California Press, 2009.

Deleuze, Gilles, and Félix Guattari. *Capitalism and Schizophrenia.* Minneapolis: University of Minnesota Press, 1977.

Dempsey, Corinne. *Bringing the Sacred down to Earth: Adventures in Comparative Religion.* New York: Oxford University Press, 2011.

Dobrowolny, Wolfgan, director. *Ashram in Poona.* Albatros Filmproduktion, 1981.

Eagleton, Terry. "Awakening from Modernity." *Times Literary Supplement,* February 20, 1987, 194.

Esposito, John L., et al. *Religion and Globalization: World Religions in Historical Perspective.* New York: Oxford, 2007.

Featherstone, Mike. *Consumer Culture and Postmodernism.* London: Sage, 2007.

Feuerstein, Georg. *Holy Madness: The Shock Tactics and Radical Teachings of Crazy-Wise Adepts, Holy Fools, and Rascal Gurus.* New York: Paragon House, 1991.

Fish, Allison E. "The Commodification and Exchange of Knowledge in the Case of Transnational Commercial Yoga." *International Journal of Cultural Property* 13, no. 2 (2006): 189–206.

———. "Laying Claim to Yoga: Intellectual Property, Cultural Rights, and the Digital Archive." PhD diss., University of California, Irvine, 2010.

Fitzgerald, Frances. "Rajneeshpuram." *New Yorker,* September 22, 1986.

Floether, Eric. *Bhagwan Shree Rajneesh and His New Religious Movement in America.* Markham, Ont.: Intervarsity Press, 1983.

Foucault, Michel. *The Order of Things: An Archaeology of the Human Sciences.* New York: Vintage, 1994.

———. "What Is an Author?" In *The Foucault Reader,* edited by Paul Rabinow, 101–20. New York: Pantheon, 1984.

Fox, Judith M. *Osho-Rajneesh—Studies in Contemporary Religion.* Salt Lake City: Signature Books, 2002.

Gerth, H. H., and C. Wright Mills, eds. *From Max Weber: Essays in Sociology.* New York: Oxford University Press, 1958.

Goldberg, Philip. *American Veda: How Indian Spirituality Changed the West.* New York: Harmony, 2010.

Gordon, James S. *The Golden Guru: The Strange Journey of Bhagwan Shree Rajneesh.* Lexington, MA: Stephen Greene Press, 1987.

Guest, Tim. *My Life in Orange: Growing up with the Guru.* New York: Harcourt, 2004.

Guha, Ramchandra. *India after Gandhi: The History of the World's Largest Democracy.* New York: Harper Perennial, 2008.

Halbfass, Wilhelm. *India and Europe: An Essay in Understanding.* Albany: SUNY Press, 1988.

Hanegraaff, Wouter J. *New Age Religion and Western Culture: Esotericism in the Mirror of Secular Thought.* Albany: SUNY Press, 1997.

Harvey, David. *A Brief History of Neoliberalism.* New York: Oxford University Press, 2007.

———. *The Condition of Postmodernity.* London: Blackwell, 1989.

———. *Seventeen Contradictions and the End of Capitalism.* New York: Oxford University Press, 2014.

Heelas, Paul. *The New Age Movement: The Celebration of Self and the Sacralization of Modernity.* London: Blackwell, 1996.

Holland, Eugene W. *Deleuze and Guattari's Anti-Oedipus: Introduction to Schizoanalysis.* New York: Routledge, 1999.

Jain, Andrea. *Selling Yoga: From Counterculture to Pop Culture.* New York: Oxford University Press, 2014.

Jameson, Fredric. *Postmodernism: or, The Cultural Logic of Late Capitalism.* Durham, NC: Duke University Press, 1991.

———. "Postmodernism and Consumer Society." In *The Anti-Aesthetic: Essays on Postmodern Culture,* edited by Hal Foster, 111–25. New York: New Press, 1998.

Jenkins, Philip. *Decade of Nightmares: The End of the Sixties and the Making of Eighties America.* New York: Oxford University Press, 2006.

Joshi, Namrata. "The Salvation Slide." *Outlook India,* October 15, 2012. www.outlookindia.com/article.aspx?282474.

Juergensmeyer, Mark. *Global Rebellion: Religious Challenges to the Secular State, from Christian Militias to al Qaeda.* Berkeley: University of California Press, 2008.

———. *Religion in Global Civil Society.* New York: Oxford University Press, 2005.

———. *Terror in the Mind of God: The Global Rise of Religious Violence.* Berkeley: University of California Press, 2003.

Keys, Scott. "Strange but True Story of Voter Fraud and Bioterrorism." *The Atlantic,* June 10, 2014. www.theatlantic.com/politics/archive/2014 /06/a-strange-but-true-tale-of-voter-fraud-and-bioterrorism/372445/.

Khanna, Sushil. "The New Business Class, Indology, and State: The Making of a New Consensus." *South Asia* 10 (1987): 47–60.

Kilachand, Shobha. "The Saffron Superstar." *Illustrated Weekly of India,* April 5, 1981, 20–24.

King, Richard. *Orientalism and Religion: Post-Colonial Theory, India, and the "Mystic East."* New York: Routledge, 1999.

Kripal, Jeffrey J. *Esalen and the American Religion of No Religion.* Chicago: University of Chicago Press, 2008.

Lash, Scott, and John Urry. *The End of Organized Capitalism.* Madison: University of Wisconsin Press, 1987.

Lechner, Frank, and John Boli, eds. *The Globalization Reader.* Malden, MA: Wiley-Blackwell, 2011.

Lincoln, Bruce. *Holy Terrors: Thinking about Religion after September 11.* Chicago: University of Chicago Press, 2006.

———. "Theses on Method." *Method and Theory in the Study of Religion* 8 (1996): 225–27.

Linden, Ian. *Global Catholicism: Diversity and Change since Vatican II.* New York: Columbia University Press, 2009.

Lofton, Kathryn. *Oprah: The Gospel of an Icon.* Berkeley: University of California Press, 2011.

Love, Robert. *The Great Oom: The Improbable Birth of Yoga in America.* New York: Viking, 2010.

Lucia, Amanda. "Innovative Gurus: Tradition and Change in Contemporary Hinduism." *International Journal of Hindu Studies* 18, no. 2 (2014): 221–63.

———. *Reflections of Amma: Devotees in a Global Embrace.* Berkeley: University of California Press, 2014.

Mandel, Ernest. *Late Capitalism.* London: Humanities Press, 1975.

Marcuse, Herbert. *Eros and Civilization: A Philosophical Inquiry into Freud.* Boston: Beacon Press, 1966.

McCormack, Win. "Bhagwan's Bottom Line." *The State of Oregon,* November 1984.

———, ed. *The Rajneesh Chronicles: The True Story of the Cult That Unleashed the First Bioterrorist Attack on U.S. Soil.* Portland, OR: Tin House, 2010.

———. "Ticking Time-Bomb?" *Oregon Magazine,* September 1984.

McKean, Lise. *Divine Enterprise: Gurus and the Hindu Nationalist Movement.* Chicago: University of Chicago Press, 1996.

Mehta, Gita. *Karma Cola: Marketing the Mystic East.* New York: Vintage, 1994.

Miller, Donald K. *Global Pentecostalism: The New Face of Christian Social Engagement.* Berkeley: University of California Press, 2008.

Milne, Hugh. *Bhagwan: The God That Failed.* New York: St. Martin's Press, 1986.

Moore, R. Laurence. *Selling God: American Religion in the Marketplace of Culture.* New York: Oxford University Press, 1994.

Mullan, Bob. *Life as Laughter: Following Bhagwan Shree Rajneesh.* Boston: Routledge, 1983.

Ortner, Sherry. "On Neoliberalism." *Anthropology of This Century* 1 (2011). aotcpress.com/articles/neoliberalism/.

Ouspensky, P.D. *In Search of the Miraculous: Fragments of an Unknown Teaching.* New York: Harcourt, Brace & World, 1949.

Padoux, André. "What Do We Mean by Tantrism?" In *The Roots of Tantra,* edited by Katherine Ann Harper and Robert L. Brown, 17–24. Albany: SUNY Press, 2002.

Palmer, Susan J. *Moon Sisters, Krishna Mothers, Rajneesh Lovers: Women's Roles in New Religions.* Syracuse, NY: Syracuse University Press, 1996.

Palmer, Susan J., and Arvind Sharma, eds. *The Rajneesh Papers: Studies in a New Religious Movement.* Delhi: Motilal Banarsidass, 1993.

Raval, Sheela. "Osho's Legacy: The Royalty Ruckus." *India Today,* July 3, 2000. www.india-today.com/itoday/20000703/religion.html/

Reich, Wilhelm. *The Function of the Orgasm: Sex-Economic Problems of Biological Energy.* New York: Farrar, Straus and Giroux, 1973.

———. *Selected Writings: An Introduction to Orgonomy*. New York: Farrar, Straus, Giroux, 1973.

———. *The Sexual Revolution: Toward a Self-Governing Character Structure*. New York: Farrar, Straus and Giroux, 1963.

Rudolph, Lloyd I., and Susanne Hoeber Rudolph. *In Pursuit of Lakshmi: The Political Economy of the Indian State*. Chicago: University of Chicago Press, 1987.

Sahlins, Marshall. *Waiting for Foucault, Still*. Chicago: Prickly Pear Press, 2002.

Shirley, John. *Gurdjieff: An Introduction to His Life and Ideas*. New York: Penguin, 2004.

Singh, Jaideva. *Vijnanabhairava Tantra or Divine Consciousness: A Treasury of 112 Types of Yoga*. Delhi: Motilal Banarsidass, 2010.

Singleton, Mark, and Ellen Goldberg, eds. *Gurus of Modern Yoga*. New York: Oxford University Press, 2013.

Smith, Jonathan Z. *Imagining Religion: From Babylon to Jonestown*. Chicago: University of Chicago Press, 1988,

Srinivas, Smriti. *In the Presence of Sai Baba: Body, City, and Memory in a Global Religious Movement*. Leiden: Brill, 2008.

Srinivas, Tulasi. *Winged Faith: Rethinking Globalization and Religious Pluralism through the Sathya Sai Movement*. New York: Columbia University Press, 2010.

Stamets, Paul. *Mycelium Running*. Berkeley, CA: Ten Speed Press, 2005.

Steger, Manfred B., and Ravi K. Roy. *Neoliberalism: A Very Short Introduction*. New York: Oxford University Press, 2010.

Strelley, Kate. *The Ultimate Game: The Rise and Fall of Bhagwan Shree Rajneesh*. New York: Harper & Row, 1987.

Swami Vivekananda. *The Complete Works of Swami Vivekananda*. 9 vols. Calcutta: Advaita Ashram, 1983.

Thompson, Judith, and Paul Heelas. *The Way of the Heart: The Rajneesh Movement*. Wellingborough, Eng.: Aquarian Press, 1986.

Turner, Bryan S. *Regulating Bodies: Essays in Medical Sociology*. New York: Routledge, 1992.

Turner, Bryan S., and Habibul Haque Khondker. *Globalization East and West*. London: Sage, 2010.

Tweed, Thomas, and Stephen Prothero, eds. *Asian Religions in America: A Documentary History*. New York: Oxford University Press, 1999.

Updike, John. *S*. New York: Random House, 2013.

Urban, Hugh B. "The Cult of Ecstasy: Tantrism, the New Age, and the Spiritual Logic of Late Capitalism." *History of Religions* 39 (2000): 268–304.

———. *Magia Sexualis: Sex, Magic, and Liberation in Modern Western Esotericism*. Berkeley: University of California Press, 2005.

———. "Osho, from Sex Guru to Guru of the Rich: The Spiritual Logic of Late Capitalism." In *Gurus in America*, edited by Thomas A. Forsthoefel and Cynthia Ann Humes, 169–92. Albany: SUNY Press, 2005.

———. *The Power of Tantra: Religion, Sexuality, and the Politics of South Asian Studies*. New York and London: IB Tauris/Palgrave, Macmillan, 2010.

———. *Tantra: Sex, Secrecy, Politics, and Power in the Study of Religion.* Berkeley: University of California Press, 2003.

———. "Tantra, American Style: From the Path of Power to the Yoga of Sex." In *Transformations and Transfer of Tantra in Asia and Beyond,* edited by Istvàn Keul, 457–94. Berlin: de Gruyter, 2012.

———. "Zorba the Buddha: The Body, Sacred Space, and Late Capitalism in the Osho International Meditation Resort." *Southeast Review of Asian Studies* 35 (2013): 32–49.

———. "Zorba the Buddha: Capitalism, Charisma, and the Cult of Bhagwan Shree Rajneesh." *Religion* 26 (1998): 161–82.

Vanaik, Achin. *The Painful Transition: Bourgeois Democracy in India.* London: Verso, 1990.

Vásquez, Manuel. *Globalizing the Sacred: Religion across the Americas.* New Brunswick, NJ: Rutgers University Press, 2003.

Ventimiglia, Andrew. "Spirited Possessions: Intellectual Property Rights in the American Spiritual Marketplace." PhD diss., University of California, Davis, 2015.

Weber, Max. *The Protestant Ethic and the Spirit of Capitalism.* New York: Routledge, 2005.

Wheelis, Mark, and Masaaki Sugishima. "The Terrorist Use of Biological Weapons." In *Deadly Cultures: Biological Weapons since 1945,* edited by Mark Wheelis et al., 284–303. Cambridge, MA: Harvard University Press, 2006.

White, David Gordon. *Kiss of the Yogini: "Tantric Sex" in Its South Asian Contexts.* Chicago: University of Chicago Press, 2003.

Winston, Diane. "Rage against the New Machine: Three Days at the Osho International Meditation Resort." *Religion Dispatches,* December 29, 2014.

Zaitz, Les. "25 Years after Rajneeshee Commune Collapses Truth Spills Out." *The Oregonian,* April 15, 2011. www.oregonlive.com/rajneesh/index.ssf /2011/04/part_one_it_was_worse_than_we.html.

Žižek, Slavoj. "The Buddhist Ethic and the Spirit of Global Capitalism." The European Graduate School: Graduate and Postgraduate Studies, 2012. www.egs.edu/faculty/slavoj-zizek/videos/the-buddhist-ethic/.

———. *Living in the End Times.* London: Verso, 2011.

Index